One of the attractions of Obama in 2008 was his tone and countenance, his willingness to engage seriously in the issues and toss out the bitter and brittle politics of all. He said we should "resist the temptation to fall back on the same partisanship and pettiness and immaturity that has poisoned our politics for so long." And millions of Americans were proud to support such a man.

But then something happened to the Obama presidency, something very disappointing. Obama stopped being the president he said he would be. And now a very real sense of regret is settling in.

—A 2008 Obama voter fearful of getting onto the Obama enemies list

First Edition
Library of Congress Cataloging-in-Publication Data

ISBN: 1478223677
ISBN-13: 9781478223672
Library of Congress Control Number: 2012912956
CreateSpace Independent Publishing Platform, North Charleston, SC

Obama's Enemies List

How Barack Obama Intimidated America And Stole the Election

by

Floyd G. Brown

Western Journalism Press
Phoenix, Arizona
WesternJournalism.com

Dedicated to

Mary Beth Brown, my loving wife. She lives Proverbs 31:10-12.

An excellent wife who can find?

She is far more precious than jewels.

The heart of her husband trusts in her, and he will have no lack of gain.

She does him good, and not harm, all the days of her life.

Contents

SECTION II: Obama Punishes His Enemies   27

The Punished: Free Trade Advocates and Business Owners........ 27

The Punished: Homeowners, the Economy and the Unemployed. . . 35

SECTION I: Obama Wins, What's Ahead?

L ate on the night of January 20, 2013, Barack Obama will be driven from the inaugural podium, parade, and festivities to the most powerful office in the world and a staff capable of anything. Since Obama won, what will he first do?

What will be his first orders to the Justice Department, Homeland Security, the IRS, INS, SEC and other agencies that can wield such comforting or crushing power over our daily lives?

Here, I'll try to answer that question.

And it could be an alarming answer, based on all that I've seen in this presidential campaign. I have some stories to tell—stories that are especially noteworthy because they involve Obama, a list, and you.

Obama Crosses the Line

Many Americans first became aware that Obama had crossed a line—a line that no president had even dared approach since Richard Nixon—when **_Kim Strassel_** of the *Wall Street Journal* dropped a bombshell in May 2012:

> *"Unlike senators or congressmen, presidents alone represent all Americans. Their powers—to jail, to fine, to bankrupt—are also so vast as to require restraint. Any president who targets a private citizen for his politics is de facto engaged in government*

intimidation and threats. This is why presidents since Nixon have carefully avoided the practice. Save Mr. Obama, who acknowledges no rules."[1]

This revelation was a slap in the face to thoughtful Americans who thought they knew this president. It was to many almost inconceivable that Obama—an historic president, so outwardly cool with inspiring promises of hope—could actually be keeping an "enemies list." And not just a list locked away safely in his desk drawer, as the infamously paranoid Nixon had done. Obama chose to publish excerpts of his enemies list right on his official re-election website—for the entire world to see. What was he thinking?

As you will see, he knew exactly what he was thinking.

Obama Has History of Making Enemies Lists

Obama's "list making" dates back much further than Ms. Strassel's public expose. In May I was already writing this book, already well aware of the existence of an enemies list. I had expected Obama to quickly begin seeing everyday Americans as "enemies" precisely because he had already done so—during his first campaign for the presidency.

Back in 2008 he called me out by name, identifying me as an enemy, and sending a signal to his supporters to actively harass me, try to hurt me.

> *"There was an ad, one in South Dakota by **Floyd Brown**, I don't think that I am off the wall here to say that, you know, a lot of outside groups that are potentially going to be going after us hard…"—Senator Barack Obama, July 2008[2]*

With these comments, Obama was able to incite his supporters to launch all kinds of personal attacks against me. As on cue, I was flooded with an onslaught of nasty, hate- filled, vulgar and obscene anonymous phone calls and emails from Obama supporters. Some included death threats, and these can be unnerving to the uninitiated. Fortunately it wasn't the first time I had felt the sting of backlash from the powerful. I am a political guy by nature. I love the rough and tumble of campaigns and elections.

My bio and personal information soon appeared on a specialized enemies list website the Obama team called "Fight the Smears". I received even more calls and the cyber-attacks increased on me and the website. The Wikipedia website that referenced me was overwhelmed with scurrilous lies.

My wife, **_Mary Beth Brown_**, began getting threatening calls at our home. She began to fear for our children.

It didn't stop until I began to record the messages and post them on the internet for all to hear. The intensity of the hatred toward me and my family was intense and ferocious.

The tactic had a clear objective. Obama and his team wanted every early opponent to know that they were being watched, and that they should fear him and his supporters. They wanted us to shut up.

If a political opponent wants to get up in my face, that's just fine…, I'll get up in theirs. That's the wonder and beauty of our American electoral process. I'll take it any day over the deadly alternative practiced in some other nations, with death squads hovering over the outcome.

As long as that is how it remains.

Obama Uses Nazi and Mob Intimidation Tactics

Early in his first term, Obama decided to stake his presidency on healthcare. He was going to be the first Democrat president since Franklin Roosevelt first tried to actually succeed in fixing the nation's broken healthcare system. He knew he was in for a fight. He knew he would be facing stiff opposition. He needed a way to get his message out, and smack down the message of his many opponents. So he made a decision: If it was good enough for the mob back in Chicago or the leadership of old Germany, it's good enough for me.

Obama put out a call to the youth of America and told them he needed their help. He needed them to be strong, and loyal, and "turn in" anybody who wasn't shouting "yes we can" to a "fundamentally changed America." The president's team went all in on the initiative.

A website was launched. Social media leaders were mobilized. Young people and old were "authorized" to listen in on conversations with family members, friends at coffeehouses, strangers on the subway. And if anything "suspect" was overheard, these newly deputized enforcement officers were to send an email to flag@whitehouse.gov, and rest easy again knowing those high-level functionaries in the White House would take appropriate action.

In 1930s Germany, this role was carried out by youth known as brown-shirts and it didn't end well. In 1920s Chicago, it was how the mob kept an iron-fisted control over the neighborhoods. Most everyone knows this. And if Obama's true believers had any sense of the historical parallels, they surely would have been appalled and declined the offer.

But they weren't, and didn't.

How many emails made their way to the White House from unquestioning loyalists? We suspect the number was substantial, but the bigger question was: How could this happen?

How could Obama do something that was, on its face, so nefarious?

Didn't he know—*instinctively know for certain*—that every American would be deeply suspect of a citizen spying operation, and view it as evil? I speculated at the time that perhaps Obama was a victim in all this. A victim of the new media structure in America where the Left-stream Media tells liberals what they want to hear, the Right-stream Media tells conservatives what they want to hear, and never the twain shall meet. If this were the case, Obama could create his own little snitch squad and count on the Left-stream Media to spin the thing into something wonderful, and who cares what the Fox viewers think?

Alarms Sounded by Both Conservative and Liberals

This is certainly a plausible explanation, but it's more likely that Obama started taking heat inside the Washington beltway—where they do know their history lessons—and he reconsidered. Maybe his change of heart was triggered by a letter from **_Senator John Cornyn_** of Texas, who reminded Obama that our nation (1) does revere our Constitution with its bill of attainder and first amendment, and (2) does abhor any kind of old-Europe "brute squad" behavior emanating from the Oval Office:

> "I urge you to cease this program immediately.... I can only imagine the level of justifiable outrage had your predecessor asked Americans to forward emails critical of his policies to the White House. [3]

Whatever the reason, Obama soon shuttered the "snitch squad." White House spokesman Robert Gibbs was left to do his best "three monkeys" pantomime in the press briefing room, hoping the press corps would laugh off the whole matter.

For the most part, they did.

Indeed, this little preview of the Obama M.O. went out with a whimper, and is mostly forgotten today. But more than one level-headed commentator was prompted to question the character of the man we'd so recently elected. Peter Wehner, of the Ethics and Public Policy Center, had this to say:

> "The Obama White House is showing a fondness for intimidation tactics that might work well in the wards of Chicago but that don't have a place in the most important and revered political institution in America. To see these impulses manifest themselves so early in Obama's presidency, and given all that he has said to the contrary, is rather startling. The danger is that as the pressures mount and the battles accrue and the political heat intensifies, these impulses will grow stronger, the constraints on them will grow weaker, and the voices of caution and reason will continue to be ignored. If that should come to pass — if what we are seeing now is only a preview of coming attractions — then the Obama administration, and this nation, will pay a very high price." [4]

Another year would pass before we learned the "price" Obama intended us to pay.

"We're Gonna Punish Our Enemies"

In October 2010, Obama met with Eddie Sotelo of the Spanish radio giant, Univision. He spoke on a number of issues of importance to Hispanics, and then added:

> *"We're gonna **punish our enemies** and we're gonna **reward our friends** who stand with us on issues that are important to us."*[5]

> *(This is, to any doubters, a direct quote. Google it! It's not taken out of context; it's not a slash-and-paste job; it's not a hoax or urban legend…sadly.)*

When Obama made these remarks, he was speaking directly to Hispanic voters about the course they should take together with him in the upcoming election. And when I heard them, I was at first moderately intrigued.

I thought Obama had to be speaking about punishing *America's* enemies, and rewarding *America's* friends. That struck me as a worthy, if unusually candid, foreign policy position for a president to take. But no, Obama was not talking about Ahmadinejad, he was talking about the American people. He was effectively declaring war on any American who would oppose his plan for a "fundamentally changed America." And likewise, he was saying he would be rewarding his friends. I wondered at the time if we were experiencing the first president in American history who viewed his job description as rewarding political allies with none of that tedious "providing for the general welfare" stuff?

Initially, I of course hoped I had just misguided, or was even completely mistaken. While I had not supported candidate Obama in 2008, I certainly support the office of the presidency.

In the days following Obama's Univision interview, I was not alone in my head-shaking. Activists of varying political stripes didn't know what to make of this young president. Was he bringing a combative new style to the presidency? Was this how they rolled in the wards of Chicago? Was Obama just one fierce competitor who fought hard for what he believed in? Each a reasonable explanation. Two years later I had my answer, and it was ugly.

Obama Launches Ominous "Truth Team" Website

To formally kick off Obama's 2012 re-election bid, his campaign created a website with the ominous title, *Truth Team*. Unless they've yanked the site out of embarrassment, you can see it at: www.keepinggophonest. com. As I write, it consists of four main pages. Here's a summary of what those pages say they do, and what they actually do:

Obama's Truth Team	Stated Objective	Actual Objective
BarackObama.com	Keep voters informed	Solicit contributions (like every politician does)
Attack Watch	Monitors opponent's campaign ads	Trash opponent's ads (like every politician does)
Keeping His Word	Showing Obama's progress first term	Posting great quotes that have little bearing on actual accomplishments (like every politician does)
Keeping GOP Honest	Showing how dishonest the opponent is	Threatening government retribution to anyone who supports the opponent (**like nobody since Nixon has dared**)

All politicians, it's fair to say, put up websites embellishing their own records, attacking their opponent's records, and claiming to be the sole emissary of "truth." But this website of Obama's goes further. So far, that it catapults into a whole other realm.

In the "Keeping the GOP Honest" section, the Obama campaign listed the names of private citizens who contributed money to Romney and then launched a brutal smear campaign against them, including slanderous character assassination based solely on their holding of opposing political views. He basically pinned a bull's eyes to their backs and implying all the power of the federal government, made them public enemies one through eight. Every political analyst capable of putting conscience before party weighed in with a swift condemnation of Obama's actions. Here is a sampling running the full spectrum from die-hard liberal to equally hardened conservative:

> *"When I see people in my city struggling with real issues, I get very upset when I see such a level of dialogue that calls us to our lowest common denominators and not the kind of things that can unify us as a nation and move us forward as a nation."[6]*

> — Newark Mayor Cory Booker

(Booker's honesty cost him his dream of serving in Obama's Cabinet, with one high ranking administration official declaring, "He's dead to us." Since a reprimand and dressing-down, Booker is back towing the party line, hoping to get back off the enemies list, to the friends list.)[7]

> *"The emergence of this list is painfully ironic in light of many of the attacks now President Obama endured as candidate Obama. And like the worst of those attacks, the Obama enemies list plays on one of the oldest and ugliest traditions in politics, one which President Obama decried regularly in his first campaign: guilt by association."[8]*

> —**Rabbi Brad Hirschfield**, National Jewish Center for Learning and Leadership

> *"[VanderSloot's] political contributions are an exercise of his rights to free speech under the Constitution's First Amendment. The Obama campaign's identification of him as 'litigious, combative and a bitter foe of the gay rights movement' as the Wall Street Journal's Kim Strassel reported, was crass, despicable, and an effort to intimidate him and others like him."[9]*

> **Peter Roff**, US News & World Report

"There seems to be a cast of mind that views critics as enemies, as individuals and institutions that need to be ridiculed, delegitimized, or ruined. Given the administration's brazen public statements, one can only imagine what is being said privately, behind closed doors, as strategies are plotted and put into effect." [10]

—**Peter Wehner**, Commentary

"It hardly seems becoming that the Leader of the Free World would try to restrict individuals' constitutionally-protected participation in public affairs.... It seems he's willing to eschew niceties like speech rights and the democratic process to keep himself competitive." [11]

—**Kate Hicks**, Townhall.com

"Politics ain't beanbag but Barack Obama took an oath to uphold the US Constitution. Any US citizen has a right to take part in the democratic process without fear of reprisal from the federal government and the top office holder in the country." [12]

— **Don Anastas**, Liberally Conservative

And on and on the reactions went. This was in every sense a new low for a president and our nation—a repulsive new low. And as Americans there is value in taking a moment to read (or re-read) the actual "Keeping the GOP Honest" webpage in its full original length, unedited. Soak it in, and think about it. Then decide if you believe this website sets an appallingly dangerous precedent in the conduct of U.S. political campaigns, and if in fact it runs afoul of the law.

The following is excerpted from Obama's Campaign, www. keepinggophonest.com:

"Behind the curtain: A brief history of Romney's donors

As the presumptive GOP nominee, Mitt Romney is relying on a cadre of high-dollar and special-interest donors to fund his campaign. Giving information about his real policy intentions

9

and high-level access for cash, Romney and Republicans are working hard to pull in as much money as they can from wealthy lobbyists, corporations, and PACs. But just who are the people that Romney has called on for campaign cash?

A closer look at Romney's donors reveals a group of wealthy individuals with less-than-reputable records. Quite a few have been on the wrong side of the law, others have made profits at the expense of so many Americans, and still others are donating to help ensure Romney puts beneficial policies in place for them. Here's a look at just a few of the people Romney has relied on:

Donors who benefit from betting against America

▶ ***Paul "Chip" Schorr:*** *Paul Schorr has given $112,500 to Romney's presidential ambitions through Super PAC and direct campaign donations. As a partner at Blackstone, Schorr closed a deal in 2007 to outsource the services of seven U.S. companies to a firm in India, boosting that firm's profits by $220 million and making millionaires of the Indian management team. In 2006, he arranged a buyout of a Colorado travel reservations company that led to 841 layoffs while Blackstone and its partners recouped the billions of dollars they invested in less than a year.*

▶ ***Sam and Jeffrey Fox:*** *Sam and Jeffrey Fox serve as co-chairman of Romney's finance operation in Missouri and, together, have donated $220,000 to Romney's presidential ambitions. They also control the Harbour Group investment firm which **bragged** about buying an automotive accessories manufacturing company in Kansas in 1997 and moving production to Mexico. In 2002, the Harbour group's Mexico operation decided to outsource to China because China was "offering incentives and making it easy to open operations there." The Chinese government awarded Sam Fox the Marco Polo Award for "his company's role in China's economic development and his humanitarian contributions to that country."*

▶ ***T. Martin Fiorentino:*** *T. Martin Fiorentino is on Romney's Florida finance team and has bundled over $140,000 for the Romney campaign. He also lobbied on behalf of Lender Processing Services, a "foreclosure mill" that paid him to lobby on legislation aimed at preventing lenders from "making loans that borrowers would have difficulty repaying." The government has **reprimanded Lender Processing Services** "for unsound practices related to residential mortgage loan serving and foreclosure processing."*

Special-interest donors

Romney's stances on social and economic issues, like his long-standing <u>alliance with Big Oil</u>, attracts the contributions of high-dollar donors who are interested in pursuing a specific agenda. Here are just a few of special-interest donors that Romney accepted money from:

▶ ***Louis Moore Bacon:*** *An early mega-donor for Romney, Louis Moore Bacon donated $500,000 to the Restore Our Future Super PAC. Bacon makes his profit off of oil, first making a huge profit from successfully betting that gas prices would rise before the Iraqi invasion of Kuwait in 1989. Bacon's firm, Moore Capital, was **fined $25 million** for attempting to manipulate certain commodity futures markets.*

▶ ***Thomas O'Malley:*** *Thomas O'Malley is the CEO of PBF Energy, America's fourth largest petroleum refining company, and gave $100,000 to Restore Our Future. Not only did PBF energy help drive gas prices up this year by curtailing gas production, but it spilled 6.6 million gallons of oil at a refinery in New Jersey. The release of toxic gas and eventual explosion at another of its refineries in Delaware also directly contributed to a spike in gas prices.*

▶ ***Kent Burton:*** *Kent Burton is one of Romney's new bundlers who raised more than $25,000 in one month for Romney's campaign. He is also **a registered lobbyist***

> *for a wide array of energy clients, including Marathon Oil and Shell Oil.*

► ***Frank Vandersloot:*** *Frank Vandersloot is the national finance co-chairman of the Romney campaign and, through his company Melaleuca, has donated $1 million to Restore Our Future. He is also a "litigious, combative, and **a bitter foe of the gay rights movement**" who "spent big" on ads in an "ultimately unsuccessful effort to force Idaho Public Television to cancel a program that showed gays and lesbians in a favorable light to school children."'*

The boldfaced passages in each donor's "bio" were actual links to the sources. I ran down those sources, and was shocked to discover that **many of the so-called "charges" against these donors were fabricated out of thin air.**

Some of the charges came from Stephanie Mencimer of *Mother Jones* magazine.[13] Now it's no secret that *Mother Jones* exists pretty much exclusively to carry water for liberal causes. That's all it does. Proudly. So it would be a source the Obama campaign is comfortable quoting, though apparently not vetting.

And it turns out that Ms. Mencimer's reporting was so disturbingly wrong that *Mother Jones* was forced to run this retraction:

> *"The original version of this article contained errors, and it has been revised for accuracy.* Mother Jones *regrets these errors."* [14]

Unnoted in the retraction was the fact that there was not just one or two errors, which can happen to the best reporter working on a deadline, there was a handful of errors. And not just on little immaterial diddlies, but on the substance of the attack- doggery. In short, stuff was just made up as if for a *Saturday Night Live* sketch—no doubt because their audience would rather laugh than think.

Obama Webmaster Keeps Errors After Proven Wrong

But after the blunders were made public, you would expect Obama's campaign webmaster to fix their own fallacious reprinting. You would expect at least as much from the highest office in the land, wouldn't you?

I do.

But no such retraction, no apology of any kind, not even a sly admission that they should have checked their facts before smearing private citizens. If those Americans chose to sue, they would have an open-and-shut case against the president (except that presidents are exempted from defamation and slander).

The existence—the continued existence of this website after all that has happened—would be insult enough but the Obama campaign was apparently aiming for injury. After singling out political opponents, the Obama campaign actively enlisted supporters in carrying out the retribution. They "tweeted" each of the names on the list to millions of unquestioning supporters, who felt empowered, entitled, and indeed authorized to go out and do whatever damage they could do.

And they did plenty.

Obama's "Plumbers" Carry Out Their Orders

Imagine you're a private citizen; you've built up a successful business through years of hard work and enterprise. And now you want to give back, by supporting a candidate for president that shares your views. You can afford to donate a million dollars to the candidate, and so you do. You even take a figurehead role in the campaign, as large donors often do, as a measure of recognition. Then you wake up one day to learn that your entire life and livelihood have been ransacked—just as surely as if identity thieves had stolen your credit card. Only these thieves are employed by a shadow company that, you learn, is employed by the President himself.

It sounds like a cheap premise for a pulp novel.

But it's not—it's exactly what just happened to Frank VanderSloot, CEO of an Idaho Falls wellness-products company named Melaleuca. Mr. VanderSloot gave $1 million to Restore Our Future, a Super PAC that supported Mitt Romney.

Soon after making his donation, Mr. VanderSloot discovered that a certain Michael Wolf was trying to dig up court records on Mr. Vander-Sloot. But not just any records; Mr. Wolf was looking for dirt. Looking for any documents on Mr. VanderSloot's past marriages, or past grievances with former employees.

This is where Kim Strassel's reporting in the *Wall Street Journal* nailed it. Her investigation revealed that Michael Wolf had sent a number of faxes to the clerk's office of the Bonneville County Courthouse, trying to find something cheap and tawdry to hang on Mr. VanderSloot.

He failed at that. But not before Ms. Strassel figured out exactly who "Michael Wolf" really was. In his document requests of the court, he listed only his name and a private cellphone number. But he had been, until just a few months prior, a law clerk on the Democratic side of the Senate Permanent Subcommittee on Investigations. Seeking the more glamorous life, apparently, he then went to work for a company named Fusion GPS—which is in the strategic intelligence business, aka, opposition research, aka, dirty tricks.

When Ms. Strassel was finally able to get someone at Fusion GPS to answer the phone, she was met with one "no comment" after another. But clearly someone at Fusion GPS was worried that they could easily be linked with the President, so they sent an email to Ms. Strassel saying:

> *"Frank VanderSloot is a figure of interest in the debate over civil rights for gay Americans. As his own record on gay issues amply demonstrates, he is a legitimate subject of public records research into his lengthy history of legal disputes."*[15]

The "gay" charge was a total fabrication, a stutter step, meant to throw off Ms. Strassel's attention and presumably that of her readers at a time when the president was taking considerable heat for his flip-flops on the gay agenda: did he support it, did he not; was he himself gay, was he not? The story was changing by the day, by the hour. And throwing out a totally unfounded but salacious comment that a supporter of Romney's is a gay basher would have exactly the effect intended: deflect attention away from Obama.

Another Disgusting Fabricated Story by Obama Campaign

However, we saw what happened when the Obama campaign tried a similar tactic a few days prior. They commissioned some hack reporter at the *Washington Post* to fabricate a story about how Romney supposedly beat-up a homosexual some 50 years ago. The story was another complete fabrication—news to just about everybody, including the boy's parents who just shook their heads in disgust.

Right after dropping that political turd, the Obama campaign moved onto its next act of treachery. **Lacking the decency gene, they kept focus on what mattered to them: keeping their and Obama's job and power.**

I think people saw as much. How could they not? I think people will see Mr. VanderSloot for exactly who he is: Someone whose only crime was to donate a million dollars to a Super PAC.

Romney Supporter and His Kids Stalked by Obama Followers

And for that 'crime' his life has been turned upside down. He's been at the center of a media whirlwind whipped up by soulless partisans like MSNBC's Rachel Maddow and columnist/blog scold Glenn Greenwald. Mr. VanderSloot has been subjected to one false allegation after another. Worse, he tells of how *"they're stalking my kids."* His children have been harassed online. Their social media accounts have been hacked. Their phone lines have been jammed by mischief makers. Wisely, the children have kept their cool and refrained from responding to the threats.

As for Mr. VanderSloot, his company has lost of a lot of business, his life has become something of a living hell, and yet he remains undeterred. In his words:

> *"The public beatings and false accusations that followed are no deterrent. These tactics will not work in America."*

Sadly, Mr. Vandersloot's admonition was not heeded in the court of public opinion on Election Day.

Rogue Bully in Oval Office

Mr. Vandersloot and other private citizens like him stand accused by the president of "less-than-reputable" records and being "on the wrong side of the law" while they "made profits at the expense of so many Americans." All the fanciful fabrication of a Red Bull-infused copywriter. But Obama doesn't care. He knows the power of money in campaigns. He's firing a shot just past the left ear of anybody who might be thinking about donating to a conservative cause. This is the Chicago way. **This was Obama trying to shut down the pipeline into Romney's campaign by intimidating donors so fiercely, they fear for their livelihoods from the rogue bully in the Oval Office.**

And consider that so far we've only seen the "public" face of the Obama cutthroat intimidation machine. With a scar face like this, what are they planning behind closed doors? He will continue these same tactics to silence and extinguish opposition of his extreme far-left agenda. Given their blithe disregard for any common standard of decency, imagine what they are saying privately, and without thoughts of re-election looming overhead, what they are planning for a second term.

In this book, we will take a closer look at those plans.

Retribution for Opposing Obama's Policies…
How Far Will They Go?

We'll look at the political and legislative retribution some groups will face for opposing Obama's policies.

We'll see how far this White House is willing to go. We do know that they ginned up an executive order that would require federal contractors to list political donations when bidding on government contracts. Companies could put in a bid, and be the most qualified, but lose out simply because they donated to Republicans. Or they could quit donating to the GOP—Mr. Obama's real aim. This is innovative political hardball on Obama's part. That is, in fact, how they do it in the Congo, and in Cuba, and old Chicago. That's not how we've done it at the national level in this country until, apparently, the Obama administration.

What's more, the Obama re-election campaign appears to be staffed with a rather arrogant bunch of amateurs. They seem to think they can con independent voters into signing-on again with Obama by simply sprinkling pixie dust on any situation.

Here's what I mean by that.

When the news of Obama's enemies list became public, the Left-stream Media's Rachel Maddow dutifully dismissed it as "faux controversy" while the Right-stream Media's **_Glenn Beck_** shook his head in disgust. And if you looked at Beck's website, *The Blaze*, and you checked out the string of Comments from listeners about this story, you found several thousand screaming conservatives and one rather serious, longwinded detractor. This 'anonymous' poster identified only as "JZS" didn't have the guts to give his or her real name—most likely because he or she works for BarackObama.com and was there at *The Blaze* to share the Obama company line.

And what was that line?

The poster was insisting straight-faced that BarackObama.com is just another Super PAC, like one of the Romney Super PACs, and free to say anything they want—thanks to the Republicans pushing the Citizens United decision through the Supreme Court.

That was a head shaker. We all know that Super PACs can and do say controversial things. But are we really supposed to believe that BarackObama.com, which is staffed by Team Obama tip to stern, is an independent Super PAC? Here's the brilliant-minded post I refer to:

> *Blaze, you're being deceptive again trying to link information that comes from a Superpac to the President of the United States. That's a lie… Corporations are people my friends, and this is a corporation, with the rights of a person, that can raise money and do whatever they want. Just like Karl Roves groups cannot legally coordinate with Romney these group are not under President Obama's control… They aren't associated with President Obama, they are simply advocating in the public interest…*[16]

Really? Is Obama supporter JZS so unhinged from reality that he or she thinks anyone with half a brain will buy this rationale cum fairy tale?

Then there's a liberal website called the Pensitor Review (www.pen-sitoreview.com). The folks behind the site seem sweet enough. They weighed in on this, and parroted the Obama campaign line that "the outrage" is way overblown—given that conservatives went after private citizens like Jeremiah Wright and Bill Ayers in the 2008 campaign. It's true what they say. Conservative activists did go after Wright and Ayers. But no president did. The 2008 race was between two senators who were, theoretically anyway, equal in their ability to marshal government resources against private citizens.

There's a glaringly obvious difference between when a campaign goes after you, and the president goes after you. That's the first difference. And when Republicans went after Wright and Ayers—they simply reported the truth. That was shocking enough. When the president, through his website BarackObama.com went after his enemies, he did it relying on the factually inaccurate reporting of a Mother Jones reporter. So two strikes.

Three strikes and you're out.

This Is THE PRESIDENT Attacking Private Citizens

Many of the people on Obama's Enemies List are wealthy, to be sure. But they are private citizens. Not politicians. Not public officials. Not criminals. They are individuals. As **_Rory Cooper_** of the Heritage Foundation points out, Obama is going after them *"at the individual level, for anyone who opposes his policies."*[7]

Obama's team, when they've deigned to respond at all, have couched their attacks in the language of "disclosure" and argued that corporations do not in fact operate under the same first amendment rights that individuals do. But that is prima facie hokum. These are individuals being targeted. And not one of them stands a chance of fighting back against the most powerful office in the world.

- ▶ At what point will the courts step in, and stop him?
- ▶ At what point will impeachment proceedings begin?
- ▶ At what point will Americans again feel they are protected against the heavy hand of governmental intimidation?

This president swore an oath to protect and defend a Constitution that gives every citizen the right to participate in the democratic process, free of the fear of government intimidation. If Obama cannot keep this oath, should he keep the office? No, he should be impeached.

This is the first of several crucial questions here. As well…

Do We Want a Nation that Tolerates No Opposition… What Some Would Call Fascism?

Can we rightly be proud of a nation that says: If you do not support [current president] then government agents will come after you, dig into your professional background and question all who know you?

Or will we call this what it is—an odious development that must be condemned by the leaders of both political parties?

If Obama needs an enemies list to win; if that's what he's willing to do for a second term; then shouldn't we question whether he should be trusted with all the powers available to the president of the United States? It's a scary and sobering thought.

A President Can Hurt You…Really Hurt You

It's no secret that a president's powers are practically unlimited. If he wants to, he can hurt you—very badly. That is why our Founding Fathers created such thorough checks and balances. More than anything, they feared the despotism of old Europe. They knew the presidency would be terribly powerful and the temptation for abuse considerable. And then if such a time would come—*a time like now*—when that president would be almost completely unchecked by the media or Congress and free to whatever he pleases—great damage could be done. A president could…

- ► Accuse you of "betting against America"
- ► Suggest that you have a "less-than-reputable" record
- ► Ask the Justice Department to look into your business dealings

- ► Tip off the IRS that something may be wrong with your tax records
- ► Ask the SEC to fine you, bury you in paperwork, or even jail you—on a trumped-up charge you're clueless to
- ► Basically post your name on a "Wanted Poster" in a thousand government offices

And this is precisely what has happened, from the highest levels of the Obama administration, right before our unbelieving eyes.

It was not anything we expected from this president. Obama was touted to be the uniter, the one who was going to listen to both sides and engage the nation in a great conversation. Instead we got a malversation—a corruptible thing. Until this administration, we have not seen this kind of behavior except from "backwoods lawyers" and third-world tyrants. Never before from a U.S. President.

And you can't help but wonder, how deep the malversation?

Many More Names on Obama's "Wanted Posters"

After the huge stink and public outcry that resulted from the enemies list, you would expect the Obama campaign to bury the thing. They've done just the opposite.

The number of people being added to the enemies list is growing—fast and furiously, according to the sources inside the Obama camp which we'll reveal in these pages. Everyday citizens like you (*and clearly me*) are being added by the thousands and being targeted for potential retribution in a second term.

The list has, according to one source, "more than four zeros and less than six." I took that to mean there are hundreds of thousands on the list. We don't know for certain. But we think it's likely ***Eric Golub*** was overstating the number a bit when he wrote in the *Washington Times*:

> "Expect his list of enemies to grow. Any conservative Republican who breathes is now a target."[18]

But the list, like a cancer unchecked, continues to grow.

Using Official Power to Intimidate Private Citizens is a Despicable
Abuse of Authority

Two brothers were targeted by the Obama campaign with the viciousness and efficiency that our government used to reserve for foreign armies attacking on native soil. The attack on ***Charles and David Koch*** was brought into brilliant clarity in an op-ed by former Solicitor General ***Ted Olsen*** in the *Wall Street Journal* recently. (Full disclosure, Mr. Olsen is the company's lawyer—but that detracts not at all from the case he makes, excerpted here:

> *"How would you feel if aides to the president of the United States singled you out by name for attack, and if you were featured prominently in the president's re-election campaign as an enemy of the people?*
>
> *What would you do if the White House engaged in derogatory speculative innuendo about the integrity of your tax returns?*
>
> *Suppose also that the president's surrogates and allies in the media regularly attacked you, sullied your reputation and questioned your integrity.*
>
> *On top of all of that, what if a leading member of the president's party in Congress demanded your appearance before a congressional committee this week so that you could be interrogated about the Keystone XL oil pipeline project in which you have repeatedly—and accurately—stated that you have no involvement?*
>
> *Consider that all this is happening because you have been selected as an attractive political punching bag by the president's re-election team.*
>
> *This is precisely what has happened to Charles and David Koch, even though they are private citizens, and neither is a candidate for the president's or anyone else's office.*

In this country, we regard the use of official power to oppress or intimidate private citizens as a despicable abuse of authority and entirely alien to our system of a government of laws.

The architects of our Constitution meticulously erected a system of separated powers, and checks and balances, precisely in order to inhibit the exercise of tyrannical power by governmental officials.

Our Constitution even explicitly prohibits bills of attainder so that Congress may not single out individual citizens or groups for disfavored treatment or unequal application of the force of government.

Prosecutorial power is rigidly constrained and judicially supervised so that government may not accuse private citizens of crimes or investigate them without good cause.

Whoever may be the victim of such abuse of governmental authority, the press and public almost invariably unify with indignation against it.

If a journalist, labor-union leader or community organizer on the left can be targeted today, an academic or business person on the right can be the target tomorrow.

If we fail to stand up against oppression from one direction, we abdicate the moral authority to challenge it when it comes from another.

This is why it is exceedingly important for all Americans to respond with outrage to what the president and his allies are doing to demonize and stigmatize David and Charles Koch."[19]

In the weeks before and after this moving Patrick Henry-like column, Mr. Olsen repeatedly petitioned Obama to stop targeting the Koch brothers, to stop misusing federal power to attack political enemies, and to stop trampling on the Constitution. His pleas have been ignored. The attacks continue to this day.

And what is the motive for these attacks? What did the two brothers do to deserve the president's most corruptible artillery?

They made money in oil.

Billions, in fact. If these boys had been Jed Clampett—liberals would love him because Jed's not real and they love that. But David and Charles Koch of Koch Industries are very real. They've created jobs for more than 50,000 people in North America. *(In his first term, with all the resources at his disposal, Obama barely topped that!)* The brothers also give millions in no-strings-attached donations to . . . hospitals, higher education, and museums. Oh, and the brothers also contribute to organizations such as ***Americans For Prosperity***. *(There's the rub.)*

Because **Americans for Prosperity exists to promote liberty and free enterprise.**

And some would say that's just unacceptable to this president.

I disagree. I've listened to Obama rail against the Koch brothers. He often has a great deal of difficulty articulating *why* the Koch brothers are on the top of his enemies list—on a "Level 5" status.

And that's the tell. Obama gets real vague in his condemnation of the Koch brothers because, as we'll see in these pages, Obama actually loves business. Oh, we all know Obama is always lashing out at free enterprise. But look behind the curtain long enough and you begin to see that, in fact:

- ▶ Obama loves big business.
- ▶ As long as they contribute to his campaigns.
- ▶ Otherwise, he hates them.

If This Paints Obama as Hypocritical and Self-serving...
That's Because He Is

Think about it. Obama and the Democratic Party received nearly a billion dollars in the 2008 campaign thanks to the behind the scenes handiwork of businessman, investor, and felon George Soros. They loved that! It's not big business or Wall Street or bankers that Obama hates—all his crowd-pleasing stump speeches to the contrary.

Obama knows that getting elected today takes money. Lots. There's only one place where this kind of money exists. Not Main Street. Wall Street. So Obama lets the fat-cats know that as soon as he's done railing against them in pubic, he wants to meet in private to discuss whether they wish to punished, or rewarded.

This gives Obama tremendous and arbitrary power over the captains of industry and the big donors. They know the power of the IRS, SEC, INS, DOJ, DEA can be used to help them, or hurt them…the choice is theirs. This is the cutthroat game Obama is quarterbacking.

Obama Takes a Page from Nixon's Playbook

There are few stains on the White House as enduring and shameful as Richard Nixon's secret enemies list. Coming as it did in the midst of the Watergate scandal, the list was the subject of justifiable scorn. And it led to the president's resignation.

Americans were shocked to discover from White House Counsel, John Dean's testimony that Nixon intended to *use the available federal machinery to screw our political enemies* by means of IRS tax audits and by manipulating *grant availability, federal contracts, litigation, prosecution, etc.*

Now Obama's re-election campaign has taken a page from the Nixon's playbook. Only in their usually audacious way, **the Obama campaign didn't even try to hide the existence of the list. They took it not a step, but a projectile missile further and published it online, seeking to publicly intimidate with impunity.**

Democrats considered it an impeachable offense, when Nixon did it. Shouldn't they consider it an impeachable offense, now that Obama is doing it?

Indeed, as we see more and more Nixonian tendencies from this White House, shouldn't we all be concerned? There appears to be a red-hot fury building against anyone who dares criticize them. It's one thing when that criticism comes from *Fox News*, the Chamber of

Commerce, or a conservative think tank. But when it comes from a liberal on the plantation and still the White House lashes out—[like they did with Cory Booker], almost eager to hurt, and to ruin, then good people can begin regretfully to conclude that their first impressions about Obama were wrong.

Not just Nixonian, but McCarthyism

When in the 1950s, Senator Joseph McCarthy launched a similar campaign of government bullying, oppression and slander; he was rightfully censured and driven out of town. "McCarthyism" went into the dictionary as the "use of unfair investigative and accusatory methods to suppress opposition." It is now synonymous with un-Americanism. In the McCarthy hearings, Army counsel Joseph Welch famously asked of the powerful Senator, *"Have you no sense of decency?"*

That is the first question that must be asked now of this president. The second is…

Who Else is on the List? Who's Next to be Punished?

I will look at all the individuals and groups in America that I believe, based on what Obama has said publicly and I've dug up privately, that Obama intends to punish in his second term.

Are you on the list to be punished?

Are you being targeted for some kind of harassment?

I genuinely hope not. But I know many thousands of people—myself included—who have been targeted, who are on the list, who have reason to be afraid.

I take no comfort in sharing these stories and lists of enemies with you. But I am printing the whole long list online for a very important reason:

The more I can shine the bright lights of public condemnation on Obama and his surrogates, the safer we'll all be. In Stalinist Russia, the people on these kinds of lists just disappeared into the gulags—because there was nobody strong enough to stand up to the regime and force accountability. I surely do not compare Obama with

Stalin. **But I am standing up now to force accountability on Obama, and censure this kind of despicable behavior, so that we're all safer and our nation's dignity preserved.**

Stand with me, won't you?

I have created a special website with the entire list of names of Obama's enemies at http://www.obamasenemieslist.com. To access the list please use the **login name**: Patriot and the **password**: wewillnotbeintimidated.

At the website you can also stand with those being targeted by adding your name to the list to tell Obama he cannot punish us all.

SECTION II: Obama Punishes His Enemies

The Punished: Free Trade Advocates and Business Owners

Obama Wants America's Free Market Traditions to End

High on Obama's list of punishes is an organization that has for nearly four decades been praised by every sitting president for enabling the business greats such as Bill Gates, Meg Whitman, and Steve Jobs.

This organization had only one group of detractors: professional agitators from the furthest left wings of the Democratic Party. Previous Democrat presidents Jimmy Carter and Bill Clinton managed to shunt these agitators off into the closet with their crazy aunts.

Attacking ALEC

But Obama has called for the punishment of the ***American Legislative Exchange Council*** (ALEC) and they are a partnership of state legislators and businesses working to advance free-market legislation.[20] Their model proposals are introduced roughly 1,000 times a year in the state capitals by some 2,000 legislators, mostly Republicans. And they are proud of their success in achieving policy breakthroughs in teacher competency testing, pension reform, and enterprise zones to advance free enterprise across the nation.

No businessman or hard-working American has any beef with this agenda.

And yet ALEC now stands accused of crimes ranging from intimidating voters to enabling the shooting of young black men. Heading up the attacks is a man named Van Jones. You may recall that he was, until recently, one of the Obama's czars, as they are known. Okay, if Obama wants czars—who are best known for having lived the good life at the expense of the peasants—that's his call. The man was elected. As for Van Jones, he was Obama's "special advisor for Green Jobs, Enterprise and Innovation" – now keep the three pieces of his title in mind. Because as it happens, back in 2005 Van Jones co-founded a group named Color of Change, and they had two missions:

1. Obtain government money for friends in the black community
2. Attack all other enterprise and business innovation

Color of Change

It says so right on their website. Color of Change has joined with other far-left groups to bring down the "fatcats" who are "massively damaging" our country according to Obama.[21] Aligned in the fight are Common Cause, ProgressNow, the AFL-CIO, and The New Organizing Institute, all following Obama's lead to "escalate" the intimidation tactics and "never relent, never let up pressure, and always increase."[22]

And what do they mean by this?

They mean to stay relevant, to keep their jobs as professional agitators, at any cost. Like the flailing, drowning fellow in the surf who will pull his rescuer under if not subdued, these Obama operatives are out to pull our nation under at any cost. We'll let one of their own, Mary Boyle of Common Cause, make her own case. She told *Bloomberg Businessweek* recently that *"the Trayvon Martin thing was like a gift"* in their fight against ALEC. Her words.[23]

She didn't even bat an eye saying them. She shamefully used a tragic shooting as a way to attack the free enterprise system. Her eagerness to make political hay from a young man's death, when there was no linkage between a local shooting and a national free-market organization, was disgraceful. She didn't know who was at fault in the shooting—nobody did at the time. But she was willing to rush to judgment, see it as a chance to advance her radical agenda, and even to refer to a young man's awful death as a "thing."

When you're this desperate, you should be left on the fringes in the swamp you play in. All presidents have known this, until Obama. He praises these groups for carrying his dirty water for him.

But this hatred of free trade is nothing new. It harkens back to the *Manifesto of the Communist Party*, where it vilifies "***that single unconscionable freedom- Free Trade. In one word, for exploitation, veiled by religious and political illusions, it has substituted naked, shameless, direct, brutal exploitation.***" [24]

Color of Change is attacking free enterprise like lions attacking the herd, trying to identify the weakest companies and "focus on a few targets at a time," says spokesman Gabriel Rey-Goodlatte. This tactic, with the full backing of the powers of the presidency allows them to harass and "create a large discussion around a small group of companies," and moreover, demonstrate to other companies how painful the punishment could be "if their brand is the next to be brought into the public conversation." [25]

In excellent reporting on these anti-business slime-balls, **CJ Ciaramella** of *The Washington Free Beacon* discovered that Color of Change is targeting AT&T, Johnson & Johnson, State Farm, and Amazon.com. They are flooding these companies with "thousands of phone calls" and will "escalate pressure" with radio ads and possibly public actions against the companies.

All with Obama's implicit blessing, and explicit when he called out the "fatcats."

ALEC's real crime was brought clearly into focus by one of its members, another on Obama's enemies list, **Texas Public Policy Foundation**:

> *"For nearly four decades, [ALEC] has been an effective, engaged facilitator of good governance and liberty-oriented legislation in statehouses across the country. Its critics don't just object to one or two of the council's programs, they object to its existence.*

Their comments may be legitimate discourse, but this ought to be called what it is. It's a debate about the role of government in a free society. ALEC is for less government and more freedom. Its opponents are for more government, and the false security that government brings. We know from the lessons of history that earned, individual success is not only the key to happiness and progress, it is the bedrock of a just society. ALEC's advocacy is really for the American dream."[26]

Others who support ALEC including, the **Mackinac Center** in Michigan, **the Freedom Foundation** in Washington State, and the **Goldwater Institute** in Arizona, are also responsible for taking conservative free market positions. That is what they do. That has made them targets of an apparently vindictive president.

Worse, it has sent a message to the people of this country. The message:

That the free market doesn't work, that only government works. That top-down government control will create a better world for you. That this assertion has never been proven true is irrelevant to these believers in government, as the answer to everything. **Government is their religion and god.**

In his wonderful new book, *The Road to Freedom: How to Win the Fight for Free Enterprise*, **Arthur Brooks** tells of his youthful days spent in Spain where he learned that even as a foreigner he would always be guaranteed a job.[27] It was there he discovered the many differences between "earned success" and "learned helplessness." Brooks writes,

"Earned success means defining your future as you see fit and achieving that success on the basis of merit and hard work. It allows you to measure your life's 'profit' however you want… Earned success is at the root of American exceptionalism. The link between earned success and life satisfaction is well established by researchers…

"'Learned helplessness,' a term coined by Martin Seligman, the eminent psychologist at the University of Pennsylvania…refers

to what happens if rewards and punishments are not tied to merit: People simply give up and stop trying to succeed."[28]

Learned Helplessness like Old Europe

This learned helplessness was the model in social-democratic Spain and most all of Europe, and the reason they remain stuck in recession, the Eurozone falling apart, unemployment at 24% and higher, youth giving up trying to find work, half of the people up to age 35 still living with their parents.

The earned success model, on the other hand, is obviously the model of the United States and it has been actively promoted by ALEC for 39 years through seven supportive presidencies. Now they are being subjected to a full on assault and punishment scheme organized right from the Oval Office, or at least it might as well be. Because Obama has put his imprimatur on the playbook. He's telling every business in America, and every worker in America, that he prefers the socialism of Old-Europe, and the learned helplessness of old-Europe. And why?

As best as I can tell, Obama naturally believes in wealth distribution models over wealth creation models. He said so with his "spread the wealth" answer to **_Joe the Plummer_** in 2008.

Obama's Punishment of Corporate America, Punishes Us All

John Hawkins of *Right Wing News* offers a colorful view of this inhospitality to business:

> *"When Uday Hussein used to run Iraq's soccer team, players who performed poorly were slapped, spit on, and beaten with electric cables until the blood flowed. This is similar to how liberals treat American businesses. They demonize them, raise their taxes, bury them in new regulations, make it easier to sue them, and harass them with regulatory agencies at every turn. Then, they become puzzled as to why those same businesses aren't creating jobs or are looking to move more of their business*

overseas. You can't cut the sparrow's throat and fry it up for dinner and listen to it sing at the same time."[29]

Or, to extend Hawkins' metaphor, you can't isolate the sparrow in a cage and expect it to grow and multiply. And what is the guiding hand of a government bureaucrat, but a cage. Sure, it keeps the business from flying away (until the door is opened). In the meantime, the business lives in a state of anxiety, not knowing what to expect. It could lose profits via new taxes. It could see huge new expenses because of regulations. It could have projects shut down by the EPA. It could face huge lawsuits for spurious reasons. It could be crippled by labor union strikes. And on and on it goes in the government cage. **The business lives in a state of anxiety long enough, and it tends to become cautious and freezes. It doesn't hire. It doesn't expand.** As Hawkins quips,

> *"It hordes cash to make sure that it doesn't get wiped out by some arbitrary decision made by a government official who has never so much as run a lemonade stand in his life." [30]*

Or it takes an entirely different tact. It learns to survive by sucking off the public teat. It gears up its lobbying efforts and discovers which of the palms in Washington need the most greasing.

Why Can't Obama Be for Business and People?

Another man who's surely on Obama's enemies list is **_David Limbaugh_**. But he shouldn't be, at least not for suggesting recently to Obama that he doesn't need to drive a wedge between businesses and individuals. Limbaugh asked in Townhall:

> *"Why can't we be pro-corporation and pro-people? Shouldn't an American president be bullish on both? The answer is yes, but Obama can't be; his class-conscious ideology forbids it, and electoral imperatives demand that he demonize his political opponents, which is why his hype about all of us coming together as one rings so hollow…[31]*

Obama's class-conscious ideology stems from the **Manifesto of the Communist Party**, where it talks about "class antagonisms. Society …splitting up into two great hostile camps, into two great classes directly facing each other -Bourgeoisie and Proletariat." (a.k.a. business vs. the people).[32]

Attacking Capitalism Sells

Someone who knows quite a bit about "demonizing" in dramatic terms is ***David Mamet***, the brilliant playwright and longtime liberal who recently woke up to political reality and wrote about it in *The Secret Knowledge*. Mamet observed,

> *"As a youth I enjoyed-indeed, like most of my contemporaries, revered-the agitprop plays of Brecht, and his indictments of Capitalism. It later occurred to me that his plays were copyrighted, and that he, like I, was living through the operations of that same free market. His protestations were not borne out by his actions, neither could they be. Why, then, did he profess Communism? Because it sold. The public's endorsement of his plays kept him alive; as Marx was kept alive by the fortune Engels's family had made selling furniture; as universities, established and funded by the Free Enterprise system-which is to say by the accrual of wealth—house, support, and coddle generations of the young in their dissertations on the evils of America...[33]*

If there is an exact opposite of David Mamet in his life path and livelihood, it is ***Edward Conard*** of Bain Capital. He's a fabulously wealthy private equity investor, and he used to work at Bain Capital for Mitt Romney. Conard also released a book recently, titled *Unintended Consequences: Why Everything You've Been Told About the Economy Is Wrong*.[34] What's fascinating about this must-read book is Conard's candor. He says the things that have been largely snuffed out—for fear of offending the refined sensibilities of the PC crowd.

Why Fat-Cats Benefit Everyone

Conard argues that the growing income inequality in this country is a good thing! He says it's a "sign our economy is working." He tells how consumers benefit from the wealthy in ways that few understand. That's because the wealthy spend only a small percentage of their money on their daily needs. **Most of their money is spent on building businesses that make life better for everyone. And those businesses return five times the value to society. That is, for every dollar invested in those companies, the public receives five dollars of value.** *"The Google founder Sergey Brin might be very rich,"* he points out, *"but the world is far richer than he is because of Google."*

In a *New York Times* interview, Conard gave some real world examples of how this "5 to 1" wealth creation ratio benefits everyday people. Conard picked up a soda pop can and pointed to the chamfered edge that makes the can stronger while using less aluminum:

> *"It saves a fraction of a penny on every can…. That means the economy can produce more cans with the same amount of resources. It makes every American who buys a soda can a little bit richer because their paycheck buys more."*[35]

Conard's point is that we all "live longer, healthier and richer lives because of countless microimprovements like that one." And that little improvement in the age old can was the result of engineers and scientists and, yes, initially, wealthy investors like Conard who was willing to risk his money to underwrite an idea that might work, might not. "While we often hear about the greatest successes — penicillin, the iPhone — we rarely hear about the countless failures and the people and companies who financed them."[36]

What's more, we don't yet know that some kid is working on in his garage, driven by dreams of glory and untold riches. But we need that kid to dream. We cannot hope to understand what he or she is dreaming of, just as we could not predict airplanes in the early 1800s, or personal computers in the early 1900s. But we know that free enterprise's often wild-paced course will take us to the next unpredictable wonder. Big government's heavy foot will not.

These ideas were accepted as central to our nation until this administration came along and decided to attack them. Whether the attack was based on principle, or the ends justifying the means, is ultimately irrelevant. Arguing whether Obama's acts are sins of omission or commission only stirs the pot, further divides, and sends an electorate spinning around in circles. Again from the artful pen of the playwright David Mamet:

> *"The Good Causes of the Left may generally be compared to NASCAR; they offer the diversion of watching things go excitingly around in a circle, getting nowhere.* [37]

The Punished: Homeowners, the Economy and the Unemployed
Homeowners Who Played by the Rules Suffer

So much has been said about the housing crash that ripped $7 trillion in equity from homeowners, it can now be chunked down into a quick 3-act play—however dissatisfying the finale.

So to be clear, Obama deserves only a third of the credit for the punishment now being meted out to hard-working homeowners who played by the rules . . . didn't cheat, didn't prevaricate . . . and are now stuck in an upside-down housing market that evidences no signs of recovery until, best case, 2020.

So yes, only a third of the blame on Obama—but it is he who asked for a performance review and to be re-elected; the historians are left to judge past office holders.

Bankers and Politicians Come Before Homeowners

Obama decided from the get-go, in hiring the banker's banker, Timothy Geithner, to run the Treasury, and that the interests of a few thousand bankers and politicians should come before the interests of the economy and homeowners. The message was clear:

The bloated incompetents on Wall Street would be allowed to grow even larger and more incompetent. And if anything ever went wrong with these private sector players—not to worry, bailout teams stood at the ready. That's what the Fed is for, right? The nation's four largest banks account for 55% of all home loans, up from 38% in 2004.[38] These banks have devolved from "too big to fail" to "too big to succeed."

And they don't mind.

They know the taxpayers and the Fed stand ready to catch their next fall. They're safe. All that's required is they take Obama's slashing populist rhetoric on the chin. He slams them by day, shakes them down at night, and everyone's happy. It's the Chicago way.

Obama Shuffle Steps with Bankers

And if by chance some reporter in the Left-stream Media gets a sudden attack of conscience, and calls either Obama or Wall Street on the scam, they have a quick reply at the ready. It's the same reply that Treasury secretary Hank Paulson opened every speech with during the Bush segment of bailouts. They just insist that the entire world's financial system would surely have collapsed had they not thrown trillions of dollars of money at the problem (yes, trillions have been spent when you add it all up). They make this claim as if it's fact, when clearly we can't ever know.

It's like saying x would be worse if not for y. Can't know. But saying the equivalent of "it's less bad than it would have been otherwise," is not leadership.

All we can know for sure is that **the Obama administration borrowed so much that there was no money left for ordinary homeowners**. Or when there was money, **the bankers had no incentive to lend to risky individuals when they were allowed to borrow from the Fed at zero interest, invest that money in bonds paying 2 to 3 percent, then leverage those purchases 20 times to get 60% return on their money—virtually risk free.**

Banks Don't Want to Lend

I contacted the main lenders – Bank of America, Wells Fargo, Citigroup, Chase – in March 2012 to ask about refinancing my mortgage. I was told that essentially the 'pipeline was full' and the lender was 'swamped with business' – they would call me back in 60 to 90 days. I wanted to give them business; they put me on a waiting list. That's when I had a V8 moment – as in, of course, banks are government wards now. They have little incentive to perform.

Fewer banks control the mortgage market now. The nation's biggest lenders take more than 70 days to complete a refinance, according to Accenture Credit Services, up from 45 days a year ago.[39] And with reduced competition, large lenders can jack-up their rates while processing fewer applications – overall boosting profits with less risk. Back before the housing crisis, the 'spread' between the cost of money to the banks and the rate they charged borrowers averaged a half percentage point. That gap has doubled since 2009.[40]

This is the kind of thing Obama rails abut on the stump, but does nothing to stop.

(Note: I'm not saying Obama *should* interfere in the free market other than with basic common sense regulation; but since he has interfered in a massive way, he should at least instruct his wards to help out the people who pay the taxes that keep the bankers artificially in business.)

Upturn Can't Come from Real Estate

Normally in a financial downturn like we're now experiencing, it is movement in real estate and refinancing that kicks the recovery into high gear. But it's not happening this time, and it's no mystery why. After four years of sleeping with the enemy, Obama is now eager for a showcase event that demonstrates how deeply he cares about his friends who owe more than their homes are worth. He's calling for legislation and calling it long-overdue. It is, and it took him four long years to do the wrong thing.

Bailing out people who can't afford their homes does not change the situation—they still can't afford their homes, whatever their reason. But those who can afford their homes, those who have been faithfully paying their mortgages, they are the ones punished.

And that's most of America.

Homes in foreclosure topped 1.1 million in 2008 at the peak of the crisis—that sounds awful until put into perspective. Looked at differently, it meant that by 2012 in Sacramento, for example, 1 in 209 homes was in foreclosure. Or Atlanta, 1 in 250 homes was in foreclosure. Or in Fort Lauderdale, 1 in 290 homes was in foreclosure. The list goes on and on, according to RealtyTrac.[41] And looked at this way, it's clear that there's a big old silent majority of homeowners who are "above water."[42] They are the ones punished here because Obama proposes to pay for his plan by taxing banks. Those banks then turn around and pass that fee onto other borrowers. All of us. The problem hasn't been solved—not that Obama could solve it if we wanted; only the market can do that. But we are still being punished.

Obama's Arrogance is Bigger than Ever Despite His Failures

Any other president would be in such hot water right now.

Except Obama's buddies in the main stream media keep giving him a break. Can you image stiff George Bush with his exasperating speaking style hopping up onto the podium before thousands of cheering partisans, and with Fleetwood Mac playing in the background, "Don't stop thinking about tomorrow," shouting out to the assembled true believers that basically, 'These first four years we're sure a bust—but the next four are going to blow your socks off!' And everyone whoops and hollers. What a charge!

Most of us would get caught with a big old guilty look on our face as we did our best to explain why just about everything we tried in the first four years . . . didn't work.

The Stimulus Was Going to Create Millions of Jobs

High on the list of people being punished by Obama are the 12.5 million Americans who are still, four years after being promised jobs, without one.

Let's be clear: No president could have driven down the unemployment rate in a short year or two—no matter which policies he pursued.

But Obama made a promise to America—a solemn promise backed by an even more solemn oath, that he would drive unemployment down to 6% by this year. And a man should keep his promises, or not make them.

Obama's promise to the nation began in January 2009 when Christina Romer, Obama's top economist, published the new administration's analysis of the jobs that would be created when Obama threw $787 billion in stimulus spending at the problem. At the time, the country's overall unemployment rate was 7.8% (Bureau of Labor Statistics). Romer told Congress that if they approved the stimulus spending, the unemployment would not rise above 8% and would in fact fall below 6% in 2012.

Let's not forget all of Obama's fear mongering and dire predictions he drummed up to get Congress to pass the failed stimulus bill.

Today the rate appears stuck above 8% and our nation's job seekers have nothing to show for nearly a trillion dollars in taxpayer spending on their behalf. That's punishing.

We have no idea how Obama manages to keep a straight face in view of this. In other forms of government, we would be asked to resign. Obama's response: the economy would be in worse shape if *"we go right back to the policies that created this mess."* When he first started trotting out this line of defense, his top economist Christine Romer decided it was time to return to academia. In resigning, she admitted that she never believed the nation's economy could be fixed with massive stimulus spending. She's even written a dissertation on the subject. But that's what Obama wanted, so she had tried her best to sell it.

Even if the Stimulus Had Worked, At What Cost?
A closer look at Obama's stimulus spending reveals even more punishment.

You will note that Obama did not mention the stimulus package in his campaign speeches, for good reason. He knows the reality of what it became. He knows that his own economist was not alone in her critique. He knows that other economists with lots of government experience, such as **_Lawrence Lindsey_** who served under George W. Bush, have made the case that the stimulus spending may have been the most reckless, economy-punishing, jobs-killing legislation in our history. Writing in the *Weekly Standard*, Lindsey said:

> *"Everyone except flacks for the White House knows that the 2009 stimulus package failed miserably to produce the promised results. But even if you buy the White House's argument that the $800 billion package created 3 million jobs, that works out to $266,000 per job. Taxing or borrowing $266,000 from the private sector to create a single job is simply not a cost effective way of putting America back to work. The long-term debt burden of that $266,000 swamps any benefit that the single job created might provide."[43]*

It's hard to swallow that kind of math: Spend $266,000 of our money to create one low-paying job for someone else. Sadly, it gets worse. Far worse.

Because the Congressional Budget Office just updated its figures. The CBO says the stimulus will now cost $831 billion . . . and end up creating between 200,000 to 1.2 million jobs that otherwise would not have been created. Taking the most optimistic number of 1.2 million new jobs, and adjusting the math, we see that Obama bought jobs for people at a cost to the taxpayers of *$692,500* per job![44]

Is there a word to describe that kind of wasteful spending? "Absurd" seems woefully inadequate.

Which is Why We're Stuck in a 60-year Economic Low

Obama took office in a terrible economy, yes. But then according to the stats guys at the National Bureau of Economic Research, the 'recession' ended in June 2009. Three years ago. Since then, America has been stumbling along at an anemic growth rate. One to two percent growth a year. In fact, no U.S. president since World War II has gone almost his entire first term without seeing at least one quarter of economic growth at 4% or higher—Obama is the first to earn that dubious distinction.[45]

And as for the people Obama promised jobs? He's still promising—trying out new rhetoric, but intending to rely on the same programs to create jobs. The same programs that, as I write, have our nation stalled at 2.2% annualized growth . . . with roughly 23 million people classified as either unemployed, underemployed, or no-longer-looking . . . and the average household being $4,300 poorer in Obama's tenure. It's a rather forceful indictment of the administration's economic policies.

Economists of the Right and Left—Both Shaking their Heads

Obama's economic policies do have a few supporters among practitioners of the dismal science. But CNBC economic analyst **_Larry Kudlow_**, himself a fierce critic of the president's policies if not the president, recently did a round-up of economic opinion among the nation's top economists. Kudlow found, in summary:

> "Stanford economist John Taylor argues that every dollar taken from the private sector and channeled to the public-sector for government spending produces a GDP multiplier of less than one . . . which is why the economy has gotten worse under Obama's big-government policies. He would have been better off leaving the money in private hands.
>
> Nobel Prize winner Gary Becker blames the current jobs deficit on the failure to resolve the budget and debt-ceiling issues, the lack of serious entitlement reform, and the absence of pro-growth tax reform toward broader and flatter tax rates.
>
> University of Chicago professor Casey Mulligan and Stanford professor Ed Lazear blame the current economic situation on the proliferation and eligibility expansion of transfer payments

such as Medicaid, Social Security, disability, food stamps, and extended unemployment benefits.

Economic historian Mike Bordo just completed a study that shows how deep recessions are always followed by strong spring-back recoveries—all except this one.

And University of Chicago professor John Cochrane argues that the failure to get a strong recovery is not because of the financial crisis, but because of stupid policies." [46]

Obama's Economic Record in Black and White

	January 2009	June 2012	Percent Change	Damage Caused
Gallon of gas (avg. nationally[1])	$1.83	$3.75	**+204%**	
Barrel of crude oil (West TX Inter[2])	$38.74	$91.38	**+135.9%**	
Gold (troy oz., London[2])	$853.25	$1,369.50	**+60.5%**	
Corn (No.2 yellow[2])	$3.56	$6.33	**+78.1%**	
Sugar (raw cane, lb. [2])	$13..37	$35..39	**+164.7%**	
Number of unemployed[3]	11,616,000	14,485,000	**+24.7%**	
Number of Federal employees[3]	2,779,000	2,840,000	**+2.2%**	
Number of food stamp recipients[4]	31,983,716	43,200,878	**+35.1%**	
Number of people in poverty[5]	39,800,000	43,600,000	**+9.5%**	
Household income (median)[5]	$50,112	$49,777	**-0.7%**	
National debt, in trillions[6]	$10.627	$14.052	**+32.2%**	

Sources: (1) U.S. Energy Information Administration; (2) Wall Street Journal; (3) Bureau of Labor Statistics; (5) Census Bureau; (4) USDA; (6) U.S. Treasury

In the Obama "Plus" Column, the Stock Market is Up

In fairness to the president, the stock market has shot up 55% under President Obama. The Dow stood at 8,077 the week after Inaugural Day, and it's at 12,930 as I write. Of course Obama took over after a spectacular crash, and the Dow has only now crawled back to where it was briefly in 2000 and 2007, but it has crawled back. Is this due to Obama's policies?

We cannot know yet because Obama has done little if anything to change the "status quo" on Wall Street. Maybe his inaction has been a good thing. Or maybe we're about to see how well investors will fare—when Obama gets what he wants on the tax front.

Obama has pledged to double capital gains rates from 15% to 30%, and that is certain to scare investors and trigger a torrent of end-of-year stock sales and falling stock prices. Then Obama wants to triple the tax on dividends—yes, triple**.** It works like this.

Obama has proposed to raise the dividend rate to match the higher personal income tax rate of 39.6% that we'll see in 2013. Then Obama wants to phase-out certain deductions and exemptions, taking the dividend rate to 41%. Then Obama wants to add a 3.8% investment tax surcharge in ObamaCare. **Add them all up, and you have a dividend tax rate in 2013 of 44.8%—nearly three times today's 15% rate.**

And don't forget, these dividends are paid only after the corporation pays taxes on its profits. So really what you have is a maximum corporate tax rate of 35%, along with a dividend tax of 44.8%, which equals a real tax rate on dividends of 64.1**%. I can't see how investors are going to be excited about risk-taking in the stock market when nearly two-thirds of any earnings are going to be snatched up by the federal government.**

And so I fully expect a stock market crash in 2013 taking the Dow back down to the 8,000 neighborhood where it was when he started.

The Fierce Psychological Punishment is Harder to Quantify...But Very Real

Obama's inability to revive the economy has had a psychological component, as well. It has turned a nation renowned for its optimism and belief in a better tomorrow, into an unruly hoard of doubters, complainers, and defeatists.

A recent poll by Scott Rasmussen's company found that 63% of the country – across all political groups – think today's children will have it worse than their parents. Though with a hint of optimism, 53% say it's still possible for people to work themselves out of poverty in this country. Looking for a silver lining in this, Michael Reagan quipped as how…

> *"That's a good thing to believe in, because by the time the Obama administration and his wrecking crew finish turning America into Greece, 53 percent of the country is going to be poor.*[47]

Are You Better Off Than You were Four Years Ago?

Roosevelt is believed to have been the first to ask this clever question in a 1934 radio fireside chat when he spoke about the upcoming election:

> *"The simplest way for each of you to judge recovery lies in the plain facts of your individual situation. Are you better off than you were last year? Are your debts less burdensome? Is your bank account more secure? Are your working conditions better? Is your faith in your own individual future more firmly grounded?"*

Ronald Reagan next used the question in 1980, and nobody in the media (which generally hated Reagan) could recall the earlier use and so they ate it up—it was so potent. This one line was a big contributor to Carter's loss—because a nation could look at their situation and see that, in fact, they were much worse off than four years earlier. Now we ask it in every election, and it is fitting that we do. It is also somehow fitting that Reagan's son Michael sums up whether we are better off today than when Obama became chief executive. **_Michael Reagan_** says,

> *"The only person I know who is better off today than he was four years ago is President Obama. He's making more money, living in a bigger house and playing more golf. And when his wife goes on a shopping spree with her girlfriends, it's to Spain on the taxpayer's dime. If you asked President Obama if he's better off today, he'd say, "Hell, yeah! And we don't want it to stop!"*[48]

I have created a special website with the entire list of names of Obama's enemies at http://www.obamasenemieslist.com. To access the list please use the **login name**: Patriot and the **password**: wewillnotbeintimidated.

At the website you can also stand with those being targeted by adding your name to the list to tell Obama he cannot punish us all.

The Punished: Paul Ryan's Budget Plan & Most Americans
Obama Goes Ballistic over Paul Ryan's Budget, Resorts to Name-Calling

In compiling Obama's Enemies List, I found a number of people who are no doubt right at the very top of the list that sits on Obama's computer, password protected. If I had to guess who Obama would paint as Public Enemy #1, it is probably the soft-spoken young Congressman from Wisconsin's 1st District and Vice Presidential candidate, **_Paul Ryan_**.

More than anybody, Paul Ryan has succeeded in demonstrating to the nation that the Emperor has neither clothes nor talent for running the country. And this assault of the very core of Obama's credibility has the president's campaign managers practically frothing at the mouth. **_Daniel Henninger_** of the Wall Street Journal had some fun in characterizing the froth—if only it was funny:

> _"With the presidential battle begun, the Obama campaign has revived the Cold War nuclear strategy of launch on warning. At any suggestion that a conservative idea might be threatening its ideological fortress, the American left now launches ICBMs of rhetorical destruction._

> _"On current course, House GOP Budget Chairman Paul Ryan himself may exhaust their entire thermonuclear arsenal before November. Once again, the Campaigner in Chief threw the switch himself, calling the Ryan House budget "social Darwinism," "a Trojan horse" and "antithetical to our entire history."_

> _"Paul Ryan's ideas are worse than wrong. They are heresy."_[49]

And what terrible deed did the Republican Congressman from Wisconsin do to deserve such spleen-ripping vitriol?

Paul Ryan offered a budget alternative to Congress. That's it.

45

Ryan's Crime was Recognizing the Depth of the Debt Hole

Paul Ryan is a smart guy. He knows the federal government is spending more than $350 billion a month, or about $1,200 per average American. And he knows that that average American only pays $550 in taxes a month, covering less than half of Obama's spending. This would send that average American to the poorhouse in no time, and it will do the same to the nation. We can't know how it will play out, only that it will—sooner or later.

Ryan has the audacity to say as much, by submitting a budget to Congress that stops the 'pretend act' and at least takes a stab of reining in future spending. And it wasn't that much of a stab. Instead of spending $47 Trillion that we don't have over the next 10 years, Ryan wants to spend only $40 Trillion that we don't have. This should have started a laugh riot—since both budgets leave future generations in a heap of pain. Ryan's budget was just 15% smaller than Obama's—around our house we make 15% cuts all the time—it's just what you do when you're spending your own money.

Obama Attacks, Calls Ryan's Budget Proposal *"Social Darwinism"*

No doubt Obama attacked because he felt embarrassed, humiliated even, that his own budget was rejected by Democrats and Republicans alike while Ryan's budget enjoyed bipartisan support. Here's a little more telling detail of the speech Obama gave in April 2012 on the subject of how nasty, brutish and short life in America would if Ryan's budget were allowed to pass:

> *"The year after next, nearly 10 million college students would see their financial aid cut by an average of more than $1,000 each. There would be 1,600 fewer medical grants. Research grants for things like Alzheimer's and cancer and AIDS. There would be 4,000 fewer scientific research grants, eliminating support for 48,000 researchers, students and teachers.*

"Investments in clean energy technology that are helping us reduce our dependence on foreign oil would be cut by nearly a fifth. [O]ver 200,000 children would lose their chance to get an early education in the Head Start program. Two million mothers and young children would be cut from a program that gives them access to healthy food.

"There would be 4,500 fewer federal grants at the Department of Justice and the FBI to combat violent crime, financial crime, and secure our borders. Hundreds of national parks would be forced to close for part or all of the year. We wouldn't have the capacity to enforce the laws that protect the air we breathe, the water we drink, or the food that we eat.

"Cuts to the FAA would likely result in more flight cancellations, delays and the complete elimination of air traffic control services in parts of the country. Over time, our weather forecasts would become less accurate because we wouldn't be able to afford to launch new satellites and that means governors and mayors would have to wait longer to order evacuations in the event of a hurricane."[50]

If you just listen to this flowery speech without filters, you can't help but side with Obama—who'd want to cut so many important programs so heartlessly?

Obama Uses a Lawyer's Sleight of Hand to Lie and Scare People

But there are people with good filters. People like **_Peter Ferrara_**, a longtime Washington insider who has served at the highest levels of the White House and Justice Department. Most recently he authored *America's Ticking Bankruptcy Bomb*—to call attention to the terrible debt reckoning we face as a nation.[51] When Ferrara heard Obama's April 3 speech to reporters, he could see that the president was employing a lawyerly sleight of noun and verb.

Ferrara noted that Obama said, *"I want to actually go through what it would mean for our country if these cuts were to be spread out evenly"* and then Obama added the caveat, *"if this budget becomes law, and the cuts were evenly applied starting in 2014."* In other words, Ferrara notes, *"Obama's speech itself tells us this is all made up."*

Obama and his speechwriters figured out *"the percentage of total spending cuts in Ryan's budget, and then applied that same percentage to every politically sensitive line item in the budget."* Of course, Ryan's budget does no such thing. His budget simply returns federal spending to its long-term *"average of 20% of GDP, which prevailed for 60 years before President Obama and his runaway spending. With that manageable federal spending, America prospered as the richest and mightiest nation in the history of the planet."*

That didn't stop Obama from attacking Ryan day after day, calling Ryan's budget *"an attempt to impose a radical vision on our country... thinly veiled social Darwinism... antithetical to our entire history as a land of opportunity and upward mobility."* Clearly Obama had no interest in an honest, intelligent discussion of the financial crisis our country faces.

Obama's scorched earth campaign strategy did not even trying to solve the huge financial problems that he and his predecessor got us into. One final observation from Ferrara:

> *"The President, in fact, does not understand the major issues facing the country, indeed, he actually can't even discuss them intelligently. Moreover, he is hopelessly, abusively dishonest about what he does understand. Thirdly, what he is demanding as policy is irreconcilable left-wing extremism. Fourthly, what the speech shows is that Barack Obama is very angry. He is angry because he has been completely shown up by Paul Ryan, who stepped up in his budget and provided the leadership that Obama promised America in 2008, and America so badly needs, but that Obama has not only failed to deliver, but refused to deliver."[52]*

When Obama's last budget proposal was put to a vote in the House, it got exactly zero votes. Zippo-Nada-Zilch. Not a single *Democrat* would vote for it. The House passed Ryan's budget instead. Last year, when Obama's budget was put to a vote in the Senate, it got the exact same zero votes. That is why Obama is so angry, and embarrassed.

Angry and Embarrassed, Obama Blames Everyone but Himself

With all that has gone wrong for him, Obama entered the re-election period with a scapegoat for everything, a growing list of perceived enemies to punish, and a shabby disregard for the dignity of the office he holds. He is not even trying to look the part of a president. Another leader of a very different sort is **_Jack Welch_**, the renowned former CEO of General Electric who built the company into a global powerhouse under his term. In looking at Obama's seemingly desperate re-election strategy, Welch comments:

> *"Obama has taken a sort of divide-and-conquer approach, amassing a list of enemies that would make Richard Nixon proud — bankers, health care insurance providers, oil companies, wealthy taxpayers, Congress and, most recently, the Supreme Court.*

> *"Gas prices are the fault of oil speculators. The failure of solar power companies is the fault of unfair Chinese competition. The bad economy is one of the many things he inherited, as is the deficit. Operation Fast and Furious was a program begun under the Bush administration that he knew nothing about. The deficit is skyrocketing because the rich aren't paying their 'fair share.'*

> *"While Obama says he wants an 'America that can last,' we long for a president who can govern, who sits in the Oval Office in this time of crisis instead of jet-setting from one fundraiser to another. Ronald Reagan worked with Tip O'Neill. Bill Clinton worked with Newt Gingrich. Obama couldn't work with Harry Reid and Nancy Pelosi to produce a budget as deficits soared."*[53]

And oh, how those deficits soared. Chew on this tidbit for a moment: In our nation's entire history through 2000, we ran up debts of $5.7 trillion in total. Then George Bush took over and spent like a madman—running the federal debt to $10.6 trillion. Then Barack Obama took over and spent like a battalion of madmen—and the federal debt is today $16.3 trillion.

When White House spokesman Jay Carney tried recently to cover up the BP-sized spill of red ink coming from this administration, the *Washington Post* Fact Checker Glenn Kessler gave Carney's performance *"three Pinocchios"* which, loosely translated, means it was an unimaginative lie.[54]

Now if Obama had spent fast and furiously, and then could today show some kind of results for his efforts, the nation could support him. But he spent fast and furiously and has very little to show for it except record numbers of people are still out of work, with no hope in sight.

I have created a special website with the entire list of names of Obama's enemies at http://www.obamasenemieslist.com. To access the list please use the login name: Patriot and the password: wewillnotbeintimidated.

At the website you can also stand with those being targeted by adding your name to the list to tell Obama he cannot punish us all.

The Punished: Taxpayers, Investors and Young People
IRS Website Reveals Fraud of "Buffett Rule"

It is becoming the accepted line that Obama is a better campaigner than leader, that he can run the 100-meter dash like nobody's business, but don't stick him in the marathon of the presidency. Obama himself hinted as much about himself in the 2008 election when he attacked John McCain by saying:

> *"If you don't have a record to run on, then you paint your opponent as someone people should run from....You make a big election about small things."*[55]

Now you could agree or disagree with McCain's record of service, but the man did have one—a long one, in fact, that had begun three years before Obama was born. But Obama lashed into McCain with these kinds of words anyway, and in so doing revealed his own insights into running for office. "You make a big election about small things," he said.

And that's what he did.

So as his re-election campaign kicked off, Obama rolled out his biggest gun: Warren Buffett—beloved investor, successful business-man, American icon. Nobody could argue with an endorsement like that. Buffett did a fine job of telling the world that his secretary is stuck with a higher tax rate than he is. That's just not fair, Buffett insisted, as Obama looked on approvingly.

From this opening salvo in the campaign came the "Buffett Rule" which Obama ensured the nation was necessary so that the 1,470 millionaires who paid no federal income tax in 2009 would begin paying at a 30% tax rate.

Several weeks would pass before we learned just how 'small' this election ploy really was.

In the meantime, Obama's legions of unquestioning supporters had their marching orders. They were going to bring a new fairness to the land—a 'bringing of fairness' that had somehow eluded Obama in this first four years, but no matter . . . *forward!*

The concept was admirable enough. If the rich are getting way too rich, and poor getting way to poor, as it was explained to Obama's supporters, then there needs to be some leveling. Some income redis-tribution. On face value, who could disagree? Lord knows that back in the times of castles and kings, the guys on the inside were gorging and the guys on the outside were starving. That wasn't right, wasn't fair. And Obama made that case as eloquently as many alive possibly could. He stood before dozens of audiences asking in earnest, if it was fair that people who are making more than a million dollars a year pay less in taxes than the average middle-class worker?

Who could argue with a question like that, if it was in fact an honest question?

A quick visit to the IRS's own website, which I've done several times now in these pages, tells us that **the top 10% of earners have been paying about 70% of the taxes, and the bottom 50% have been paying about 3% of the tax load**. Not exactly a picture of serfs handing over all the fruits of their labor to the overlord on the hill.

But let's keep at this. Let's stipulate that there are things government does that are good, and they have to be paid for. The citizens have to pay taxes. The government has to collect the taxes. They have to be forceful about it—since as we'll see shortly; nobody ever pays a dime more than they're legally required to. We don't want our government to roll out the "brute squad" but we do need to have taxes collected and federal coffers filled. So what have Obama and the Democrats who control the Senate done in these last four years to fill the coffers with such badly needed revenue?

Nothing.

How Many Tax Loopholes Has Obama Closed?

Has Obama tried to close any of the loopholes in the tax code that the rich are notorious for leaping through? Actually no. Not a single loophole closed and the tax code is still, after four years of Obama's fairness rhetoric, a complete and utter abomination. It's 3.8 million words long—about 50 times longer than this book. We spend an estimated 7.6 billion hours in addition to hundreds of billions of dollars trying to comply with federal tax requirements. Bottom line:

- ▶ The dishonest are rewarded for cheating on their taxes
- ▶ The ultra-wealthy have moved trillions of dollars to offshore tax havens
- ▶ The hard-working middle class are punished for trying to do the right thing

The current tax code is utterly broken and almost beyond repair. Unfortunately, neither the Democrats nor the Republicans are proposing that we should get rid of it. No politician yet elected seems willing to tackle the IRS monster head-on. Any hope of change seems likely to come from legislation in Congress.

So we ask, what legislation has been advanced to bring the fairness Obama says he seeks?

Obama and the Senate Democrats did write some legislation seeking to subject America's taxpayers to a little fairness. The bill was known as the "Paying a Fair Share Act." Sounds pretty good, but the bill died a quick death when the Democrat-controlled Senate threatened to filibuster it.[56] Hmmm. The bill never even made it to the floor to be argued. It just died in some back room . . . which is why I suspect that the whole act was a show piece. A big dirty shovel full of hornswoggle for the unquestioning faithful back home.

"Buffet Rule" Re-election Gimmick

Let's return to the cameo performance Warren Buffett gave Obama. When Obama first announced his 'Buffett Rule,' he said it would help *"stabilize our debt and deficits over the next decade."* Okay. So the bean counters went to work and try as they might, they found that the new 30% millionaire's tax would raise only $46.7 billion over 10 years, and would leave about 99.5% of the deficit intact in 2013. A far cry from "stabilizing the debt."[57]

So Obama did a quick stutter step. He came out with a new fairness tax . . . a *new* Buffett rule. His goal, as we suggested from the start, was to keep people distracted by the "small things" so they wouldn't notice the big failures. Or the lies.

For the truth is, the wealthy *do not* pay a lower tax rate than the middle class. Glenn Beck's producer and head writer, ***Stu Burguiere***, proved as much. He went to the IRS website—hard to argue with that source. He quoted the *Associated Press*—as nonpartisan source as exists in our world. "Stu" as he's known, wasn't trying to entertain, as he often does, but to educate. And in so doing he broke down the truth from the convenient fictions Warren Buffett was telling. [58] A few of them merit a mention here:

The typical person making between $50,000 and $75,000 a year pays an effective rate of about 14%, or if married 7.6%. This is according to the IRS. And this is far less than the 30% Buffett claims his secretary was paying—even if you add in payroll tax.

Rich people pay more than the middle class in both total dollars and percentage terms. A third-party analysis from Stephen Ohlemacher of the *Associated Press* concluded: "This year, households making more than $1 million will pay an average of 29.1% of their income in federal taxes, including income taxes and payroll taxes... Households making between **$50,000 and $75,000 will pay 15%** of their income in federal taxes."[59] Those numbers aren't even close to what Buffett is claiming.

Obama Admits "Buffet Rule" Won't Help

When you read all of this, and run down the sources, and see how credible they are, you can see why Obama felt he had to face reporters and admit that, in fact, the Buffett Rule had been one big election-year gimmick. This is the president speaking:

> "There are others who are saying: 'Well, this is just a gimmick. Just taxing millionaires and billionaires, just imposing the Buffett Rule, won't do enough to close the deficit. Well, I agree."[60]

Really?

Did the President of the United States just admit that he was trying to run a grand ruse past the American people? Apparently so. And in the press room, you'd expected even that jaded bunch to be stunned, and then to hop up and run out to the TV cameras to report: "President calls self liar."

But none of that happened.

The press practically yawned in unison when **Obama made this startling admission that millions of dollars of taxpayer money had**

been devoted to selling the Buffett Rule, and it was all a ruse, a ploy, a stunt—call it what you will.

Everyone assembled already knew the truth.

Before the president spoke, reporters had been herded into the room through hallways filled with campaign photos showing Obama touring factories and kissing babies. Then up on stage there were heavyweight props: four millionaires, and their four middle-class assistants. All smiling and nodding at just the right cues, and with such precision, that *Washington Post* reporter Dana Milbank wondered if Obama was *"sharing the stage with eight bobbleheads."*[61]

Obama's Phony Fairness

"You make a big election about small things," Obama said. He knew he had to keep voters focused on dead-end, phony fairness junkets so that they didn't spend too much time asking the big important questions. Questions such as:

> *"Mr. President, when you create this special whopper of a tax for the 4,000 taxpayers making more than a million a year—how will that help the nation's economy and create jobs that are needed?"*

I suspect the whole Buffett Rule charade, not to mention all the time and money the White House spent trying to foist that charade on the American people, actually backfired on Obama. It put into black and white clarity the elitist snobbery of Obama and Buffett. Those two would tell us how to do the right thing for our country when they themselves have yet to ante up. Journalism Mark Landsbaum of the *Orange County Register* gave a big appropriate shout-out to Obama and Buffett on this:

> *"We agree with President Barack Obama. If any millionaires or billionaires don't feel they are paying enough in federal taxes, they should pay more. We don't wish to see really rich people wallowing in guilt. Warren Buffett and friends, get out your checkbooks. Nothing's stopping you. Patriotic millionaires, get out your checkbooks."*[62]

The Truth about Tax Increases under Obama

Stumping for his 'Buffett Rule' tax increase on the wealthy, Obama said over and over again to audiences in state after state:

> *"For those people who make under $250,000 a year – like 98% of American families do – then your taxes don't go up."[63]*

And in fact one of Obama's central campaign promises in 2008 was a "firm pledge" against "any form of tax increase" on families making less than $250,000 per year. **But since taking office, Obama has increased taxes *seven* times, and he did it all with the single stroke of the pen—when he signed the "Affordable Care Act" into law.** The watchdogs at Americans for Tax Reform identified seven violations of Obama's pledge—all attributable to Obamacare legislation. Here are the violations, straight from **John Kartch** at Americans for Tax Reform:[64]

1. The Obamacare Individual Mandate Excise Tax: Starting in 2014, anyone not buying "qualifying" health insurance—as defined by Obama-appointed bureaucrats—must pay an income surtax according to the higher of the following:

	1 Adult	2 Adults	3+ Adults
2014	1% AGI / $95	1% AGI / $190	1% AGI / $285
2015	2% AGI / $325	2% AGI / $650	2% AGI / $975
2016	2.5% AGI / $695	2.5% AGI / $1390	2.5% AGI / $2085

[AGI = Adjusted Gross Income}

2. The Obamacare Medicine Cabinet Tax: This tax took effect in January 2011 and prevents Americans from being able to use their health savings account (HSA), flexible spending account (FSA), or

health reimbursement (HRA) pre-tax dollars to purchase non-prescription, over-the-counter medicines (except insulin).

3. The Obamacare Flexible Spending Account Cap—aka "Special Needs Kids Tax": Starting in January 2013, Obamacare imposes a cap on FSAs of $2500 (now unlimited under federal law). There is one group of FSA owners for whom this new cap will be particularly cruel and onerous: parents of special needs children...

4. The Obamacare "Haircut" to the Medical Itemized Deduction from 7.5% to 10% of AGI: Currently, those facing high medical expenses are allowed a deduction for medical expenses to the extent that those expenses exceed 7.5% of AGI. Beginning in January 2013, this new Obamacare provision imposes a threshold of 10% of AGI.

5. The Obamacare HSA Withdrawal Tax Hike: This provision, which took effect in January 2011, increases the tax on non-medical early withdrawals from an HSA from 10% to 20%, disadvantaging them relative to IRAs and other tax-advantaged accounts, which remain at 10%.

6. The Obamacare Tax on Indoor Tanning Services: Since July of 2010, Americans using indoor tanning salons face a new 10% excise tax.

7. Obamacare Excise Tax on Comprehensive Health Insurance Plans: Starting in 2018, this provision imposes a new 40% excise tax on "Cadillac" health insurance plans ($10,200 single/$27,500 family). Higher thresholds exists for early retirees and those in high-risk professions.

In case you just breezed through this section, the one big takeaway is this: **Nowhere in these coming tax increases is there any exemption for families making less than $250,000 per year. Taxes will go up**—considerably. If the president wants to create a costlier healthcare system, okay. He won in 2008 and 2012. But the President lied to us about the costs of that healthcare system, and the need for higher taxes to pay for it, and the voters believed his lies.

One man has been sounding this theme particularly forcefully in the last year. His actions as a high-profile publisher have surely earned him a Level 5 position on Obama's enemies list…

The Invisible Tax being leveled on Young Americans

I'm speaking of **_Joseph Farah_**, publisher of WND, who has been writing tirelessly on behalf of the biggest losers of the Obama years—ironically, the young. For when the government spends about a dollar for every 50 cents it collects in taxes, where does the other 50 cents come from? In Farah's words:

> *"We've approached the sad state of affairs during the last four years in which nearly half the money spent by Washington is raised without the consent of the governed through an insidious form of taxation not on the voting public, but on their posterity, on their children and their children's children…*

> *"That's done through borrowing. Nearly half the money being spent by Washington, well over a trillion dollars a year, with much more planned for next year and the year after that, is raised not through taxation by elected representatives of the people, but through fiat borrowing specifically disapproved of by vast majorities of Republicans, independents and Democrats who essentially have no say in the matter.*

> *"The borrowing has to stop. A line in the sand must be drawn. The kind of courage our founders exhibited must be exhibited once more—by the people of the United States, by you. It's time to recognize it's one of the roots of the problem we have in America. It's downright immoral...*

> *"It's with that in mind that I devised the 'No More Red Ink' campaign to put Republicans on notice that we see through their broken promises, too, and to show them we know they have the power to say no, to show them they are part of the problem and not part of the solution…*

"Obviously this campaign has not yet been successful, though it has been ongoing since January 2011. However, it has shown potential for returning America to its principles. Nearly 1.5 million letters have been targeted to Republicans…

"That's why I urge you, as I have many times in the past, to support the 'No More Red Ink' campaign to force Washington to retrench – not 10 years from now, not five years from now, not three years from now, but right now.[65]

Obama Punishes Investors, even though it also Slams the Economy

Obama plans to let the Bush capital gains tax cut expire at the end of the year. He may face opposition, and may fail. But that's his plan—to pursue what he calls "fairness." And when he was selling the plan, he had the audacity to compare himself to Ronald Reagan and claim his plan was no different than Reagan's.

Even the *Washington Post* Fact Checker gave Obama "two Pinocchios." Here's the greeting Obama will have for investors on January 1, 2013: The tax rate on long-term capital gains will increase from the current 15% to 20%. In addition, a number of itemized deductions for income above a threshold will no longer be allowed, taking the rate to 21.2%. Then there's the additional 3.8% tax for Obamacare, taking the rate to 25%. **When the Buffett Rule is enacted, the average investor is going to be punished—er, greeted—with a capital gains tax rate of 30%.**

And it's not just the 50% of Americans who own stocks who will be impacted. **The 50% of Americans who don't own stocks, will also be impacted.**

If history is any guide, the repeal of the Bush tax cuts will depress economic growth. Looking back, we see that **capital gains taxes and gross domestic product (GDP) have something of an inverse relationship: when the rate goes up, the economy goes down; when**

the rate goes down, the economy goes up. Here's how this dynamic has played out recently:

- ▶ 1968 to 1981: RATE INCREASED from 25% to 40% and GDP DECREASED from 3.8% to 3.1%
- ▶ 1987: RATE INCREASED from 20% to 29% and GDP DECREASED from 3.5% to 3.1%
- ▶ 2001 to 2003: RATE DECREASED from 21% to 16% and GDP INCREASED from 1.8% to 2.8%
- ▶ 1997: RATE DECREASED from 29% to 21% and GDP INCREASED from 3.1% to 4.5%

If you look closely, this is not a Democrat-Republican struggle, this is straight economics. It's one of the easier lessons in the economics texts in college—soon forgotten by many, apparently. **When capital gains taxes are raised, investors grow wary, businesses take their profits overseas, the economy slows down, people lose jobs.**

Obama surely knows this. So what is he thinking?

Perhaps Obama is not as interested in creating jobs and economic growth as he is in increasing federal revenues. Maybe the growing of the government is his top concern. It appears so. In fact, that is the one thing that cannot be taken away from him—he has grown government.

Obama Picks and Chooses Who's on His List

Apple should be at the top of Obama's enemies list—but the president hasn't said word one about 'America's biggest tax cheat.' Apple computers avoids billions in taxes—far more than Exxon Mobil, AT&T and others that Obama regularly excoriates for "shirking their corporate duty." So what gives?

Why does Apple get a pass, when other companies which actually provide a higher coefficient of societal equity—that is, we need them more—get verbally abused on a regular basis by Obama? Isn't this just a bit hypocritical?

Of course it is. Obama knows that it would look bad to all of his fawning young supporters if he were to publicly tar Apple with the label "America's biggest tax cheat." So he zips it. He turns his attention to easier targets. When talking about Apple, he talks about *"building an America that can last"* as if (1) he is playing some role in that, and (2) Apple is playing a role in that.

Neither is true, actually.

If Obama were providing the kind of leadership America needs if we hope to remain competitive in the global marketplace, he would be honest about Apple. He would begin by pointing out that the Cupertino, California, based company avoids hundreds of millions in California taxes. Apple designs its iPhones in California. Apple runs AppleCare customer service from California. Apple has some 37,000 employees with most of them in the California headquarters. Yet by placing a handful of employees in a small office in Reno, Nevada, Apple avoids California's corporate tax rate of 8.84% and basks in the sweetness of Nevada's tax rate of zero.

Does that upset me?

No, but is sure should upset Obama based on the speeches he gives. And avoiding state taxes is only the beginning of Apple's corporate tax strategy that ought to have Obama seething. Because Apple also slashes its federal tax bill by billions of dollars every year. They do it through a fancy accounting scheme known as the "Double Irish With a Dutch Sandwich." Stripped away all the complexities—and there are plenty—this scheme allows Apple to reduce taxes by routing profits through Irish subsidiaries and the Netherlands and then to the Caribbean.

If Apple paid taxes like other companies pay taxes, their bill would have been about $2.4 billion higher last year, according to former Treasury Department economist, Martin A. Sullivan. [66] That's a lot of money—or it used to be, anyway. Now it's enough to fund about four hours of federal government operations. But hey, every penny counts! And Obama should be making the case that Apple has to "do their fair share."

But no such case was ever made to Steve Jobs.

And it's wasn't just Steve Jobs and Apple pulling these clever tax tricks. A *New York Times* investigation found more than 70 'high-tech' companies in the S&P 500 biggest companies pay a full third less in taxes than 'old-tech' companies.[67] Dollar for dollar on earned income, companies like Apple pay only 66% as much in taxes as companies like Caterpillar. This is due largely to the fact that our tax system is ill-equipped to handle modern electronic commerce, software and royalties-based earnings. But whatever the reason, don't you think it's an imbalance that Obama should have tried to fix in his first term?

Shouldn't Obama have instructed the IRS to close these loopholes?

If the government is losing billions in tax revenues because companies like Apple, HP, Cisco and now Facebook are playing on an uneven field, then shouldn't Obama be trying to fix the issue rather than angling for the best photo-op on their Silicon Valley campuses? Of course he should. But then he would lose all those corporate contributions. See, the guys in charge in Silicon Valley are one smart bunch. They figured out that they could align with the Democratic Party, work that relationship to seek protection from them, get special favors that would make them much richer than otherwise possible, and even stave off attempts to tax internet commerce which has become 10% of retail and now should be taxed. But by burrowing in tight with the Democrats, becoming something of a sacred cow and a very hip and cool one at the same time, Silicon Valley has created something of a modern fortress for itself.

And Obama Looks the Other Way

Worse, on every campaign stop in this election Obama ripped into the fat-cat companies for avoiding taxes. He didn't mention that U.S. corporate taxes are now, thanks to a recent rollback in rates in Japan, the highest in the world. He didn't mention that in 1950 in this country, corporate taxes accounted for about 30% of all federal revenue. But in 2012, corporate taxes will account for less than 7% of all federal revenue. Think maybe we're doing something wrong . . . that Obama should be addressing?

Fact is, no U.S. company has an incentive to keep operations in this country—particularly in a time when two-thirds of their global sales are in overseas markets. Our government tax structure is sending an unmistakable message to these big S&P500 companies: *Go overseas, outsource jobs, expatriate profits.* But Obama didn't mention this on the campaign trail. He says: *forward!*

To what?

I have created a special website with the entire list of names of Obama's enemies at http://www.obamasenemieslist.com. To access the list please use the login name: Patriot and the password: wewillnotbeintimidated.

At the website you can also stand with those being targeted by adding your name to the list to tell Obama he cannot punish us all.

The Punished: Christians, Traditional Women, Pro-lifers, and Preborn Babies

Obama's "Fundamental Changes" Opposite to Christian Beliefs

Obama calls himself a Christian. Fine.

Obama went to church regularly in Chicago and a lot of commentators have jumped on Obama's pastor, the America-hating Jeremiah Wright, and suggested that Obama too must hate America. I don't see it that way. I think Obama dozed through it all, wishing he was home watching a Bulls game. But Michelle told him he would meet the right people in this hate-spewing congregation, so Obama did his husbandly duty. And scored political points to boot. A small price to pay, I imagine him confiding to Rahm Emanuel.

And for my proof? Well, Obama was not long in his first term when he made it clear that all of the religious liberties that had been observed by forty-three previous presidents were fair game under his rule. He had "fundamental changes" in mind and if they flew in the face of Christian values—well, maybe he could sneak it past them.

Obama's first big sneak-attack came buried on page 747,356 or so of the Obamacare enabling legislation. Religious employers and institutions were "mandated" to provide contraceptive and abortion services for free to their employees or students. The mandate isn't even in the law itself but in guidelines issued by Kathleen Sebelius, the Secretary of Health and Human Services (HHS).

Clearly, the Obama Administration wants to force all religious institutions in America to provide abortion services – and even sterilization options – for their employees and students. **This is a violation of the First Amendment's protection of religious liberty** and flies in the face of our Founding Father's belief that **the government has no right to violate the freedom of conscience of American citizens.**

As Thomas Jefferson declared in 1809:

> *"No provision in our Constitution ought to be dearer to man than that which protects the rights of conscience against the enterprises of the civil authority."* [68]

But this doesn't matter to Obama. In his cold calculus, the abortion lobby is bigger and better funded that the more conservative Christians who might vote for him. So his bed is made. **He'll use the power of the federal government to force Christians to provide services that violate the theology and conscience of believers.**

Church Leaders Organize in Protest Against Obama

The mandate has awakened Catholic Church leaders to the dire threat that this poses to religious liberty. In fact, a coalition of forty-three Catholic and Protestant institutions has filed twelve separate lawsuits against ObamaCare's abortion mandate – even as the Supreme Court reconsiders the constitutionality of the entire law.

Cardinal **_Timothy Dolan_**, the Archbishop of New York has taken a key leadership role in fighting back against Obama's assault. Cardinal Dolan says:

> *"Never before have we faced this kind of challenge to our ability to engage in the public square as people of faith and as a service provider."* [69]

It's not just Catholics who are outraged by Obama's attack. The Southern Baptist Ethics and Religious Liberty Commission (ERLC) has enjoined the fight against Obamacare. ERLC leader **_Richard Land_** says:

> *"…this issue is not about contraceptives. Instead, it is about consciences and religious freedom. And we must not allow this assault on our First Amendment freedoms to stand."[70]*

The mandate, if allowed to stand, will violate the freedom of religion and conscience of millions of Southern Baptists at their schools and charities.

Assault on the First Amendment's Protection of Religious Freedom and Conscience

Ken Blackwell, co-author of *The Blueprint: Obama's Plan To Subvert The Constitution And Build An Imperial Presidency*, spoke to the conservative Family Research Council in May 2012 on the subject of Obama's authoritarian impulses:

> *"One of the most unprecedented and ominous assaults on religious freedom is the proposed Health and Human Services contraception mandate. As I have written in a variety of opinion pieces, there has been nothing comparable to this in 225 years in this country. There is truly no precedent for the threat embodied in the HHS Mandate.*
>
> *"If the federal government can force not only Catholic institutions, but those of many other faith communities, and small businesses, and family-owned firms to provide drugs that can cause abortions or chemical contraceptives that violate their beliefs, then the First Amendment to the Constitution has effectively been repealed."[71]*

Blackwell also raises a larger question: **If the federal government is free to force religious institutions to provide abortion and contraceptive services, what's to keep them from mandating that Christian hospitals perform abortions or sex-change operations?**

And, if Obamacare can force American citizens to purchase a government-approved health insurance package, what's to keep Obama from forcing us to buy a government-subsidized car from GM – or to buy certain foods approved by his wife Michelle?

After the firestorm of controversy erupted over the HHS abortion mandate, Obama announced a compromise: He would only force the insurance carriers to provide the abortion services, not the religious institutions. But, this is meaningless. It still forces religious groups to participate in practices they deem sinful. In addition, many religious groups are self-insured, so Obama's belated olive branch bears no fruit.

In yet another meaningless compromise, Obama has given religious institutions one year to figure out how to violate their consciences before the mandate goes into effect. And he calls that "accommodating."

A year before HHS's Sebelius issued her infamous abortion mandate, Obama had been working quietly to *overturn* a policy created by his predecessor. The policy had been meant to protect the freedom of conscience of doctors, nurses, and health care aides. Those healthcare workers could not, under the policy, *be forced* to perform abortions or other medical procedures that violated their religious or moral beliefs. And they could not be denied employment based on those beliefs. The Bush policy went into effect in 2008. By the February 2009, the Obama administration was "reviewing" it. In 2011, the policy was killed.

Apparently, **Obama wants to force pro-life Christians to perform abortions . . . or resign.** When this turnabout happened, the head of the Christian Medical Association, *J. Scott Ries*, told reporters:

> *"The Obama administration's regulatory action today diminishes the civil rights that protect conscientious physicians and other healthcare professionals against discrimination. Any weakening of protections against discrimination against life-affirming healthcare professionals ultimately threatens to severely worsen patient access to health care."*

> *"Losing conscientious healthcare professionals and faith-based institutions to discrimination and job loss especially imperils the poor and patients in medically underserved areas. We are already facing critical shortages of primary care physicians, and the Obama administration's decision now threatens to make*

the situation far worse for patients across the country who depend on faith-based health care." [72]

No pro-life Christian medical professional should be forced to assist or perform an abortion – or risk losing his or her job! Yet, that's the Hobson's choice, or rather, Obama's choice they face.

And that's fine with Obama. He long ago decided in his own mind that the First Amendment is a section of the Constitution that can be ignored if it conflicts with his own personal ambitions.

Obama seems to believe that religious institutions and individuals exist to serve the purposes of the secular state and an imperial president. The implied warning to Christians is: Obey or find work elsewhere.

But a deeper agenda may be that Obama is using a backhanded maneuver to try and put religious institutions out of business, and quiet Christians.

For this is the method used in communist countries to limit religion; by putting extremely difficult restrictions on them. In a draft of a *Communist Confession of Faith*, (the original name for the *Manifesto of the Communist Party*) it says ***"communism is that stage of historical development which makes all existing religions superfluous and supersedes them."*** [73]And the Manifesto says, ***"There are, besides, eternal truths, such as Freedom, Justice, etc., that are common to all states of society. But Communism abolishes eternal truths, it abolishes all religion, and all morality..."***[74]

Atheism is at the center of communism; a doctrine that denies the existence of God and thereby removes God from our purpose for life. The brilliant Christian apologist, Chuck Colson, explained in his book, *Kingdoms in Conflict*, that Christianity and communism are at odds because "each is a religion and each is inherently expansive and evangelistic."

The abortion mandate firestorm isn't dying down – and it shouldn't. **This is government overreach at its worst – and is a direct assault on the First Amendment's protection of religious freedom and conscience.**

The entire Obamacare law is a blatant attack on the freedoms we hold dear.

EEOC is Obama's Hammer, and Religion a Rusty Old Nail

The Equal Employment Opportunity Commission (EEOC) is being used by Obama as a sledgehammer to destroy religious freedom. The assault is being spearheaded by lesbian activist Chai Feldblum, who was nominated to the EEOC in 2010. When at Georgetown Law School professor, Feldblum wrote extensively on one subject: the gay rights agenda *must* trump religious freedom concerns.

To wit, Feldblum has authored the Employment Non-Discrimination Act (ENDA) which turns some people into federally protected minorities based solely on their sexual orientation. ENDA was on a fast-track for passage in 2009, but then Democrats lost control of the House of Representatives and the act stalled.

If passed, ENDA would affect every business owner and religious institution in America with 15 or more employees. It would make it a crime for Christian groups or Christian businessmen to "discriminate" against gays, lesbians, bisexuals, or transgendered God-knows-what-they-are's. Due to Feldblum's ballsy tenacity, the EEOC recently "discovered" that Title VII in the 1964 Civil Rights Act was originally intended by its writers to protect "transgenders" in the workplace. (*Who knew?*) According to the EEOC, these troubled individuals now enjoy federal protections . . . and the stream of obligation-free payments and business-killing regulations implied by such protections.[75]

In short, religious institutions can be sued by the DOJ . . . with their unlimited legal pool . . . if some jagoff claims he, or she, or it was discriminated against on the day he wore a dress to work or she stepped out at lunch to have a sex-change operation.

But, it's not only hip cross-dressers egged on by Hollywood's finest who are benefitting from Obama's attacks on religious liberty.

The EEOC also recently took on the case of Emily Herx, who had taught literature and language arts at ***St. Vincent de Paul Catholic School*** in Fort Wayne, Indiana since 2003. Herx was fired from the

Catholic diocese for undergoing in vitro fertilization (IVF), which is contrary to Catholic teachings.

One may disagree with the Catholic Church over this particular teaching, but there's a larger principle at work here. It is the principle that a religious institution has the right to hire people who adhere to the teachings of the institution or to be fired if they violate those teachings.

The EEOC, however, ruled in favor of Herx in January 2012. The high (clearly) commission found that Herx had her rights violated under Title VII of the 1964 Civil Rights Act and Title 1 of the American Disabilities Act. Oh, by the way, Herx was infertile, and so she was considered "disabled" under the act.

These people are running our government!

Obama's EEOC also got involved in a dispute between an employee of the ***Hosanna-Tabor Evangelical Lutheran Church*** and the church leadership. [76] The issue involved a teacher named Cheryl Perich who was a minister in the church and taught fourth grade. Perich was fired for being disruptive and insubordinate. The church followed all labor law guidelines, using the well-known "ministerial exception" which permits the firing and prohibits ministers from suing. The EEOC, however, decided that a longstanding religious freedom would no longer apply and ministers should be free to sue.

The case went all the way to the Supreme Court and the EEOC was voted down 9-0! Not 5-4 with conservative justices prevailing. But nine to zero. The Justices rejected the EEOC claims as "extreme" and "untenable." In its decision, the Court observed:

> *"The interest of society in the enforcement of employment discrimination statutes is undoubtedly important. But so too is the interest of religious groups in choosing who will preach their beliefs, teach their faith, and carry out their mission. When a minister who has been fired sues her church alleging that her termination was discriminatory, the First Amendment has struck the balance for us. The church must be free to choose those who will guide it on its way."[77]*

Despite being roundly defeated by the highest court, Obama's EEOC has continued to attack religions freedoms, and will continue to do so.

Minorities More Important than Majorities in Obama's Military

In 2011, Obama pressured Congress and the military to overturn the "Don't Ask, Don't Tell" policy on gays serving in the military. That's when military chaplains knew they were in trouble. It took less than a year for the attacks on chaplains to surface in the media.

Chaplains started getting orders: keep your mouth shut about homosexuality. And those who didn't follow these orders were soon threatened with the loss of their careers.

The situation has become so serious that **_Ron Crews_** with the Chaplain Alliance For Religious Liberty has gone public with the organization's concerns. He represents 2,500 military chaplains. According to Crews:

> "[The Obama administration] has created an environment in the Department of Defense that if you are in favor of same-sex relationships, you may speak. If you are not in favor, you cannot speak."[78]

He describes the plight, for example, of one chaplain who was told that if he can't get in line with the support of homosexuality, he should resign his commission. Others are being threatened with forced retirement if they don't shut up.

So today we have a situation in the military where one individual's civil rights become more important than the corps' interests. Who cares if our military is prepared to defend our vital interests – little Johnny feels put upon. We're devolving at a furious pace, allowing the perceived slights of one man control the fates of all men.

Former Navy Chaplain **_James Klingenschmitt_** told the _Christian Post_:

> *"There are dozens of active duty chaplains who have been*
> *pressured to not speak against homosexuality. I know of one*
> *Army and one Navy chaplain who have already resigned.*
> *Another active duty chaplain has been silenced, threatened,*
> *and punished against speaking against 'Don't Ask, Don't Tell.'"[79]*

Responding to this threat to religious liberty, Rep. **_Todd Akin_** from Missouri added an amendment to a defense bill that would protect the right of conscience of chaplains who don't want to be forced into performing gay marriages or other such ceremonies for homosexual couples. Akin was roundly attacked by Obama. Apparently its okay for gays to get whatever their hearts' desire, while those who "cling to their guns and religion" get the shaft. The thing is, Akin's amendment was pretty straightforward, and respectable of the rights of one group, without being disrespectful of another. It simply dictated that no member of the armed forces may:

> *"…direct, order, or require a chaplain to perform any duty, rite,*
> *ritual, ceremony, service, or function that is contrary to the*
> *conscience, moral principles, or religious beliefs of the chaplain,*
> *or contrary to the moral principles and religious beliefs of the*
> *endorsing faith group of the chaplain."*

But that kind of talk is just unacceptable to Obama.

Disagree with Obama, and Get Uninvited

Within the past two years, three conservative Christian leaders have been "uninvited" to prayer events and military events because of their policy disagreements with Obama. This is, by the way, unprecedented. Things like National Prayer Breakfasts have a long and storied bipartisan tradition in Washington. But Obama the Uniter can't seem to stand the company of anyone but fawning acolytes.

And so it was in 2010 that **_Franklin Graham_**, who runs Samaritans Purse, was uninvited to the Pentagon's National Day of Prayer service. Graham was the honorary chairman of the event—a rather high post—until uninvited! Graham was banned from the event because a couple of Muslim agitators had complained about his view that Islam as widely practiced is evil.

Graham later explained that he has no quarrel with Muslim people, but he believes Islam is a serious threat to women's rights. He is, of course, right. But that doesn't matter to a Pentagon eager to please the current overlords.[80]

In early 2012, three-star retired General **William Boykin** was pressured into dropping out of a West Point prayer breakfast. Boykin was a founder of Delta Force; commanding officer in the famous "Blackhawk Down" incident in Mogadishu.

Boykin is also an outspoken Christian and a critic of Islam and Islamic terrorism.

It was his Christian beliefs and views on Islam that made the far left and Muslim Brotherhood front groups like the Council on American-Islamic Relations (CAIR) go berserk over his appearance at West Point. They caused such a firestorm of controversy over his plans to speak, he opted to withdraw.

Was Obama directly responsible for stirring up controversy about Boykin? I don't know. What I do know is that Obama has created a climate of hostility in the military against outspoken critics of Islam like Boykin and critics of the gay agenda inside the military.[81]

Officials at the Pentagon understand that they're to distance themselves from anyone like Franklin Graham or William Boykin who actually tell the truth about the dangers of the totalitarian political system known as Islam.

And, then there's the incident involving **Tony Perkins** of the Family Research Council. Perkins is an outspoken critic of the gay agenda, political Islam, and Obama's policies. In 2010, Perkins was drop kicked out of a prayer event at Andrews Air Force Base.[82] Obama could have met with Perkins there, and used the opportunity to discuss their differences like leaders have always done. But that kind of open-minded tolerance is lost on this president.

Obama had previously demonstrated his disdain for the whole National Day of Prayer concept. In 2009 the annual event was chaired by ***Shirley Dobson***, the wife of Christian author and radio talk show host ***Dr. James Dobson***. Obama didn't say, "I don't want anything to do with these people," but he might as well have when he refused to participate and didn't attend the Catholic prayer breakfast the day after.[83]

Of course a few months later, Obama hosted an "Iftar" (dinner) to celebrate the Islamic holy month of Ramadan. In his speech to his assembled Muslim guests, Obama crowed:

> *"The contribution of Muslims to the United States are too long to catalog because Muslims are so interwoven into the fabric of our communities and our country."[84]*

Apparently Obama thinks more of Islam rising than our Judeo-Christian heritage—that, despite the relative emptiness of the Muslim "catalog" and the fullness of the Judeo-Christian catalog. I'm reminded, in this context, of an interesting list—a very different kind of list than the one Obama is keeping…

A Very Different List—the One Obama Should Be Keeping…
Muslims are 20% of the world's population, and have received 7 Nobel Prizes.

Jews are .02% of the world's population, and have received 129 Nobel Prizes.

The Jews are not brainwashing children in training camps, teaching them how to blow themselves up. The Jews don't hijack planes, nor kill athletes at the Olympics, or blow themselves up in German restaurants. The Jews don't traffic slaves, nor have leaders calling for Jihad and death to all the Infidels.

Regardless of your feelings about the crisis between Israel and the Palestinians and Arab neighbors, Benjamin Netanyahu really says it all:

> *"If the Arabs put down their weapons today, there would be no more violence. If the Jews put down their weapons today, there would be no more Israel."*

Obama should know this in his heart. And yet somehow he does not. His record of hostility toward Jews and Christians is clear. And, it will get worse now that he has another four years in the White House.

Women with Traditional Values are Less Than...

Perhaps most surprising is Obama's disdain for women who don't think like him. He's made enemies of stay-at-home moms and strong conservative women. Of course, he won't openly say this but his surrogates will.

One of those surrogates is Hilary Rosen who works with former White House communications official Anita Dunn at an outfit known as SKDKnickerbocker. (If the name "Dunn" sounds familiar, she's the one who was shown the back door of the White House after being exposed for being an admirer of Mao, who of course murdered 30 million people while ruling China with an iron fist.)

For her part, Rosen has visited the Obama White House pretty much every month – including five visits to the Oval Office. It is likely that these were not social visits; they were undoubtedly strategy sessions on how best to slime Obama's political opponents – including Ann Romney.

After one of those meetings, Rosen emerged to say of Ann Romney: "What you have is Mitt Romney running around the country saying, 'Well, you know, my wife tells me that what women really care about are economic issues. And when I listen to my wife, that's what I'm hearing. Guess what? *His wife has actually never worked a day in her life.* She's never really dealt with the kinds of economic issues that a majority of the women in this country are facing in terms of how do we feed our kids, how do we send them to school, and why we worry about their future. There's something much more fundamental about Mitt Romney. He just seems so old-fashioned when it comes to women. And I think that comes across. And I think that that's going to hurt him over the long term. He just doesn't really see us as equal."

How does Rosen know so much about Romney's thoughts on women? She's doesn't. She apparently thinks she can say anything she wants, and that makes it true. But in reality, her communist beliefs that deride traditional families and values were shining through: ***"The bourgeois sees his wife a mere instrument of production. He hears that the instruments of production are to be exploited..."*** [85]

And what's more, the *Communist Confession of Faith* states**, "We will only interfere in the personal relationship between men and women or with the family in general to the extent that the maintenance of the existing institution would disturb the new social order."** [86]

This explains one reason why the Obama administration is attacking and interfering with traditional families: They want them to fall apart so that people will be dependent on the government, and run for everything to Big Brother, as a family substitute, instead of their own family!

The truth is that Ann Romney raised five boys quite well, while undergoing breast cancer treatment and being treated for multiple sclerosis.

For Rosen to say that Ann Romney hasn't worked a day in her life is a slap in the face to every mother who has chosen to stay at home, rear children and be a loving home maker. To liberals, homemaking is a waste of time and demeaning to feminists. Only working outside of the home is valued – except if you're **_Sarah Palin_**. Then, you're supposed to stay at home and keep your mouth shut.

Of course, when former Alaska Governor Sarah Palin was running for Vice President with John McCain, the Hilary Rosen's of the world were suggesting she should stay at home and care for her Down's Syndrome child.

Rush Limbaugh was outraged by Hilary Rosen's attack on Ann Romney and her motherhood. He pointed out on his radio show that it's not just conservative women who get slimed by Obama operatives like Rosen. Limbaugh noted:

> *"... that there is genuine hostility for women who do not work, who only stay at home and raise their families. So the Obama administration has just effectively, whether they know it or not,*

*launched a War on Motherhood via Hilary Rosen on CNN last
night. Obama and the Democrats are not content to just divide
men and women. They want to go deeper and divide working
mothers from stay-at-home mothers, and they want to attach
the virtue to working mothers and assign no virtue to stay-at-
home moms.*[87]

Obama Targets Sarah Palin and Mama Grizzlies

Sarah Palin and her family has been mercilessly persecuted and
ridiculed by the Hollywood's script-reading beauties as well as Obama
operatives. Yet rather than give in, Palin is smart enough to turn the
attacks into a wake-up call for traditional values women:

*"The comments that Hilary Rosen made today certainly have
awakened mama grizzlies across the nation....Why is it that
some on the left choose to divide to incite with comments like
that instead of just respecting women's choices and what they
want to do with the gifts that God has given them?"*[88]

Sarah Palin has been the victim of what conservative commentator **Michelle Malkin** calls the "Female Conservative Derangement
Syndrome."

It is known that prior to the 2008 election, Obama operatives set
up a series of anonymous web sites to spread vicious rumors about
Palin. Among those rumors – known to be false – were that Palin was
a member of the Alaskan Independence Party and a member of an
anti-American separatist group.

The Jawa Report did some digging into who produced these web
sites and lies and found that the sites were linked to a PR firm that
has direct ties to the Democrat Party – and that the guy who did the
voiceovers for the smear videos of Palin has ties to Obama operative
David Axelrod – a man who is well-known for engaging in phony
"astro-turfing" activities. This same guy has worked directly for the
Obama campaign staff.[89]

It is clear that Sarah Palin was at the top of Obama's enemies list in 2008 because she was doing such a great job of energizing conservative grassroots activists. They had to do whatever they could to ridicule, marginalize and destroy her – the typical strategy used by Saul Alinsky followers!

Arizona Governor Jan Brewer Stands Up to Obama

Obama and his Department of Justice Attorney General Eric Holder have relentlessly attacked Arizona Governor **_Jan Brewer_** for trying to control illegal immigration, on Arizona's borders.

Brewer is clearly on Obama's enemy list – especially after publication of her book, *Scorpions for Breakfast: My Fight Against Special Interests, Liberal Media, and Cynical Politicos To Secure America's Border.*

Brewer and Obama got into a well-publicized spat on the Arizona tarmac. There's the famous photo of Brewer pointing her finger in Obama's face as they discussed her book. They sparred over the contents of her book (of which he had only read excerpts) and Arizona's tough immigration law – which seeks to actually deal with illegal immigration since the Obama Administration won't.

According to Brewer, "He was a little disturbed about my book. … I said to him that I have all the respect in the world for the office of the president." For his part, Obama was seen stalking off while Brewer was in mid-sentence. Obama later complained that Brewer hadn't treated him civilly. You know, it's just hard to imagine Obama lodging that kind of complaint. But he did.[90]

Obama had attacked the Arizona immigration bill as threatening "basic notions of fairness that we cherish as Americans." And his Attorney General Eric Holder attacked the bill as well, only later admitting that he'd never even read the text of it!

The Department of Justice is sued Arizona for passing the bill. The DOJ is also harassing Arizona **_Sheriff Joe Arpaio_** for his efforts to enforce both state and federal immigration laws. The DOJ accused him of "racial profiling" – and violating the "civil rights" of illegals. That surely landed Arpaio high on Obama's enemies list as well. Arpaio has since been cleared of the DOJ charges.

Arizona is simply trying to enforce federal immigration laws—something Obama doesn't want done. And why not, is a good question. We suspect that Obama champions wide open borders because he knows that homeless, non-English-speaking, welfare-bound illegals are more likely to vote Democrat.

You're on Obama's enemies list if you dare try to protect your state borders from illegals and from Islamic terrorists who are known to be infiltrating into the U.S. from Mexico.

Michele Bachmann and other Conservative Leaders

An outfit named Media Matters does opposition research for Obama and his operatives. Their specialty is smearing conservatives and conservative media outlets like Fox News with out-of-context quotes and character assassination. Media Matters recently created their own subset of the Obama's enemies list, in fact, populating it with a long list of conservatives to smear.

They then funnel these hit lists to anyone in the Obama Administration charged with launching baseless attacks on the enemy. In fact, according to an investigative report published by *The Daily Caller*, **Media Matters has weekly calls with the Obama White House to coordinate messaging on Obama's socialist agenda and to craft talking points against conservatives.**[91]

In addition, Media Matters founder David Brock met regularly with Anita Dunn while she was still in the White House communications office. Internal documents from Media Matters reveal a plan called "Project 2012" which is designed to drive conservatives like ***Rush Limbaugh*** off the airwaves.[92]

Media Matters has also set up a searchable database of individuals it considers enemies at a sub-site called "Political Correction." This information is provided to Obama operatives to help them smear opponents.

Along with **_Michele Bachmann_** in the enemies database are **_Carly Fiorina_, _David Vitter_, _Eric Cantor_, _John Boehner_, _Mitch McConnell_** and **_Steve King._**

Carly Fiornia is considered a Media Matters/Obama enemy for running against Barbara Boxer for Boxer's Senate seat. And, of course, she's a businesswoman who became successful without government handouts.

And, of course, **_Senator David Vitter_, _Rep. Eric Cantor_, _Rep. John Boehner_, _Rep. Steve King_**, and **_Senator Mitch McConnell_ are all on the Media Matters/Obama enemy list because they all aggressively oppose the Obama socialist political agenda.**[93]

Bachmann and her husband have been the subject of repeated smears in the press – undoubtedly orchestrated by Obama and Media Matters operatives.

One of the most infamous smears of Bachmann, when she was running for president, came from *Newsweek*, which ran a cover photo of her looking like a crazed lunatic with the headline: "The Queen of Rage."

The feminist who runs *Newsweek* is Tina Brown, who's been rightly called "The Queen of Sleaze" for her tabloid journalism and practice of smearing conservative women. And, of course, she nearly drools all over herself when talking about Barack or Michelle Obama.

Tina Brown is one of the most shameless supporters of Barack Obama – recently dubbing him the "first gay president" for supporting gay marriage.

Brown despises conservative women and lamented the political victories by Republican women in 2010 by calling it a "blow to feminism." According to Brown:

> *"The only trouble with this one is, it almost feels as if all these women winning are kind of a blow to feminism. Because, each one of them, really, most of them, are, you know, very much, uh, uh, you know, against so many of things that women have fought for such a long time....Women, too, can be wing nuts, is the point."*[94]

79

Brown explains why she picked the photo of Michele Bachmann looking crazy: "You know, there was one picture of her praying, which frankly we rejected because we thought that seemed somehow some kind of a commentary on her religiosity that maybe would be offensive. There was another picture of her sitting kind of sideways and I thought she looked extremely strange."

The smear-merchants have also attacked Michele Bachmann over reports that she has migraine headaches. This became a huge media event until the drive-by media moved on to attacks against her husband.

Obama's operatives have gone into orbit over Bachmann's husband Marcus, who is a therapist who treats individuals with unwanted homosexual desires. Immediately, the leftwing media swung into action and began accusing Dr. Bachmann of being a closeted homosexual and a bigot.[95]

Clearly, Michele Bachmann is on Obama's enemy list.

What Kind Of Woman Does Obama Approve Of?

Barack Obama wants the kind of woman portrayed in his creepy slideshow about "The Life Of Julia," a fictional character that lives a government-subsidized existence.

In this slideshow, Julia is followed from age three until she goes through college and has her own child – apparently without a husband.

Julia is totally dependent on the federal government from the moment she's born. At three, she heads off to a federally-subsidized Head Start program. She breezes through high school with Obama's "Race to the Top" program and goes to college with a government provided student loan. She then ends with free Obamacare health coverage and later in life she gets her Social Security check and Medicare coverage.

Commentator *Marybeth Hicks* provides more details about this government-dependent woman:

"Conservative commentators point out that 'The Life of Julia' is creepy and condescending. Graphic Julia has no facial features, all the better to be led blindly down the path to socialism. Insultingly, she achieves nothing on her own, nor is there any mention of her personal support network (you know, a husband or family). Rather, her feminist triumphs all are achieved with the help and support of the ultra-generous Mr. Obama.

"More telling about the 'Julia' meme is not only what it conveys about the president's vision of women's needs and priorities, but also his under-lying belief about his personal role in the lives of American citizens."[96]

Obama is being patronizing to women. He clearly thinks they can't survive without his help every step of the way through life. And, since there's no mention of a husband or father in the slideshow, it is apparent that Obama considers the federal government to be Julia's husband and the benevolent father to her child Zachary.

The kind of woman Obama approves of is the perfectly obedient, submissive subject in his socialist utopia.

The Republican National Committee (RNC) expressed outrage against the "Life Of Julia" slideshow and countered with their own facts about what Julia's life will be like in Obama's socialist-welfare state.

The RNC pointed out that Julie would be paying record high tuition to attend college; and when she graduated, she wouldn't be able to find a job in Obama's failing economy. In addition, she'd be saddled with a $25,000 loan – the highest in history and rising under Obama.

As a 23-year-old college graduate, she'd likely end up living with her parents – and be paying double for gasoline compared to what she would have paid before Obama took office.

But, it gets worse for Julia as she ages under Obama's regime. Julia, the mother will have to pay higher health insurance premiums under Obamacare than with a private insurance company. Social Security and Medicare will be gutted as well.[97]

She-PAC Counters Obama & His Surrogates
Who Demean Women

Suzanne Haik Terrell and **_Teri Christoph_** are on Obama's enemy list. They are the co-founders of She-PAC, which helps elect conservative

Republican women to Congress. (Terrell was the first woman to be elected as a state representative in Louisiana in 1999.]

This political action committee worked to help elect Mia Love, a black Mormon Tea Party candidate for a newly created House seat in Utah! But sadly she lost.

Mia Love is clearly on Obama's enemy list. She said she would "elect a shoe over the current president."

She-PAC also supported **_Linda McMahon_** in Connecticut; **_Deb Fischer_** Nebraska's new conservative Senator; **_Sarah Steelman_** in Missouri; and **_Martha Zoller_** from Georgia. Zoller, is a radio talk show host. "I'm really tired of having liberal women speak for me," said Zoller. "Any time there's a women's issue, the first person the media goes to is people who represent liberal points of view."[98]

All of these women are undoubtedly on Obama's enemies list. Why? Because they're bright, conservative, independent, support capitalism, traditional values, and love America.

I have created a special website with the entire list of names of Obama's enemies at http://www.obamasenemieslist.com. To access the list please use the **login name**: Patriot and the **password:** wewillnotbeintimidated.

At the website you can also stand with those being targeted by adding your name to the list to tell Obama he cannot punish us all.

The Punished: Border Defenders and US Citizens
Try to Protect America's Borders and "I'll Sue You"

Barack Obama has made it clear through his policies and political appointments that he's an advocate of "open borders" and has no intention of keeping illegal aliens and potential terrorists from entering our nation through Mexico.

As governor of a state that is being overrun by illegals, Arizona Governor Jan Brewer, had to take action on her own. She signed into law a measure in 2010 that gets tough on illegals, and assists the federal government in securing our borders. When she did so, U.S. Attorney General Eric Holder's response was swift and heavy-handed: He sued her. Yes, the AG filed lawsuit against the people of Arizona and claimed that the state was interfering with federal immigration responsibilities and must be stopped. In an official statement, Holder appeared to try and take a reasonable position:

> "Arizonans are understandably frustrated with illegal immigration, and the federal government has a responsibility to comprehensively address those concerns. But diverting federal resources away from dangerous aliens such as terrorism suspects and aliens with criminal records will impact the entire country's safety." [99]

In expanding on this, Holder expressed his concern that a *"patchwork of state laws"* like ones in Arizona could *"create more problems than it solves."* Holder's point was a good one on face value—if in helping Arizona fight illegal immigration the federal government would have to divert precious resources from the fight on terrorism, then that's a hard choice to make. Or if Holder offered some alternative form of assistance to help states like Arizona with a mounting public safety problem—that, too, would be good. But Holder was making a straw man argument, plain as day. And that's when the war between Arizona and Washington pitched forward.

Governor Brewer shot back at the AG defending Arizona's rights and exposing the Obama administration's failure to protect Arizonians and enforce existing laws:

> "It is wrong that our own federal government is suing the people of Arizona for helping to enforce federal immigration law. As a direct result of failed and inconsistent federal enforcement, Arizona is under attack from violent Mexican drug and immigrant smuggling cartels. Now, Arizona is under attack in federal court from President Obama and his Department of Justice." [100]

Arizona Senators John McCain and **_Jon Kyl_** then joined in backing their governor—as both knew how dangerous the borders in Arizona had become. They issued this joint statement:

> *"The Obama administration has not done everything it can do to protect the people of Arizona from the violence and crime illegal immigration brings to our state. Until it does, the federal government should not be suing Arizona on the grounds that immigration enforcement is solely a federal responsibility."*[101]

Showdown at the AZ Tarmac

There are often tensions between the state and federal governments, and understandably. But we expect our leaders on both levels to work together to make the big decisions, like adults. Or at least we hope for as much. In this case, AG Holder never even notified Governor Brewer that he was suing her state. She learned about it watching Secretary of State Hillary Clinton on an Ecuadorian TV station.[102] You would think the Obama administration would have the cajones to inform the governor before informing the citizens of another nation. But no.

The Obama administration became so churlish in their communications that Governor Brewer went ahead and authored a book to fight for her case. Titled *Scorpions for Breakfast: My Fight Against Special Interests, Liberal Media, And Cynical Politicos To Secure America's Border*, the book made a powerful case for the Arizona law. Bu this point, relations between Brewer and Obama were in the tank. And when Obama's plane next sat down on Arizona tarmac, and Brewer gamely went out to meet him, the cameras famously caught the tense discussion and Obama angrily turning away from Brewer when she was in mid-sentence. Was he unable to have an intelligent conversation with this woman? Was he too thin-skinned? Or was he stunningly rude? Whatever the reason, he was not very presidential.

Governor Brewer has argued that the Arizona law compliments federal law, and does not preempt federal statutes in any way. Attorney **_Kris Kobach,_** who helped write the Arizona law is now the Kansas Secretary of State. He points out:

"The Supreme Court has ruled multiple times that states have spheres of activity where they can operate to discourage illegal immigration. It's an area of shared authority."[103]

Arizona argues that their law is needed because Obama isn't enforcing its own law. Local officials cite as evidence an Obama administration memo in April 2012 that discourages Immigration and Customs Enforcement officers from going after illegals if they're enrolled in an education center or have relatives who have volunteered for the military.

Kobach has been on the frontline of the immigration battle, and like the governor he once served, he is hard-pressed to understand Obama's policy position on border security:

"They're pushing the agents to be even more lax, to go further in not enforcing the law.... At a time when millions of Americans are unemployed and looking for work, this is more bad news... [if the administration] really cared about putting Americans back to work, it would be vigorously enforcing the law. The deliberate non-enforcement of our immigration laws in this administration certainly seems politically motivated [but] how exactly they expect to win votes by doing this is beyond me."[104]

A Re-election Ploy, or a Border Security Policy, Or...What?

In 2010, Arizona Senator Jon Kyl had a private meeting with Obama on this very issue. And afterward, Kyl reported to constituents:

"Here's what the president said. The problem is, he said, 'if we secure the border, then you all won't have any reason to support comprehensive immigration reform.' In other words, they're holding it hostage. They don't want to secure the border unless and until it is combined with comprehensive immigration reform."[105]

Immediately after Kyl revealed this at a Townhall meeting in Arizona, the White House issued a denial and claimed Kyl was lying. Kyl stuck to his guns. Who would you believe?

Follow the evidence, and see. Obama's appointment of Cecilia Munoz as director of his Domestic Policy Council is exhibit one. Munoz is the daughter of Bolivian immigrants—that is good, she knows the turf. She is also the former vice president of the National Council of La Raza—not so good. La Raza is the most radical of the Hispanic groups—the ones you see tearing down U.S. flags and putting up Mexican flags. Since the 1960s, La Raza has agitated for everything from racial preferences, to mass immigration and amnesty for illegal aliens. Says Ms. Munoz: *"Ultimately my career is about making sure the doors are open in this country for everybody."*

She's entitled to her opinion, but that opinion has become a part of Obama administration policy and the flag-burners are now actually getting taxpayer money to fund their activities. I could not make this up. La Raza received $11 million in federal funds in 2010.[106] Of course this sum of money is not even a rounding error in Washington parlance, but what is the federal government doing funding a private political group in the first place?

When you dig deeper, we begin to get a clearer picture. One expert on immigration issues, **_Mark Krikorian,_** has written the book, *How Obama Is Transforming America Through Immigration.* And the title says it all—but it suggests that Obama's aims are simply policy oriented. But in reading this fascinating book we learn that the 645-page immigration bill that Obama is trying to pass is intended to working on two levels. On one level:

> *"[this bill] makes very clear the true aims of the Obama Administration and the Democratic Congress: Easy amnesty, little enforcement, and more immigration."* [107]

Supporting his point, Krikorian notes how under Obama, work site raids to find illegals have been suspended. **Obama has also redefined the term "illegal" to only mean those who commit violent crimes – and not so-called minor crimes like drunk driving, shoplifting, or domestic abuse.** What really reveals the Obama end-game is that the only group 100% committed to supporting the immigration bill is the

Congressional Progressive Caucus—the only openly socialist caucus in Congress, and proudly so.

Obama's bill also lays the groundwork for a series of recurring amnesties—allowing pretty much everyone now in country to stay in country. **That would increase the number of people dependent on Obama's cradle-to-grave social service programs by almost 10% — clearly not affordable**, but Obama plans to be long out of office and set for life before the bill comes due on the amnesty travesty.

If Obama's bill is passed, it will ban states and municipalities from participating in the enforcement of immigration laws. **It adds new *"rights* for illegals** – including "legal orientation programs" and limits who may be detained – including illegals who have dependents here or in their home countries who have *"medical or mental health needs"* or who *"intend"* to apply for asylum.

The bill also restricts the ability of our border patrol to build border fencing under the guise of protecting the environment. It also **ends the E-Verify system**, which is currently an effective way of determining who's legal and who's not.

There are dozens of other absurdities in this bill – all designed to hamstring law enforcement and create an environment that **permits illegals to enter the U.S. at will**.[108]

Fortunately, the bill hasn't gone anywhere in the Republican-controlled House, and let's hope it stays that way in the face of intense pressure on House Speaker John Boehner. Obama would sign it at once if Republicans cave. And the Bill would effectively destroy any semblance of protected borders.

Which brings us to the second front in the Obama immigration war, and this does appear to have higher priority to Obama. **Open borders will provide the Democrats with more disgruntled constituencies, more voters, and more reasons to expand the welfare state – thus creating more dependent subjects.** As Krikorian puts it:

> *"To exaggerate only a little, the Obama crowd's immigration strategy is to replace the American electorate with one that is more receptive to a statist agenda. Overall, new immigrants are*

voting 60 percent to 80 percent in favor of the Democrats. It's not just Hispanic immigrants either; there is evidence that Asian, African, European, and Middle Eastern immigrants are also voting mostly Democratic."[109]

What's at Stake in this Border Security Battle?
Aside from increasing the welfare rolls, changing the character of our nation, overwhelming our emergency services systems, burdening our schools, spending billions to deal with illegals, and seriously jeopardizing our nation's internal security, nothing is at stake!

To many Americans living in the heartland or far from border crossing hotspots, the "immigration" issue is a distant concern. Or at least we wish it were. But we also know that Mexico has become a Narco-State run by drug cartels vying to supply Americans' insatiable appetite for marijuana and, increasingly, cocaine and heroin. And U.S. intelligence has linked these drug cartels to Islamic terrorist organizations with their operations spread all across the Latin America jungles.

Hezbollah, the Iran-backed terrorist group is known to be operating in Mexico. In 2010, a Hezbollah cell being set up in Tijuana was exposed and broken up by Mexican authorities. A report in 2010 by *The Washington Times* found that some 200,000 Lebanese and Syrians have relocated in Mexico. And a good number of them want to hit the U.S.

A jihadist cell in Mexico was recently found to have a weapons cache of 100 M-16 rifles, 100 AR-15 rifles, 2,500 hand grenades, C4 explosives and antitank munitions.[110]

In 2011, Representative **_Sue Myrick_** described a conversation she'd had with a Mexican military official. He informed her that Hezbollah was giving explosives training lessons to members of the drug cartels – including lessons on how to create car bombs.

There is also evidence that an Al-Qaeda-linked Somali terrorist group known as al-Shabaab is operating south of our border. In 2010, a terrorist named Anthony Joseph Tracy was arrested in Virginia. He is thought to have smuggled at least 270 Somalis into the U.S. through

Mexico. Another member of the Somali terrorist network was arrested in San Antonio. He admitted to smuggling terrorists into the U.S. from Mexico.[111]

Obama knows all this. It's all in his daily briefing. So why would he weaken our border security at a time when we are clearly facing a terrorist threat coming up from Mexico? Obama believes Hispanic voters care more about open borders than they do about terrorism on U.S. soil. Hispanic voters value a strong economy—just like everyone else. But sadly, they seemed to buy Obama's excuses on the economy. Obama's pro-amnesty positions simply became icing on the cake.

Border Security Is a Mess

Sara Carter is _The Washington Examiner's_ point journalist on border security, and she has over the years developed many contacts with border patrol agents. She's been told that these agents are under strict orders to _not_ make arrests of non-criminal illegals and not to patrol areas of high traffic along the 2,000-mile southwest border. One agent told her the administration is deliberately failing to document what is actually happening on the border:

> _"In many cases my supervisors make it clear that they don't want increased apprehension numbers, which means no arrests."_ [112]

According to Carter, the Administration is also failing to patrol hundreds of miles of federal wildlife preserves that fall under the jurisdiction of the Department of the Interior. This gives smugglers and potential terrorists a clear corridor to use in entering the U.S.

In fact, very little of the southern border is actually patrolled by U.S. border patrol. Richard Stana, the Government Accountability Office's expert on this, told a House committee in February 2011 that the **border patrol has control over only 129 miles of the 1,994-mile long border.** By this, he means there are only 129 miles where agents can actually detect illegals with a high probability of actually apprehending them.[113]

The situation is so bad, border patrol agents are openly admitting that drug cartels have taken control of key crossing zones. Customs and Border Protection Deputy Commissioner David Aguilar says:

> *"The cartels are turning into more of a Mafia-like organization that are specializing not just in any one crime, not in the singular fashion. Now they may have a focus of narcotics, but they will expand very Mafia-like into other criminal opportunities, one of them being the smuggling of people . . . the exploitation of young men, young women, children for human trafficking, slavery, forced labor . . . any crime that will get them that profit."[114]*

With Drug Smuggling Becoming Human Trafficking, Will Obama Now Act?

Former Border Patrol agent **Zachary Taylor** talked with Glenn Beck in 2012, and shared a chilling slide show of what's actually happening on our vulnerable southern border. Taylor described a firefight in 2009 between Border Patrol agents and bandits near Ramanote Canyon in Arizona. Armed smugglers opened fire on the agents, wounding one in the ankle. A helicopter arrived on the scene, but was forbidden by the Department of Homeland Security rules from landing to pull the wounded agent from the fight. Instead, the agent had to be loaded on to a horse and brought out of the area!

Why is this happening? Obama's rules.

Taylor also told how in December of 2011, the Department of Homeland Security cancelled Close Air Support helicopters – even though they are very effective in helping capture illegals and potential terrorists. According to Taylor:

> *"[The Obama Administration is] killing the operation through policy and how they deploy assets… it's about spending money and making the show, not about effectiveness."[115]*

In addition, Border Patrol agents aren't permitted to enter or pursue on federal wildlife refuges without permission. In Taylor's view, *"this administration is trying to facilitate the entry of illegal aliens into the United States."*

And what about the border fence that was supposed to be built to protect us? In late 2011, the Obama administration—which views taxpayer money like an unlimited spigot—somehow couldn't find the funding for the border fence. The 2011 budget for border fencing and infrastructure technology was cut in half—leaving 1,300 miles of the Mexico border effectively unfenced.

At this point, only 649 miles of the 1,954 mile border have been fenced. After spending $1 billion on fencing over a five year period, **the Obama Administration has now scrapped the project** and is embarking on a new technology surveillance plan that's estimated to cost $1.5 billion over a 10-year period. Based on what we've seen so far, we can expect this new project to be quietly dropped as well after a billion or so has been dumped into it.

Obama does not even view the illegal border crossers as enemies of our national sovereignty (despite having a lengthy list of domestic enemies). He avoids describing illegal aliens for what they are: Criminals who have broken our laws. He'll only refer to them as "immigrants" and pretend that there's no distinction between those who have entered our country by criminal means and those who played by the rules and entered lawfully to become part of America's melting pot.

Obama has even issued "proper speech" rules dictating how administration officials will talk. **There will be no using terms like "Islamic terrorism," "Muslim terrorism," or "Islamic Jihad." Instead, Obama officials must use terms like "man-caused disasters" to refer to Islamist attacks on civilians**. The Global War On Terror is now called "Overseas Contingency Operations" to deal – not with Islamic terrorism, but with "religious extremism"—and thus, by insinuation, equating Islamic fascists with Christian fundamentalists.

Who Does Obama View as His Enemies?

Arizona Governor Jan Brewer and Kansas Secretary of State ***Kris Kobach*** are Level 5 enemies—that we know. They're both on the list for the "crime" of trying to defend our southern border from illegals – including drug and human traffickers and Muslim terrorists who seek to kill Americans. And, of course, there are the Border Patrol agents who are working under unbearable restrictions to actually enforce our immigration laws.

Obama's enemies list also includes Arizona's Maricopa County Sheriff Joe Arpaio, who was sued by AG Eric Holder for his "crime" of arresting and jailing illegals. Arpaio was accused of "racism" – a tired old accusation freely thrown around by Holder. The fact is that Arpaio is enforcing federal immigration laws, while Holder and Obama are not.

Arpaio explained his philosophy and his concern about illegals on his re-election website:

> *"There are few nations in the entire world where people are allowed to enter, work and live without registering or receiving a visa from that nation's government. Every country has a right to protect its borders and to demand to know who is living there. Why do some people feel that is an unreasonable position?*
>
> *"The United States has been a country that is far more lenient with its population of illegal immigrants than many others. We are and always have been a generous country. By and large, we take care of people in need of medical care, education and a whole host of social services. Few other nations are so generous to their non-citizens.*
>
> *"But our generosity has brought us to a breaking point. We cannot continue to ignore the millions of people who are sneaking into the United States to live and work, no matter how heartbreaking their stories of family hardships are back home. Our tax supported systems and many private businesses could be brought to their knees by the weight of so many people requiring services.*
>
> *"We have an obligation to enforce the laws of this land. And laws exist, both federally and locally, making it a crime to illegally enter the United States.*[116]

Joe Arpaio clearly understands the importance of border security and the Arizona immigration law, and the majority of Americans support his position. A recent Quinnipiac University poll asked 2,500 Americans if they supported the Arizona law that Obama and Holder are attacking in court. The poll found that 68% in support of the law! Only 27% said they disapproved.[117]

Should Obama's enemies list also include the 68% of Americans who support the Arizona immigration law? Does he rail in private against these Americans as he does in public against Brewer and Arpaio? If so, then we should all stand as co-defendants in the government's heavy-handed attack lawsuit.

I have created a special website with the entire list of names of Obama's enemies at http://www.obamasenemieslist.com. To access the list please use the login name: Patriot and the password: wewillnotbeintimidated.

At the website you can also stand with those being targeted by adding your name to the list to tell Obama he cannot punish us all.

The Punished: Energy Users and Energy Producers
To All the Efficient, Productive Energy Producers—*Frack You*

Are you an **oil, natural gas, or coal executive?** You're definitely on Obama's energy enemies list. Do you **work in the fossil fuel industry?** Consider yourself on the menu too, as you're an accessory to human-caused climate change. Are you associated with a **think tank** or **do you dare criticize Obama's environmental policies**—such sophistry definitely **puts you high on his hit list.** Do you work at a hydroelectric plants, or worse, in the nuclear power sector? Even though you supply the United States with close to 20% of our electricity—all emission free, you too are on Obama's roster of antagonists because **the president is a radical environmentalist who despises a cheap and abundant source of electricity.**

Fossil Fuels Have to Go—Whatever the Price

At least 3 in 10 American households receive electricity from coal-fired power plants. We *all* rely on gasoline or diesel powered transportation. Natural gas is used for electricity, heat, or hot water in 67% of all homes. Even the most modest of retirement plans is invested in fossil fuel-based companies. The hopes of millions of Americans for a decent retirement are threatened by Obama's war on the fossil fuel industry, not to mention by his mishandling of the economy.

Let's begin with coal.

Obama first revealed his "green dreams" in his first campaign. In a January 2008 interview with the *San Francisco Chronicle*, Obama divulged:

> "If somebody wants to build a coal-powered plant, they can;
> it's just that it will bankrupt them because they're going to be
> charged a huge sum for all that greenhouse gas that's being
> emitted." [118]

Apparently the *Chronicle* was too embarrassed by Obama's quote since it ran only in the online edition and was omitted in the print edition the next day. It can be hard speaking your true thoughts when you're a radical liberal—so much of it sounds silly in print.

Coal is an inexpensive energy resource, and abundant. The United States has the world's largest known coal reserves, an estimated 489 billion tons, enough to last at least another 100 years at today's level of use.[119] Coal is a native resource in 27 states and the industry directly employs some 170,000 blue-collar workers.[120]

But coal has a bad rap for being "dirty." It's a rap that people like Obama perpetuate because it serves them. The truth? Beginning in the 1960s, the harmful pollutants in coal and the dangerous impurities such as sulfur and nitrogen oxides, and particulates (soot) have been reduced by 90% through advances in technology, even though the use of coal tripled during this time.[121] Nonetheless, **regardless of the obvious benefits produced by this inexpensive, abundant source of energy, Obama's Energy Secretary, Steven Chu, has repeatedly stated, "Coal is my worst nightmare."[122]**

Obama's war on King Coal has taken a remarkable toll. Thanks to draconian new regulations issued from his Environmental Protection Agency, older coal plants are being shut down. In May 2012, the Energy Information Administration reported that coal-fired power plants are now generating just 36% of U.S. electricity, versus 47% when Obama took office.

That same month, PJM Interconnection, the company that operates the electrical grid in thirteen states (Delaware, Illinois, Indiana, Kentucky, Maryland, Michigan, New Jersey, North Carolina, Ohio, Pennsylvania, Tennessee, Virginia, West Virginia and the District of Columbia) held what's known as its 2015 capacity auction. According PJM, the market-clearing price for new 2015 capacity was 800% higher than today—$136 per megawatt.

The reason for these massive price increases coming to a utility bill near you very soon? The reason is Obama's forced retirement of key coal-fired plants.

In some states the 2015 price is even higher; for example in northern Ohio the bill skyrocketed to $357 per megawatt. Those increases will be felt by millions of Americans who will see their power bills rise by eye-popping amounts now that Obama was re-elected.

Cheap coal power has always kept energy rates low—but not anymore. Obama meant what he said in that same interview with the *Chronicle* I referenced earlier:

> *"You know, when I was asked earlier about the issue of coal, uh, you know—under my plan of a cap and trade system, electricity rates would necessarily skyrocket."*

The Great Natural Gas Flimflam

In what I hoped was Obama's last State of the Union address, the president told a whopper:

> *"We have a supply of natural gas that can last America nearly 100 years, and my administration will take every possible action to safely develop this energy,"*

It was a bald-faced lie because less than two weeks after that speech, Obama's Interior Department proposed new rules that add layers of bureaucratic regulation to companies using hydraulic fracturing—also known as "fracking"— to harvest natural gas. To cover for this obvious deceit, the Left-stream Media dutifully began running stories on the horrific life-threatening dangers of "fracking." All the pretty liberals began worrying aloud about spoiled groundwater, freak earthquakes, and the spooky connection between fracking and global warming. Left unsaid was the simple fact that: **Fracking is neither new nor risky technology.**

Over the last 60 years, the fracking process has been conducted more than one million times in the United States alone. There have long been regulations in place—as there should be—to ensure that natural gas exploration is conducted in a safe, productive way.

The point of fracking is to fracture a shale formation below the earth's surface, so that trapped natural gas can flow to a wellbore and be brought to the surface.

Fracking is a very orderly process. Simply described, a large drilling rig is used to dig far below the earth's surface with surgical precision. Next, a truck snakes a large reel of coiled steel hosing into the well. A device known as a "perforating gun" is then lowered into the well, punching pinholes into the shale strata. Another truck mixes water, sand and any additives needed to aid the fracturing process, pumping the mixture at high pressure through the hose into the well. Huge pumps drive water mixed with silica sand down into the horizontal leg of the casing—forcing the sand and water through the tiny holes to make hairline cracks in the shale. The microscopic grains of sand "prop" open the cracks, to allow the gas into the well and to keep the cracks from closing.

Once fracked, the well is "pumped back" for several days until enough water is removed and gas is flowing. The well is then capped until pipelines are built to connect to larger transmission lines. All of the fluids utilized in the process are reused, and the water is recycled.

Again, this brilliant technology has been used successfully for decades. Last summer, the MIT Energy Initiative released a 170-page report on natural gas which directly addressed the fracking, stating:

> *"The fracturing process itself poses minimal risk to the shallow groundwater zones that may exist in the upper portion of the wellbore."*

But listen to Obama and his surrogates and you might think the natural gas industry had just secretly brewed a deadly virus.

In May 2012, the EPA and Department of Interior announced new rules designed to hamper the fracking process, and thus drive up the cost of energy for most Americans. The EPA's new rules require that any air pollutants released at the fracking sites—primarily methane and the starter compounds in smog—have to be captured. This capturing procedure is a costly one. It was already required in Colorado and Wyoming. Now it's a nationwide federal mandate—further driving up prices.

While it is true that methane is a greenhouse gas that is 21 times more potent than carbon dioxide, it's relevant to note the most prolific methane emitter on the planet is the . . . termite. Is the EPA on top of that menace? Traditionally, the most efficient way of ridding the atmosphere of fracking emissions was to burn the toxic gases at the point of origin—a process known as flaring. But forget efficiency. The EPA would rather punish the natural gas industry and its users with considerably more expensive technologies.

The second move the administration has made to inhibit fracking is to require the disclosure of chemicals used. Had this king of rigorous disclosure been required of Obama's favorite "green" companies such as Solyndra, perhaps the taxpayers wouldn't have footed that half billion dollar boondoggle. But I digress.

Additional new federal rules require government testing of oil and gas well construction—as if these private enterprises have no clue what they've been doing for decades.

These new Obama strictures are clearly meant, as Obama promised, to punish the natural gas industry for its success. And again it's the thousands of company shareholders and 174,000 industry workers who are punished as industry profits tumble, and jobs are slashed, while the net salutary effect on the environment is negligible, at best. Of course, the strictures do create more federal jobs to write and administer a tangle of new regulations. That makes it a win-win in Obama's eyes, and a lose-lose to the nation.

Obama's Public Enemy Number One: Big Oil

It's certainly no secret: The Obama Administration is on a campaign to destroy Big Oil. This was completely confirmed in April 2012 when a video of an Environmental Protection Agency official revealed the White House's vicious attitude toward the very industries that supply the American people a reliable, affordable energy source. The video revealed EPA Region VI Administrator Al Armendariz describing his agency's *"philosophy of enforcement"* with respect to the regulation of the oil industry, likening it to brutal tactics employed by the Romans to intimidate its foes into submission. With a mocking grin, Armendariz detailed how the EPA inflicts punishment on its enemies:

> *"It was kind of like how the Romans used to, you know, conquer the villages in the Mediterranean. They'd go into a little Turkish town somewhere and they'd find the first five guys they saw and they'd crucify them. And then, you know, that town was really easy to manage for the next few years."*[123]

Even though the Constitution prohibits cruel and unusual punishment, as well as bills of attainder, it obviously doesn't apply to the eco-thugs at the EPA. None of this should be a surprise coming from the most anti-energy administration in history. Let's set the record straight.

In the days following the terrible 2010 British Petroleum oil spill in the Gulf of Mexico, Obama remained quiet. He offered absolutely zero presidential leadership at a time that demanded it. Even when other countries were offering help, Obama refused. Then on May 6, three weeks later, Obama leapt into exploitation mode and slapped a 30-day moratorium on new deep-water drilling operations in the Gulf. He also suspended drilling on rigs working in water deeper than 500 feet. This mandate immediately froze operations on 33 operational oil platforms, and another eight that were under construction, pending an investigation into the explosion that generated the BP leak.[124]

But the Obama administration didn't just limit its anti-drilling dictates in the Gulf. Simultaneous to that abeyance, the administration also suspended applications for exploratory drilling in the Alaskan Arctic, until an unspecified date in 2011. This extreme action was taken despite the fact that, in 2009, preliminary permits had already been issued by the Interior Department to Shell Oil to drill five wells in the region—three in the Chukchi Sea and two in the Beaufort Sea.[125] The suspension was a shock to Shell, who had been planning the projects for a year. **Obama's decision shot that plan down for another year ... and consumers wonder why prices at the pump continued to rise.**

But Obama's exploitation was still early stage. Prior to the expiration of the 30-day Gulf drilling moratorium, on May 27, the stay was extended for an extra six months. Then Obama ordered the Atlantic Coast off limits to energy development or exploration through 2017. This was a stunning reversal of the promise Obama made to the people of Virginia just two months earlier, on March 31, when he announced the lease-sale of nearly three million acres off their coast, a move that would enable America to harness some 130 million barrels of oil, and over a trillion cubic feet of natural gas. According to Virginia Governor **_Bob McDonnell,_** the offshore projects would "*speed our economic recovery.*"[126] McDonnell estimated that the plan would have added 2,578 full-time jobs annually, brought to the state capital investment of $7.84 billion, yielded $644 million in direct and indirect payroll, and resulted in $271 million in new state and local revenue. But none of that happened.

It was an opportunity lost for creating real American jobs and economic progress.

Meanwhile, the Gulf freeze was challenged in Federal court twice, with the Administration losing both times. In the first loss, U.S. District

Judge **_Martin Feldman_** of New Orleans stated the Interior Department _"acted arbitrarily and capriciously"_ when it incorrectly assumed that because one rig failed, all companies and rigs doing deep-water drilling pose an imminent danger.[127] Feldman went so far as to suggest the administration's motives were _"driven by political or social agendas."_[128]

Unfazed, the Interior Department issued a second challenge, but that appeal was rebuffed by a three-judge panel in the 5th District Court of Appeals. The panel stated it was open to a further hearing on the merits of the appeal in September. However, the government wasn't interested in waiting for that. Instead, Interior Secretary Ken Salazar painted the getaway car a different color and quickly sped away to pull his next caper. On July 12, Salazar issued, not a moratorium, but a "suspension" on all floating-type rigs, like the one used by BP, in any depth of the Gulf's waters, through November 30. About 36 rigs were instantly impacted.[129]

What followed was an unpublicized meltdown of the Gulf oil industry.

Getting a permit from the feds to drill anywhere became nearly impossible. As for the 36 floating rigs that were commanded to cease operations, the majority packed up for other waters. Each of these massive rigs (the larger structures are 800 feet wide, 150 high and weigh some 70,000 tons) cost up to $600 million to build, and are constructed under strict debt-financing terms that require the owners to have long-term drilling contracts secured in advance. If those contracts are not generating revenue to pay back their loans, the rig owners must wind-up operations and go to where the money is.

Eric Smith, a business professor at Tulane University, calculated that the **Gulf moratorium and suspension caused a combined loss of 137,000 jobs, with the state of Louisiana forfeiting up to $400 million in oil tax receipts.**[130] Professor Joseph Mason of Louisiana State University estimated that the **overall economic loss for the Gulf region—not because of damage from the BP spill, but because of Obama's decisions—at $3 billion.**[131]

As the suspension drew toward its expiration, the administration had the audacity to make it appear as if they were graciously lifting the ban. Ken Salazar took the stage bogusly boasting, *"The policy position that we are articulating today is that we are open for business."*[132] However, this was yet another ruse. A company could drill, but first they had to locate a floating rig, and then jump through the myriad of brand new rules and regulations contrived by Salazar for obtaining a new permit. Executives in the oil industry refer to Salazar's de facto moratorium, as a *"permitorium."*[133] Six months after Salazar's supposed reboot, only four permits had been issued—all to projects that had been suspended a year earlier.[134]

Because of the Obama's real, and de facto, moratoriums, the United States lost an estimated 360,000 barrels of oil production per day from the Gulf of Mexico in 2010 and 2011.[135] According to the Energy Information Administration's Annual Energy Outlook, released April 26, 2011, the combination of the new permitting rules and the lasting effects of the drilling moratoria will cause offshore oil production to continue lower than expected *"throughout most of the projection period,"* which extends to 2035.[136]

Meantime in the Arctic, where drilling applications were essentially suspended, Shell conceded defeat. Speaking on a conference call with investors and media in February 2011, Shell CEO ***Peter Voser*** urged the Department of Interior to stop the stonewalling and speed up the permitting process:

> *"There will be no drilling offshore Alaska in 2011…. We need urgent and timely action on permitting to go ahead with the 2012 drilling program."*[137]

If Mr. Obama really wanted to make good on not leaving our energy problems "for the next president," then he needs to make friends—not enemies, with Big Oil and its users.

Obama Saved by the Tsunami

Japan's Fukushima nuclear disaster provided Obama with the cover he desperately desired; he had long wanted to replace nuclear power with …

with . . . well, with something as yet uninvented. Back in 2008 Obama leaked his nuclear sentiments to a New Hampshire newspaper's editorial board. Asked about his stance on nuclear power, Obama showed off his sarcastic side:

> "I don't think there is anything we inevitably dislike about nuclear power, we just dislike the fact that it might blow up, and irradiate us, and kill us! That's the problem."[138]

Of course, that hadn't been a problem outside of Russia—where the only flows stronger than nuclear are vodka-based—until Fukushima. Japan's atomic energy companies and regulators were shown to both be wildly negligent. And Obama was quick to draw an American parallel and cautionary warning. It's a warning that would have earned him a rebuff from even his liberal supporters at the *New York Times*— because **the U.S. nuclear power industry has enjoyed more than 50 years of error-free operation** and, after all, Mr. Obama, **we've got to get energy somehow!**

And forget that there are 440 nuclear power reactors operating around the globe in 47 different countries, accounting for 14% of the world's electrical production.[139] In Lithuania, 76 percent of the electrical grid is supplied by nuclear power; in France, it's 75 percent. In the United States, 104 nuclear power plants supply 20 percent of the electricity, with some states benefiting more than others. Worldwide there are 64 nuclear plants under construction; none of those are located in the U.S.[140]

In 2005 the chairman of the Federal Nuclear Regulatory Commission, **_Dr. Nils Diaz_**, recommended building 100 American nuclear power plants.[141] He became the instant laughingstock of the Democratic Party . . . which is why the last successful order for a U.S. commercial nuclear power plant was in 1973, and the last unit to be turned on in the U.S. was the Watts Bar Unit 1 reactor in East Tennessee in June 1996.

If the Democrats would stop catering to the concerns of the radical, uncompromising environmental lobby and allow the nuclear industry to construct new facilities, we would see a more

stable energy grid, reduced energy costs, a massive increase in good jobs, and America would regain competitiveness with the rest of the world. But poppycock to all that, say the sanctimonious twits as they scoot off in their Prius cars, blissfully unaware that when they plug in at night, coal is being burnt for the electrical recharge.

In 2009, Senator **_Lamar Alexander_** of Tennessee asked,

> *"So why not build 100 new nuclear power plants during the next 20 years? American utilities built 100 reactors between 1970 and 1990 with their own (ratepayers') money. Why can't we do it again? Other countries are already forging ahead of us."[142]*

As **_Brian Sussman_**, author of *Eco-Tyranny: How the Left's Green Agenda Will Dismantle America*, says:

> *"The Senator makes an excellent point. There is no coherent reason we cannot replicate what we've already accomplished in past decades. We are a nation of doers. In 1961 President John F. Kennedy called for a moon landing by the end of the decade. In eight years we went from launching a rocket carrying a chimpanzee, to watching men to walk on the moon. There's no reason we can't build 100 nuclear power plants in the next twenty years, and then keep on constructing them.*
>
> *"Census data indicates the U.S. population will rise by some 50 million people come 2032; that's a 16% increase. By 2050 the population will expand by 100 million, or roughly 33% from today. Given the push by environmentalists to tear down hydroelectric dams and prevent new coal-fired electrical generating plants from being constructed—simply to avoid rolling blackouts and incredibly expensive energy from becoming the norm—we need to begin constructing a fleet of new nuclear power plants now! Wind and solar are not going to provide baseload electricity—they'll only help reduce peak energy demands. Thus, just to maintain parity within our nation's energy portfolio, we need 200 nuclear power plants by 2032; that will provide America with about 20 percent of its energy output—roughly the same amount that nuclear energy provides today…*

"We must plan ahead if we want to meet the needs of our citizens and provide the basic energy infrastructure to support our industrial base. Obama's nuclear policy goes hand-in-hand with his overall anti-energy policy, which is destined to dismantle America."

One hundred new reactors would be a boon to American industry and would create thousands of excellent, permanent jobs. It would also help us keep pace with the increased demands of a growing population.

According to Admiral **_Frank Bowman_** of the Nuclear Energy Institute, peak employment per reactor during construction could be as many as 3,000 to 4,000 full-time jobs.[143] Assuming it takes five years to build a nuclear plant, if 20 such facilities were built every five years, that's 60,000 to 80,000 jobs per five-year construction cycle. Once the plants are online, there will be at least 700 permanent, high-paying jobs with great benefits—real "green" jobs that cannot be shipped offshore. In the surrounding community, each plant would then naturally spur many more employment opportunities providing goods and services necessary to support the primary workforce.

If Obama would pull the trigger to expand our nuclear portfolio and reinstate our ability to recycle our nuclear fuel, tens of thousands of Americans could find honorable careers. On top of this, each year, the average nuclear plant generates $430 million in sales of goods and services in the local community and nearly $40 million in total labor income.

And then there's total state and local tax revenue of almost $20 million from every plant to benefit schools, roads, and other state and local infrastructure, which equate to more jobs. Add to that annual tax payments of roughly $75 million per plant to the federal government, and you have billions to use to pay down our exploding national debt.[144]

America clearly needs a sound energy plan. **We need to stop the rabid environmentalists who are purposefully instituting policies and laws aimed at decimating our power portfolio, including yet another form of emission-free electricity: hydroelectric dams.**

Is an EPA Goon Squad at Your Door Next?

Larry Keller is a patriotic American, probably a lot like you. One day this spring, after voicing his concerns about Obama's Environmental Protection Agency, a team of armed government agents showed up at his home, unannounced, to "question" him.[145]

Keller runs a computer consulting business in North Carolina. On April 27, he sent an email to the EPA in an attempt to reach Al Armendariz, the EPA regional administrator who, two days earlier, had been caught in the YouTube video boasting about crucifying Big Oil executives. After watching the video, Keller told the *Carolina Journal* that he was troubled by the comments and wanted to express his concerns to Armendariz, a public official whose salary is paid by taxpayers. Keller said,

> *"I wanted to know why someone in his position would say what he did. I wanted to question his reasoning and principles. It's all about freedom of speech…"*

In an effort to locate Armendariz's email address, Keller contacted David Gray, an EPA director of external affairs and sent the following brief email:

> *"Hello Mr. Gray. Do you have Mr. Armendariz's contact information so we can say hello? Regards, Larry Keller."*

Following the uproar generated by the video, Armendariz resigned, appropriately. However on May 2, the two EPA agents, accompanied by a six-foot-six armed police officer, knocked on Keller's door. According to Keller, the agents *"presented very official looking badges and asked if we could sit and chat awhile. We moved to the back porch and took our seats with the exception of the armed officer who stood by the door to the house the entire time."*

Keller was asked by EPA agent Michael Woods if he had sent an email to an EPA employee. Initially Keller answered *"No,"* but soon recalled the email to Gray. Woods then produced a copy of the email and asked if it was the email Keller sent. Keller answered, *"Yes."* The second agent said Keller's email was *"suspicious"* and could be interpreted in *"many different ways."* Keller asked the agent to be specific, saying he didn't have anything to hide. He also pointed out that the email clearly revealed all of his contact information. Irritated, Keller told the agents that surely *"they have bigger fish to fry"* than to drive across the entire state to follow up on an unthreatening email. He also reminded them that he is a taxpayer who contributes to their salaries.

When Keller heard his wife arriving in the front driveway, he asked the agents to remain so she could meet them and *"see what all the fuss was about."* Immediately the agents announced they had to quickly depart. Keller asked for their business cards, but they said they had none. Keller insisted they give him the name of their supervisor in Atlanta.

Keller later made several attempts to reach the supervisor, Michael Hill. Finally, Hill returned Keller's phone call and explained that orders had come directly from the Obama administration to investigate every communication with Armendariz. Hill presented Keller with the impression that everyone who had tried to reach Armendariz received a special visit from EPA agents, complete with an armed accomplice.

Larry Keller is a patriot, who responded to a pompous EPA eco-thug. For that, he was threatened with Gestapo-like representatives sent at the behest of Obama, and found himself on an enemies list for daring to publically criticize the president's anti-growth, economy-busting, green crony-promoting agenda.

Climate Change Skeptics—High on the Hit List

Many more Americans have made Obama's green enemies list, particularly the outspoken skeptics of global warming and climate change who vigorously oppose taxpayer funds being used to front a controversial, policy-driving, faulty scientific theory. Some of the more notable skeptics include:

> ► The "Chief Denier" (as christened by Al Gore), **_Dr. Fred Singer_**, founding director of the U.S. weather satellite program.

▶ **_Dr. William Gray_**, the world's premier hurricane forecaster, whose team has been unable to receive funding from the Obama administration to provide his life-saving annual storm prognostications.

▶ **_Dr. Willie Soon_**, a 47 year old solar physicist who is slowly being squeezed out of the Harvard-Smithsonian Institute because he won't back away from his powerful research indicating that the sun drives climate change, not human activity.

▶ **_Marc Morano_**, a former aide to Oklahoma Senator James Inhofe. Morano runs the website climatedepot. com, where he constantly exposes the green schemes of the Obama administration.

▶ **_Chris Horner_** of the Competitive Enterprise Institute and author of the bestseller, *The Politically Incorrect Guide to Global Warming*. Chris is an attorney who has put significant legal pressure on Obama's EPA for their draconian carbon dioxide regulations.

▶ The aforementioned Brian Sussman; an award-winning meteorologist turned radio talk show host in San Francisco, and author of *Climategate: A Veteran Meteorologist Exposes the Global Warming Scam* and *Eco-Tyranny: How the Left's Green Agenda Will Dismantle America*. Sussman was also the first to reveal the infamous Solyndra scandal, detailing how Obama brokered a sweetheart deal with political cronies, loaning their failing solar firm easy money, only to have the green darling financially crash a short time later.

▶ **_Joseph Bast_**, President of the Heartland Institute, a non-profit organization that hosts an annual international climate change conference which draws hundreds of scientists, academics, and former federal employees (note, *former*) including astronauts—all skeptical of anthropogenic global warming.

▶ **_Daniel Noe,_** Editor-in-Chief of **EPA Abuse.com,** a spunky daily blog about the threats to freedom posed by the EPA.

Also likely on Obama's green enemies list are many of the 31,000 scientists who have signed The Oregon Petition, (including more than 9,000 with Ph.D.'s), which states:

> There is no convincing scientific evidence that human release of carbon dioxide, methane, or other greenhouse gasses is causing or will, in the foreseeable future, cause catastrophic heating of the Earth's atmosphere and disruption of the Earth's climate. Moreover, there is substantial scientific evidence that increases in atmospheric carbon dioxide produce many beneficial effects upon the natural plant and animal environments of the Earth.

In the end, we are all on Obama's enemies list because no matter our politics, we are paying a dear price for Obama's unwavering desire to replace proven, low-cost energy programs with, er, something.

I have created a special website with the entire list of names of Obama's enemies at http://www.obamasenemieslist.com. To access the list please use the login name: Patriot and the password: wewillnotbeintimidated.

At the website you can also stand with those being targeted by adding your name to the list to tell Obama he cannot punish us all.

The Punished: Gun Groups, Gun Owners and Their Families
According to Obama, None of You "Nuts" Should Own Guns

You already know this, but it bears repeating in the clearest terms possible:

If you're a member of the **_National Rifle Association_**, the **_Gun Owners of America_**, the **_Second Amendment Foundation_** or a local bunch of guys and gals who like to shoot at things, or even if you just **believe strongly in the Second Amendment to the Constitution, you are high on Obama's enemies list.** This is too high for comfort in a second term when Obama has clearly formulated plans to complete **his vision of a disarmed public.**

In fact, it goes deeper than that. Senior officials in the Obama administration made it clear decades ago that they consider it their life's work to rip away two centuries of American rights and try to actually brainwash you into believing that all the problems in our modern world can be laid at the feet of gun owners, that in fact gun owners are the real menace to the enlightened society they seek to create.

This is a weighty charge, this charge of ours that the Obama administration is out to "brainwash" people that gun owners are a "menace" to society. But this is not an exaggeration, not a breathless hyping of the situation meant to provoke or startle you for some partisan purpose.

Holder Thinks Second Amendment
Doesn't Pertain to Private Citizens

Attorney General Eric Holder is Obama's point man on guns and the Second Amendment. Holder's views were made clear in May 2012 at Breitbart.com with a video of Holder giving a speech to the Woman's National Democratic Club back in 1995. At that time, Holder was a U.S. Attorney for Washington, D.C. In his speech to the ladies, he laid out a goal he would pursue through two Democratic administrations, first Clinton's and then Obama's:

> *"What we need to do is change the way in which people think about guns, especially young people, and make it something that's not cool, that it's not acceptable, it's not hip to carry a gun anymore, in the way in which we changed our attitude about cigarettes."* [146]

Guns and cigarettes—pretty much the same things in Holder's view. Again, this was not just his wishful thinking on display; this was his policy implementation. He told his audience that he had made requests of the District of Columbia's School Board:

> *"…to make a part of every day, some kind of anti-violence, anti-gun message. Every day, every school, at every level…. We need to do this every day of the week, and just really brainwash people into thinking about guns in a vastly different way."* [147]

Holder also explained that he wanted to use then "influential" Democratic leaders such as Washington D.C. Mayor Marion Barry (*convicted junkie*) and the Rev. Jesse Jackson (*extortion artist*) as well as TV shows like "The Fresh Prince of Bel Air" (*messing with whitey*) and "Martin" (*teaching cusswords to kids*) to push his anti-gun message.[148]

Holder's anti-gun accomplishments continued to mount and he must have felt proudest when in 2008 he filed a legal brief in *D.C. v. Heller*. Here Holder argued, and I'm not making this up, that the Second Amendment right of the people to keep and bear arms does not apply to private citizens! The summary page of their argument read as follows:

> "The Second Amendment Does Not Protect Firearms Possession or Use That Is Unrelated To Participation In A Well Regulated Militia"
>
> [and on page 42 of the brief]
>
> "(concluding from review of modern scholarship that there are "many adherents" of the view that the Second Amendment does not protect an individual right to keep and bear arms for private purposes)
>
> [and on page 43 of the brief]
>
> "...the text of the Second Amendment, its drafting history, and the historical context in which it was enacted support the conclusion that the constitutional right to keep and bears arms is limited to the possession or use of firearms that is reasonably related to a State's operation of a militia regulated by state and federal law. [149]

Holder and his law firm of the time were basically claiming that the Second Amendment could be and should be tossed into the dustbin, and that a nationwide ban on gun ownership would not be any kind of violation the Constitution.[150]

__David Kopel__ is an expert on the Second Amendment and head of the Independence Institute, and he has written extensively on Holder's contempt for the Second Amendment and the right of private citizens to keep weapons in their homes:

"As Deputy Attorney General, Holder was a strong supporter of restrictive gun control. He advocated federal licensing of handgun owners, a three-day waiting period on handgun sales, rationing handgun sales to no more than one per month, banning possession of handguns and so-called 'assault weapons' (cosmetically incorrect guns) by anyone under age of 21, a gun show restriction bill that would have given the federal government the power to shut down all gun shows, national gun registration, and mandatory prison sentences for trivial offenses (e.g., giving your son an heirloom handgun for Christmas, if he were two weeks shy of his 21st birthday). He also promoted the factoid that 'Every day that goes by, about 12, 13 more children in this country die from gun violence' — a statistic that's true only if one counts 18-year-old gangsters who shoot each other as 'children.'" [151]

Kopel went on to detail Holder's arguments before the Fifth Circuit Court that the Second Amendment should not be viewed as a barrier to gun confiscation, not even to the confiscation of guns from on-duty National Guardsmen.

Obama's Biggest Scandal, Lives Lost, Cover-ups

Holder could be seen as a man, sort of, on a mission. And be became something of a kid in a candy shop when Obama appointed him the highest attorney in the land. Only a few months would pass before Holder would put himself dead center in the first major scandal of the Obama presidency. This scandal was detailed in stunning detail in Townhall.com columnist **_Katie Pavlich's_** bestselling book, *Fast And Furious: Barack Obama's Bloodiest Scandal And Its Shameless Cover-Up.*

The "Fast and Furious" program was run by the Bureau of Alcohol, Tobacco, Firearms and Explosives (ATF). Federal agents encouraged and even ordered American gun shops to sell guns to 'straw man' buyers who then funneled the weapons to Mexican drug gangs. The idea, in all its ivory tower theory, was that the agents could then locate the drug kings. But there was no system in place for tracking the weapons sales, and agents who tried to follow the purchasers were told to "back off."

For his part, Holder was quick to claim that he was unaware of the "Fast and Furious" program until just a few weeks before it all blew-up. But follow-up investigations revealed that he was plainly lying, and that he had received numerous memos about the program much earlier. When this information came out, Holder adjusted his story to say that he knew about the memos but hadn't read them. And he's sticking to that story.[152]

Pavlich was interviewed by **David Limbaugh**, and she explained the real reason for "Fast and Furious:" to push for tough gun control laws:

> "Operation Fast and Furious is the deadliest and most sinister scandal in American history. A scandal so big, it's worse than Iran-Contra and makes Watergate look like a high school prank gone wrong.

> "In the early days of the Obama Administration, President Obama claimed his goal was to stop the trafficking of guns from the United States into the hands of violent Mexican drug cartels. He claimed gun dealers in the United States were responsible for sending guns to Mexico. Both of his claims were lies.

> "In order to push his lies and policies built around them, with a goal of implementing harsher gun control laws and reinstating the assault weapons ban, President Obama packed his administration full of anti-Second Amendment zealots. After all, personnel is policy.

> "I document the conspiracy of senior Obama officials to subvert the Second Amendment, which led directly to the murders of Border Patrol Agent Brian Terry, I.C.E. Agent Jaime Zapata and countless, faceless lives in Mexico. It debunks the Obama administration's lies, denials and excuses. This administration was willing to use humans as collateral damage to push a

political agenda, and had no shame in doing so. Now, the administration has no shame in covering up their reckless actions."[153]

Pavlich's book should become required reading for every liberal of conscience—because she exposes the intensity of the corruption in Holder's Department of Justice and how Holder himself was very centrally involved in the scandal which resulted in the death of one border patrol agent, Brian Terry, and the murder or wounding of some 200 Mexican citizens.

Even after Holder was held in "contempt of Congress" for stonewalling the congressional investigations, he doesn't care. Obama also doesn't care. With Obama in the White House, Holder knows the bloodstains on his hands will not matter until Obama does not.

Obama, of course, has been a long-time enemy of the Second Amendment and things will get far worse if Obama has a second term. **_Wayne LaPierre_**, the Executive Vice President of the NRA explains it this way:

> *"Barack Obama spent his entire political career proudly and publicly pushing for the most radical anti-gun positions you can imagine. He endorsed a total ban on the manufacture, sale and possession of handguns. He opposed right-to-carry laws. He voted to ban nearly all commonly used hunting-rifle ammunition.*
>
> *"During the presidential primary debates, Obama even vowed to re-impose the discredited Clinton gun ban, which banned many commonly owned firearms used for hunting and self-defense."[154]*

LaPierre also predicted that during his political campaign, Obama would try to neutralize gun owners and NRA members by pretending to be pro-gun or by avoiding any mention of his anti-gun agenda. He was right on. Since his reelection, he is preparing to launch an all-out assault on the Second Amendment through legislation, litigation, regulation, executive orders and international treaties.

In short, **Obama will use every lever of power at his disposal to undermine and even terminate the right to keep and bear arms.**

Using International Law to Take Away American Rights

For now, the Obama Administration is working through the United Nations to pass laws that would have legal bearing on American citizens. His United Nations Arms Trade Treaty (ATT) includes language that will, according to Gun Owners of America: [155]

- ▶ Require the registration and licensure of American firearms;
- ▶ Ban large categories of firearms;
- ▶ Require the mandatory destruction of surplus ammo and confiscated firearms;
- ▶ Define manufacturing so broadly that any gun owner who adds an accessory such as a scope or changes a stock on a firearm would be required to obtain a manufacturing license;
- ▶ Require "micro-stamping" of ammunition.

The treaty could be "self-executing" which means that it could achieve its anti-gun objectives without implementing legislation from Congress. For her part, Secretary of State Hillary Clinton has committed the U.S. to accepting and being bound by the terms of the treaty. And a committee at the United Nations is (as I write) working on a final draft of the treaty to submit to Obama for a "look see" before putting it to a vote at the UN.

Bottom line: Obama has resorted to an end-run; he is working around the U.S. body of laws and using international law to take away from Americans a fundamental constitutional right. (Echoes of the Communist Manifesto ring in our ears, ***"The Communists are further reproached with desiring to abolish countries and nationality"*** and ***"United action, of the leading civilized countries at least, is one of the first conditions for the emancipation of the proletariat."***)[156]

At the local level, Obama's ATF is also quietly working to obtain lists of gun owners (for what reason, we can only guess, except to add the 47% of U.S. households that own guns to the enemies list?). They are trying to get names of gun owners now in Alaska – even though it is illegal to do so. A report in the *Alaska Dispatch* on April 25, 2012 describes how several owners of gun shops in Alaska were visited by ATF officials to get their lists of gun owners.[157]

Again we ask why?

Alaska Congressman **_Don Young_** also asked why; he put his question to the head of the ATF. Young concedes freely that ATF has a responsibility to run routine compliance inspections of gun sellers. But it has been illegal for ATF to seek access to gun owner lists since 2011. According to Young:

> *"The ATF has some serious explaining to do. Congress has been unequivocal when it comes to gun registries or anything that resembles one – they are against the law. I expect a full and complete response from the ATF in a timely fashion. In the time-being, I will continue do everything in my power to ensure Americans' Second Amendment rights are not trampled on."[158]*

Illegal or not, in 2011 Holder's Department of Justice sent out a memo to gun shops in California, Texas, Arizona and New Mexico instructing them to "notify the AFT" about "frequent buyers" of high-power rifles. The edict also required gun owners to report the purchase of two or more pistols or revolvers. Fortunately, Congress blocked this edict in May 2012.[159]

What is Obama's End-game?

A good insight into Obama's real intentions comes from **_John Lott,_** author of *More Guns, Less Crime*. Lott has made a responsible case for arming the citizenry, and that has put him squarely in the sights of Obama, who uses his meetings with sadly unfortunate victims like Sarah Brady to make his point:

> *" 'I don't believe that people should be able to own guns…. I just want you to know that we are working on [gun control]. We have to go through a few processes, but under the radar.' "[160]*

Hmm. Sounds an awful lot like what Obama told Soviet President Dmitry Medvedev, and no doubt others—he could work with them;

he just couldn't do it or admit it publicly because only a few would support him and so it has to happen through "flexible" means, through "back channels" and "under the radar."

So there's a liberal dilemma—having to create smokescreens and artifices to mask policy aims, since so few would support those aims if they knew the full truth about them. But understanding the dilemma, and accepting it, are not the same.

In his end-game of disarming America, Obama's most effective strategy is appointing anti-gun judges to the federal courts. Obama has already appointed two anti-gun zealots to the Supreme Court—Elena Kagan and Sonia Sotomayor. Justice Kagan pushed an anti-gun agenda while working for President Clinton. Justice Sotomayor affirmed a Supreme Court decision stating that there is no individual right to private self-defense in America (basically parroting AG Holder's position, discussed earlier).

Obama tried, but failed, to get Caitlin Joan Halligan appointed to the U.S. Court of Appeals in Washington, D.C. Ms. Halligan opposes private gun ownership and was a key player in the lawsuit against gun maker Sturm & Ruger, arguing that gun makers should be held liable for the criminal acts of third parties.

Now that Obama is reelected to a second term, he could end up appointing over half of the federal judges in our court system. That's worth repeating. **Now that Obama is reelected to a second term, he could end up appointing over half of the federal judges in our court system. And based on his appointments to date, he would pick anti-gun fanatics who would in turn issue edicts that effectively disarm us.**

None of this can be considered surprising.

This is the man who, in a moment of honesty in his 2008 campaign, expressed disgust with those who *"cling to their guns, cling to their religion."* That his description fits the majority of Americans should have been a flashing yellow warning back in 2008. And it's certainly a red light today.

Why Was the Second Amendment Added to the Bill Of Rights?

Obama's desire to disarm Americans can be better understood in a historical context. **Those who seek to control others, must first disarm them.** The American Revolutionaries understood this well.

James Madison's *Federalist Papers* explained that standing armies could forever threaten the new nation's liberties—but not if opposed by a *"militia amounting to near a half-million citizens with arms in their hands."* This "militia" he referred to was not the National Guard. It was every able-bodied American who owned a gun and could use it effectively.

As John Lott said of the Founding Fathers:

> *"[They] believed that an armed citizenry is the ultimate bulwark against tyrannical government. Possibly our trust in government has risen so much that we no longer fear what future governments might do. Having just fought a war for their independence against a government that had tried to confiscate their guns, the founding fathers felt very strongly about this issue."* [161]

Ken Blackwell and ***Ken Klukowski*** have written a most chilling book—another must read. Titled *The Blueprint: Obama's Plan to Subvert the Constitution and Build an Imperial Presidency,* this book begins with the events at Concord Green in 1775—because it bears on today's situation. The incident that started the Revolutionary War was the attempt by Britain to seize arms and ammunition from the colonists – in other words to do exactly what Obama is trying to do today. From *The Blueprint*:

> *"On April 19, 1775, the Shot Heard 'Round the World was fired on Lexington Common. Seven Americans lay dead after the shooting. Word of British soldiers firing on civilian colonists spread like wildfire, and anger reached a critical mass among the American people. The colonists decided that the split with the British couldn't be mended, and that war was inevitable.*

"What fewer people know, however, is what the British were doing that day. They were marching to Concord, Massachusetts, on orders from Lieutenant General Thomas Gage, who was in charge of the growing unrest in Massachusetts, to seize the firearms and ammunition kept in an armory at Concord. The act that sparked the American Revolution was an attempt by the government to take away our guns. So when the Constitution was ratified and the Founders resolved to amend the Constitution to include a Bill of Rights (without promises for which the Constitution would never have been ratified), the right to keep and bear arms was among the specific rights enumerated in the amendments. The Second Amendment reads, 'A well regulated militia, being necessary to the security of a free state, the right of the people to keep and bear arms, shall not be infringed.'"[162]

Chilling Words from Someone Who Knows

The right of the American people to keep and bear arms is enshrined in the Bill of Rights and is inviolable. It is an essential right of a free and independent people. Or, at least, it was for two centuries prior to this administration. Again from *The Blueprint*:

*"Perhaps the most powerful exposition we've ever read for the reason for the Second Amendment is the one written by Chief Judge **Alex Kozinski** of the Ninth Circuit. For those who would dismiss his statements as fear-mongering or alarmist, know this: Kozinski was born in Romania, under communist tyranny. His parents were Holocaust survivors. So when he speaks of Jews being herded into cattle cars for mass extermination, he's not invoking some bogeyman; he's speaking of his own family. His words are so profound that we have nothing to add; we'll just close with the insight he and his family have gained from their own nightmarish experience.*

"Writing in dissent on the denial of rehearing the case Silveira v. Lockyer, which challenged the California assault weapons

ban, Kozinski wrote: [Some believe] that ordinary people are too careless and stupid to own guns, and we would be far better off leaving all weapons in the hands of professionals on the government payroll. But the simple truth—born of experience—is that tyranny thrives best where government need not fear the wrath of an armed people....

"All too many of the other great tragedies of history-Stalin's atrocities, the killing fields of Cambodia, the Holocaust, to name but a few-were perpetrated by armed troops against unarmed populations. Many could well have been avoided or mitigated, had the perpetrators known their intended victims were [armed] ... If a few hundred Jewish fighters in the Warsaw Ghetto could hold off the Wehrmacht for almost a month with only a handful of weapons, six million Jews armed with rifles could not so easily have been herded into cattle cars. [Many forget] these bitter lessons of history. The prospect of tyranny may not grab the headlines the way vivid stories of gun crime routinely do. But few saw the Third Reich coming until it was too late.

"The Second Amendment is a doomsday provision, one designed for those exceptionally rare circumstances where all other rights have failed—where the government refuses to stand for reelection and silences those who protest; where courts have lost the courage to oppose, or can find no one to enforce their decrees. However improbable these contingencies may seem today, facing them unprepared is a mistake a free people get to make only once."[163]

These are sobering remarks from someone who is very familiar with tyrants and why tyrants fear an armed citizenry.

If you're a member of the NRA, Gun Owners of America, the Second Amendment Foundation, gun shop owner, or just own a firearm, you're on Obama's enemies list. He wants your weapons and he's going to do everything he can to disarm you. It's the way of tyrants, petty and otherwise.

Obama has a perfect record in undermining and seeking to eliminate our Second Amendment rights. **Obama has:**

- **Voted to ban common ammunition**
- **Supported lawsuits against gun makers if one of their guns is used by a criminal**
- **Supported increased federal taxes on guns and ammunition**
- **Stated he wants to force every gun owner to get a license**
- **Stated he wants to force every gun owner to register their guns**
- **Stated he wants to outlaw concealed carry laws**
- **Voted for the government to keep secret records on gun owners**[164]

I have created a special website with the entire list of names of Obama's enemies at http://www.obamasenemieslist.com. To access the list please use the login name: Patriot and the password: wewillnotbeintimidated.

At the website you can also stand with those being targeted by adding your name to the list to tell Obama he cannot punish us all.

The Punished: Young People, College Students, Future Generations
So What if I'm Screwing over Future Generations… They're Not Voters Yet

President Obama has had nearly four years now to "fix" our economy, but he's only made things worse. During two of those years, he controlled both the House and Senate – so he can't honestly blame Bush for his failures (but lacking any semblance of integrity, he does, anyway). Those suffering *most* from Obama's failed economic policies are young people.

By punishing businesses with over-regulation, handing out millions of tax dollars on failed stimulus programs, and railing against the "rich," Obama has effectively destroyed any potential growth in our economy. Businesses are fearful of expanding and face uncertain taxation problems. Obamacare has thrown companies into chaos and they're dealing with unexpected increases in the cost of health insurance for their employees.

Obama's war on energy production is going to have an immense impact on the future of young people's ability to buy homes, buy cars, and lead productive lives. Obama's decision to destroy the coal industry is killing jobs and hope for hundreds of thousands of Americans. His decision to block the Keystone XL oil pipeline has killed thousands of construction jobs – jobs which could be filled by young men and women.

Obama's goal of bankrupting the coal industry will result in power outages, blackouts, and a reduced standard of living for all Americans. As he attacks the oil industry and prevents us from drilling on our own land, he's killing jobs for hundreds of thousands.

His energy policies will result in higher food costs, higher gas prices, higher trucking costs, and more unemployment.

Those already in the workforce face layoffs and uncertain futures. And as the job market shrinks, who suffers the most? High school graduates, followed by college graduates, who are finding job postings few and far between, and then countless applicants for those postings. **Young job seekers today are competing with an estimated 20 million *older* Americans who have experience in the workplace and no interest in ceding their job**—since there's little upward opportunity for them, either. Not only that, **older Americans are forced to continue working because they lost so much value in their houses and money in the stock market that they were counting on using for their retirement years.**

Obama has effectively put every young person seeking work on his enemies list. One of those is ***Chris Cocchi***, a 27-year-old who currently lives in Philadelphia with his father. He's unemployed and no matter how hard he looks, he can't find a job. Another victim of Obama's economy is 22 year old ***Elijah Little***, also of Pennsylvania. He left one job for a better one unloading trucks at a warehouse. But before long, he was laid off—because of a slow economy. He's been trying to get work ever since, without success. He's started taking classes at a community college to complete an associate degree, but now he can't—because he can't afford the tuition.

Andrew Sum, a professor at Northeastern University, tracks unemployment trends among the young. He says:

> *"I've never seen the world so bad for young people. The only way I can describe it is as a Great Depression."* [165]

Barely half of Americans between 16-29 were working in 2010.

The hardest hit jobs have been manufacturing and construction jobs – jobs that are usually filled by men with high school educations. College graduates are also having difficulty finding work – especially if they've majored in the humanities instead of computer science or health care.

Youth Helped Re-elect Obama

The youth vote was a key to Obama's victories in 2008 and 2012. Obama won 66% of the 24 million voters between the ages of 18-29 in 2008. For instance in 2012, although the president's support among white, young voters declined from 54% to 44%, he nevertheless managed to win the under-30 block by 24 points due to an unusually high turnout of minorities. Latinos comprised 18% of young voters this year while blacks made up 17%, compared to 10% and 12% in 2008. These groups backed the president by 74% and 91%, respectively.

Tracking on these young voters is a group called Generation Opportunity. **_Paul Conway_** runs the group, and says:

> *"These vocal young voters are even more digitally connected— and politically potent—for 2012 than they were in 2008."* [166]

Those that turned away from Obama realized that he may be cool, may be fun to shoot some hoops and have a beer with – but he's definitely not their friend and in fact he personally has never known hardship and seems somehow unable to understand their situation. He needs to be taken off their Facebook page, because he's systematically destroying any chance they have of a productive future in America.

According to studies done by Generation Opportunity:

44% are delaying buying a home
28% are delaying saving for retirement
23% are delaying starting a family
18% will wait to get married

Interestingly, this study found that 69% of young people say the current leadership in Washington, D.C. fails to reflect their interests; 59% of the Millennials agree that the economy grows best when individuals are allowed to create businesses without government interference. This is sound economic sense, but it runs counter to Obama's own utopian vision for America. Generation Opportunity's Conway is former chief of staff of the Labor Department and Office of Personnel Management, so he knows his way around statistics and outcomes. His own analysis of young people's attitudes is.

> *"Young Americans continue to suffer the impacts of the President and his administration's bad economic policies, the resulting poor economy, and the overall lack of opportunity. The administration has failed to listen closely to the needs of young adults – they want meaningful, full-time jobs in a career path of their choice to get on with their own lives.*
>
> *"Instead, the Obama administration continues to push a vision that offers less hope and less opportunity. Nearly every week, administration officials appear on college campuses and at gatherings of young Americans to brag about how the federal government is expanding to take over more of their healthcare, education, job training, and other decisions – where is the hope in that?"*[167]

Samuel Bain is a young conservative, and likely to be more critical of Obama than many of his age. Yet his critique of Obama's 2012 State of the Union message resonated with many of his fellow young Americans when he said on *Fox News*:

> *"Young people worked tirelessly to put Obama in office by a 2 to 1 margin over McCain. Obama returned the favor with a bogus*

trillion dollar stimulus that only benefited his personal circle of the one percent. Next, he passed Obamacare which looks more like a new tax code than it does healthcare legislation. Over 20 new taxes and fees imposed that hurt small businesses and drive up the costs of health coverage.

"Young people are getting over this Obama fad. We don't believe that our success is determined by another individual. We don't believe in this false mantra of jealousy and class warfare. What we believe in is liberty and independence and the chance to succeed on our own without an overbearing and over reaching government getting in our way and telling us how to live our lives.

"My generation and America deserve a man in the Oval Office committed to the well-being and unity of every American. Last night's speech contained no such rhetoric. The most ironic part of Obama's address was the audacity of his self-comparison to Lincoln. Mr. President, you are no Lincoln. He saved the union. You're dividing it."[168]

I couldn't have said it better than Samuel Bain, who clearly understands that young people are on Obama's Enemy List. He doesn't want independent productive young adults – he wants obedient subjects who are totally dependent on him for their livelihoods. Sadly, Obama seems to be getting the type of young person he wants. They still overwhelming supported him, even when it was clearly not in their best interests.

A Lot of Young People Lost their Innocence These Last Four Years

Another student skeptical of Obama's failed promises is ***Harry Graver***, a Yale University student who published a scathing critique of Obama's speech to young women at Barnard University in May 2012.

Graver noted how Obama portrayed himself as a 'struggling student' in the class of 1983. Interesting. Since it was 1983, Obama entered an economy shaped by the Reagan recovery, an economy

Reagan took credit for rather than lamely continuing to blame his predecessor, an economy that lifted the wealth of Americans greater than any previous period, adding roughly 400,000 jobs per month, growing GDP at high 7% a year levels. But in his speech to the ladies at Barnard who are not taught to question the liberal orthodoxy, but to obey, Obama won cheers for blaming everyone else for his failed economic policies. Graver concluded:

> *"This sort of finger pointing is not uncharacteristic for Obama, who always seems ready to construct a culprit other than himself, be it a Republican Congress, the Supreme Court, Wall Street, Super-PACs, and even now, with an equal amount of irony and desperation, the mainstream media."*

> *"Cloaked in empathetic anecdotes and an admirable personal story, the President has redefined his failings as virtuous opportunities…. His economy is our defining struggle–yet, miraculously, he is the shepherd, not the villain. With the economy in tatters, Obama's message has gone from 'Hope and Change' to 'Grin and Bear It' in the course of four short years.*[169]

So Obama somehow has these college kids to believing he'll somehow turn things around for them in another four years in the White House, when he couldn't do it in the first four years. That's quite a leap of faith. We can only hope someday they realize what the conservative commentators like **_Mark Steyn_** have known all along. Here's classic Steyn from *After America:*

> *"Obama himself is not about 'doing:' Why would you expect him to be able to 'do' anything? What has he ever 'done' other than publish books about himself? That was the story of his life: Wow! Look at this guy! Wouldn't it be great to have him … as Harvard Law Review editor, as community organizer, as state representative, as state senator, as United States senator. He was wafted ever upwards, staying just long enough in each 'job' to get another notch on the escutcheon, but never long enough to leave any trace–until a freak combination of circumstances*

(war weariness, financial meltdown, divisive incumbent, inept opponent, the chance to cast a history-making vote) put Obama in line for the ultimate waft."[170]

And on that "ultimate waft" Obama has failed America's youth—effectively turning every young American into an enemy on the day they wake up and smell the coffee and discover that their future ain't pretty. And that it didn't have to be.

Obama's Student Loan Scheme—Good Intention Gone Bad

Who can argue with the idea of investing in our future, one college student at a time? Certainly not me. So let's look at how the student loan program will play out.

Obama has chosen to extend the interest rate that students pay – a rate of 3.4% which is lower than just about all other loans – for federally subsidized student loans. Okay, but Obama has to pay for this extension. And to do so, he worked with Senate Democrats to cover the costs by *raising* payroll taxes on employers. So the logic of the plan appears to be: Let's increase the cost of doing business for employers, so they have less money to hire new college graduates, who then can't payback their subsidized loans.

Hmm.

It doesn't matter how low interest rates go on student loans, if students can't find jobs because businesses are struggling to pay higher payroll taxes and compete in a global marketplace, where corporate taxes are already the world's highest.

In 2010, Obama seized control of the student loan program; prior it had been backed by private loan companies. But Obama made it a wholly federal program, cut private enterprise out of the deal, and put the taxpayers on the hook. And what a hook...

Until the Obama takeover, about 15 million of the 19 million outstanding student loans were private loans. Now they're public, amounting to nearly one trillion dollars in obligations. Yes, that's a thousand billion dollars, give or take a few billion. Now we know that students are just about the worst credit risks, a step above alcoholics with a gambling problem. Only a few of these loans will ever be fully paid back. That job of "paying down the bad debt" will fall to the taxpayers, thanks to Obama. He'll have to raise taxes yet again, and he'll have to crank the printing press yet again. And those actions will be like a wet wool blanket laying over the economy, making it even harder for recovery to break out.

What's more, **the old student loan program was working. Private enterprise had student loans under control. But now the 31,000 Americans who work at community banks and non-profit lenders in the student loan business are looking at pink slips.**[171]

Once again this situation sounds exactly like what Karl Marx and Frederick Engel had in mind when writing about necessitating **"further inroads upon the old order."** Some of their ten measures of doing this, include, *"A heavy progressive or graduated income tax"* but also, *"Centralisation of credit in the hands of the state, by means of a national bank with State capital and an exclusive monopoly"*[172]

What a deal! Obama managed to destroy thousands of private sector jobs, while making college students dependent on him for their student loans – and we're borrowing more money from China to drive future generations into unbelievable debt.

But Obama is not satisfied with this. Simply controlling student loans and putting private loan companies out of business is not enough. He also wants to "fundamentally change" the for-profit colleges and training institutes that he accuses of abusing the GI bill and deceiving military veterans. White House talking points tell of Obama as going after "diploma mills" that exploit GIs returning from war. Sounds noble. Fighting for veterans! Defending the taxpayers from fraud.

But, that's not what's going on.

Maritza Vega is a *single mom* who attended for-profit schools and eventually earned a BA at the University of Phoenix and finished her MA in September 2011. She says Obama's attack on for-profit schools (such as the University of Phoenix) are harming students like her who must work and have flexible hours to attend classes. Writing in *The Daily Caller*, Vega noted:

"While Americans have been focusing on other things, the Obama administration has been quietly waging a war on for-profit colleges — a war that could end up destroying necessary opportunities for people like me.

> *"Recently, the Department of Education, under pressure from not-for-profit community colleges and education policy institutions, has proposed a 'gainful employment' rule that would place a heavy burden on students who decide to go to for-profit schools. These new rules would limit federal grant money to schools whose students have low post-graduation income, and could eliminate financial aid to as many as 360,000 students. Many of those students are single mothers like me — women who depend on the flexibility of for-profit institutions to pursue their dreams while still caring for their families."*

> *"The Obama administration does not seem to understand how their actions will impact the lives of thousands of low- and middle-income students who need the flexibility and opportunity that these schools offer. Not to mention, graduates of for-profit schools have a 38% higher completion rate than their counterparts at community colleges and over the next several years will provide almost 1.6 million new employees to some of the fastest-growing industries in America. Driving these institutions out of business would deal a crushing blow to the aspirations of thousands of students who know this is their best option."*[173]

However, Obama driving these private institutions out of business is right in line with Marx and Engels, who wrote they want *"to rescue education from the influence of the ruling class,"* and get all children into public schools. [174]

If you're someone like Maritza Vega who attends a **for-profit college or training institute, you made Obama's Enemies List in spirit. If you actually *run* a for-profit educational institution, you made it for real.** *(Unless you're a super-liberal trust fund baby like*

University of Phoenix's Peter Sperling, in which case a blind eye is turned—just keep those cards and donations coming Pete!)

"Pretend" Jobs for Those Summertime Blues

In an effort to be seen driving down youth unemployment in time for the election, Obama has been rolling out a pretend-plan after another. His latest was a plan to create 300,000 summer jobs and employment for what he calls "disconnected" youth. Of these, 90,000 will be paid jobs. Obama budgeted $1.5 billion to pay for these jobs, calling them *"high-impact summer jobs"* for youth aged 16-24. But even his partisans in Congress recognized this was wasteful spending on useless make-work jobs, and they blocked the legislation.[175] Federally-created "summer jobs" aren't real jobs, of course. They do nothing to help America's youth find gainful, productive employment. They do nothing to contribute to a chronic problem, except to make it worse. What they do accomplish, and apparently well, is convince gullible voters that Obama is taking action.

On an allied front, Obama has been trying to raise the minimum wage because in his worldview, it helps the youth of America. But as we've seen, Obama's understanding of economics and the free enterprise system is rather limited—academic at best. Any one of his economic advisors could tell him—if they dared (and he would listen)—that every time the minimum wage is raised, teens and poor people experience a net job loss.

The Wall Street Journal reported in 2009 on an exhaustive study done by a Federal Reserve economist on the impact of raising the minimum wage. The economist reviewed more than 100 academic studies and found overwhelming evidence that: The least skilled and young suffer a loss of employment whenever the minimum wage is increased.

When Congress raised the minimum wage in July 2007 to $5.15 an hour, it resulted in the loss of 691,000 fewer teens working by October 2009.

A minimum wage increase in July 2009 to $7.25 an hour resulted in the loss of 300,000 youth jobs by September of that year. That's 300,000 jobs lost in two months—because of wrong-headed economic policies that fly in the face of marketplace realities in a global era.[176]

In a second term, Obama can be expected to keep banging the drum for a higher minimum wage . . . leading to fewer jobs but more government control. He's okay with that.

I have created a special website with the entire list of names of Obama's enemies at http://www.obamasenemieslist.com. To access the list please use the login name: Patriot and the password: wewillnotbeintimidated.

At the website you can also stand with those being targeted by adding your name to the list to tell Obama he cannot punish us all.

The Punished: The Sick, The Elderly, The Military, Everyone who needs Medical Care
Healthcare is Getting Messy—Starting with the Elderly

Americans born before 1945 are soon to face the most uncertainty they've known since the year they were born, and war was raging on six continents. They are about to see the true face of Obamacare, and the cold hard truth that they are expendable in the eyes of the 26 year old former sociology majors charged with administering an impossible mandate.

When Obama first started "selling" his healthcare plan, he trotted out Andy Griffith in a TV media blitz to push Obamacare as a savior for the elderly. And he paid off the AARP leaders to get their endorsement; the payoff was a "waiver" of some of the plan's more onerous provisions.[177]

This waiver was a tell—one of many to come—that the plan was deeply flawed, however admirably intended, at the outset. And who could argue that healthcare in America didn't need fixing. It did. But at this point, the country didn't yet know that the solution would be worse than the problem.

The second tell was the ease at which Obamacare sailed through the legislative process—especially in view of the obstacles Hillary Clinton faced when she tried a similar thing. Why didn't we hear the big bad pharmaceutical companies crying bloody murder, undercutting, fighting, and lashing out?

Because it is **the pharmaceutical companies, and not the American people, who will be the biggest beneficiaries of Obamacare.**

They crafted a deal with Obama.

In return for rolling over, Obama promised them hundreds of billions in prescription revenues, and a free ride on the regulation train. By some estimates, the consumer will see a $3.5 billion a year bump in drug prices. A hefty price tag for a flawed program. But as we said, America didn't know that in 2009…

Fast-forward to the present. Obamacare has been shown to be such a mess at the most fundamental level; the Supreme Court had to decide its outcome. This should have been a big sign to Obama. A sign to go back to the drawing board. But rather than do that. Obama dug in and launched a scare campaign to divert attention. A favorite tactic of his, as we've seen again and again. This time he stuttered-stepped on Obamacare and then started blasting evil Republicans for trying to eliminate Medicare and Medicaid and kill-off wheelchair-bound grannies.

One liberal group even produced a video showing Republican Congressman Paul Ryan pushing an elderly woman in a wheelchair up to a picturesque cliff overlooking a lake. He then throws her off the cliff. As "America the Beautiful" played in the background, ominous text claimed that Ryan was going to eliminate Medicare altogether.

The video was an amateurish canard, of course, but what do you expect from a radical socialist named Erica Payne, who runs the outfit? Payne is the co-founder of the Democracy Alliance, a group that spawned Media Matters, a group that exists solely to invent stories about conservative legislators, reporters and conservative principles. Payne is buddies with John Podesta, who ran Obama's transition team and served briefly as his Chief of Staff. Podesta now heads the Center for American Progress, which is a George Soros front group. Payne is now employed as an Obama surrogate to try to scare the elderly into supporting his left-wing agenda. The message is clear:

Vote Republican and you'll be executed!

No Republican has any intention of throwing grandmothers over a cliff, of course, but grandma has a rough wheelchair ride ahead. One can even argue that Obamacare itself may be the single greatest threat to the future health and safety of the elderly. And unfortunately, because the whole issue is so complex, most people don't understand how bad it will be for them...

Robbing from Medicare to Pay for Obamacare

One of Obama's first moves was to take $500 billion from Medicare and transfer it to the Obamacare program. This means seniors will see a reduction in services and in many cases, doctors will simply stop accepting Medicare patients.

Obama intends to eliminate another $300 to $500 billion from Medicare and Medicaid—by streamlining and eliminating waste, fraud and abuse. This sounds peachy. But once again, this will inevitably harm seniors. Because every president promises to eliminate waste, fraud and abuse. And every president—especially those who want more government, not less—fail. So the cuts won't get made, and the health programs will become even more financially unstable.

The biggest threat to seniors through Obamacare is the inevitable rationing of healthcare. The healthcare law that Obama's surrogates rammed through Congress – without anyone actually reading the document – includes what's known as the Independent Payment Advisory Board (IPAB). This is a 15-member unelected panel that is given the job of imposing price controls on Medicare costs. [178]

This panel was modeled after the British National Institute for Health and Clinical Excellence (NICE . . . but it sure isn't) because it routinely rations healthcare for patients who are trapped in England's socialist system.

Obama's first pick to run his new health control system was Dr. Donald Berwick. The doctor is a great fan of NICE, and made it clear he would use it as a model for Obamacare. In his words:

> "…the decision is not whether we will ration care; the decision is whether we will ration with our eyes open."[179]

But Dr. Berwick's tenure was short-lived. When he learned that he would have to endure Senate confirmation hearings, "something" in his past worried him enough to turn down the most prestigious job an admitted "socialist," like himself, could ever hope to attain.

Obama's next pick to run the Social Security Advisory Board was Henry J. Aaron. He stated from the outset that the Independent Payment Advisory Board (IPAB) should have the authority to ration payments to acute and long-term care hospitals, hospices, and inpatient rehabilitation and psychiatric facilities. He has publicly lamented that the IPAB isn't yet in the rationing business, and has urged that this restriction be repealed *"as soon as possible."*[180]

If Dr. Berwick follows the British rule of thumb, we'll find that hospitals cannot spend more than $22,000 to save six months of life. As a result of this rule now, 25,000 British cancer patients die prematurely each year. Expect the same thing here.

Dr. Scott Gottlieb, a practicing physician and resident fellow with the American Enterprise Institute, testified before Congress in March 2012 on IPAB and was asked if healthcare will be affected by reimbursements being cut for particular services? He replied:

> "I think it absolutely will…. You're going to have payment driven so low in some settings that certain services won't be available. Physicians won't be available to take patients."[181]

Inevitably, medical services will be rationed and unelected government bureaucrats will also be making life and death decisions over who lives and who dies. **The losers will be the elderly and the disabled**—who are considered less valuable to those who are still young and can work. When you heard tell of "death panels," this is what they were talking about.

Now if it were necessary to ration healthcare to get expenses under control, and to create the best healthcare solutions for all, we'd be all for it. Americans would support it. But that's not what Obama did.

Fewer Health Choices, Fewer Everything Choices

However Obamacare finally bedpans out, seniors are in for some tough years ahead—as a direct result of Obama's policies and his unwillingness to effectively manage the federal government's purse strings.

In February 2012, **_Forbes_** published a depressing article, "Obama's 'Sneak Attack' On Senior Citizens." It details how seniors have been hoodwinked by the millions in believing that Obama's plans for them are well-intentioned.

The impacts on the elderly are going to be painful, and include:

- ▶ **Depressed Interest Income:** Obama's economic policymakers in concert with the Federal Reserve are artificially holding down interest rates so that seniors on fixed incomes are earning very little interest from their savings accounts, money market funds, and bonds.
- ▶ **Draining Remaining Social Security Funds:** In Obama's desire to buy votes, he created a "Payroll Tax Holiday" that reduced the employee's portion of payroll taxes by 2% (good for employees to a small extent) but also means those payroll taxes do not go onto the Social Security Trust Fund, and it goes belly-up sooner (bad for seniors, to a large extent).
- ▶ **Dry Up Dividends, Gut Capital Gains:** Obama has proposed doubling the tax rate on dividends and capital gains to help pay for his $5 trillion in deficit spending.
- ▶ **New Taxes Hidden In Obamacare:** The President buried a 3.8% tax on "unearned income" – which includes dividends, interest and proceeds from the sale of homes. Seniors who are downsizing could use that money – but he wants it.
- ▶ **Reduced Funding In Medicare And Rationing Health Care:** Obama has cut Medicare benefits by $500 billion over a period of years.[182]

Seniors are also being stressed economically by the high cost of gasoline and food! Thanks to Obama's refusal to permit our energy producers to exploit our nation's abundant natural gas, oil, and coal industries, the price of transportation, electricity and food are constantly going up. This directly impacts seniors who live on fixed or limited incomes from diminishing investments and savings accounts.

Just watch.

Gasoline prices moderated temporarily before the November election because of agreements Obama has made with the Saudis. But now that he won the election be guaranteed that gasoline prices will go up relentlessly.

Jim Martin heads up the 60 Plus Association, another spokesman for seniors that was not bought off by Obama, like AARP was. Martin writes:

> *"The biggest Medicare fraud ever was committed by this President and former Speaker Nancy Pelosi when they conspired to gut Medicare by half a trillion dollars to help fund Obamacare. If he were serious about prosecuting those who would harm seniors then both of them would be in the back of a paddy wagon. The President is telling a lot of whoppers lately to wipe the slate clean on his record, but saying that he is a protector of Medicare is the biggest whopper of them all. What a cruel, even craven, way to treat seniors with this totally false claim.*

> *"Seniors will not be fooled by Obama's paid attempts to rewrite history and cast himself as a hero to America's elderly. In over three years in office he has not proposed a single policy to help preserve Medicare, which his former Chief of Staff Bill Daley said would be broke in five years. In fact President Obama has sped the demise of Medicare by slashing its trust fund, proposing the health care rationing IPAB, and expanding Obamacare.*

> *"Come November, I promise that America's seniors will treat President Obama with the same regard he has treated Medicare over his four years."[183]*

Dan Weber, head of the Association of Mature American Citizens, writes on behalf of his members:

"The steep hike in gas prices has all kinds of negative implications for the nation's seniors. But it seems President Obama doesn't care who gets hurt this election year, as long as he appeases his ideological base of supporters and gets reelected.

"Obama nixes the Keystone pipeline and imposes a moratorium on drilling and then says 'it's not my fault' that gas prices are where they are. Does this make sense? I don't think so. We have more than enough oil reserves under our feet and off our shores to make us self-sufficient and able to stabilize prices at reasonably lower levels.

"Perhaps he thinks that we'll all forget that his hand-picked Energy Secretary, Stephen Chu, has already admitted that: 'Somehow we have to figure out how to boost the price of gasoline to the levels in Europe'". [184]

Obama is dedicated to forcing up the price of fuel in order to make "green" energy more attractive. And that's making life increasingly miserable for seniors.

If You Love British and Canadian Health Care, You'll Love Obamacare

Dr. David Gratzer is a Canadian with first-hand experience in the healthcare fiasco Obama is leading us into. In his book, *Why Obama's Government Takeover Of Health Care Will Be A Disaster,* Dr. Gratzer explains why both the British and Canadian health care systems are failing, and how the citizens of those nations are being denied medical coverage, thanks to long waiting periods and rationing policies. He sees this same cruel and unnecessary pain arriving soon in America. Every American will suffer from Obamacare, he says, but seniors and the handicapped will bear the brunt. Writes Dr. Gratzer:

"In countries like Canada, the approach to health care has not been reengineered. Primary care doesn't focus on wellness; chronic disease management is not more sophisticated than anything found in the United States. Rather, governments have simply rationed care, restricting the supply of providers, diagnostics and new drugs, and leaving people to suffer and, in the words of the Canadian Supreme Court justices, sometimes die."[185]

This is what seniors face under Obamacare: Rationing, drastic limits on drugs and tests, and all too frequent deaths from waiting too long for medical procedures.

Obama's ultimate goal is to drive private insurance companies out of business and shove everyone into government-run programs – managed by bureaucrats. In his second term, he may very well get there.

Obama Targets Military Retirees and Their Dependents

Obama intends to be an equal-opportunity healthcare rationer. And so he is also targeting military retirees and their benefits. He recently tried to raise Tricare enrollment fees and deductibles for military retirees and their families. He also pushed to hike prescription drug fees for veterans. However, both the House and Senate Armed Services Committees blocked his plan in May 2012. Drug costs will continue to rise, though. And there's no guarantee that the House or Senate will have the courage to fight Obama in a second term.

Under Obama's plan, Tricare costs would double or even triple for military retirees. According to one congressional estimate, Tricare costs would have increased between 30% and 78% in the first year alone! After that, the plan imposed five-year increases ranging from 94% to 345% — these are the real numbers, not the feel-good talking points issued by the White House. Moreover, it is certainly a far cry from Obama's *original* promise to provide quality healthcare for all Americans for less than we now pay.

And so if you are a **retired Army colonel with a family currently paying $460 yearly for health coverage, you're set to pay $2,048** under Obama's plan (and Obama conveniently planned it so this increase wouldn't be noticed until *after* the 2012 election.)

When retired Colonel **_Allen West_**, a former Republican Congressman for Florida, learned of Obama's attack on retired military personnel, he let fly the outrage felt by many veterans:

> *"It is unconscionable, utterly disrespectful and obviously evidences the disdain the Obama administration has for our warriors, to whom he should apologize.... President Obama believes healthcare should be free for his union cronies and entitlement-centered political base, but not for those exceptional men and women who serve or have served to keep us free."*[186]

As I said, for now Congress has blocked Obama's plan to punish military retirees, but now that he has another term – and the Senate remains in liberal hands, he'll push this attack on retired military personnel again.

I have created a special website with the entire list of names of Obama's enemies at http://www.obamasenemieslist.com.

At the website you can also stand with those being targeted by adding your name to the list to tell Obama he cannot punish us all.

The Punished: Entrepreneurs and Small Business Owners
Somebody Has to Pay for All This Spending...
Why Not Small Business Owners?

Ever heard of the **New Party?** Most people haven't. **It's a proudly socialist group whose stated goal is to convert America from a free enterprise system into a European socialist state – where government controls the economics of a nation.** (*"Never mind how Europe turned out,"* is not their official slogan, though it should be.) The New Party is, in fact, the political arm of ACORN—the proven-corrupt organization that has elevated voter fraud to a science. You may recall that Obama trained ACORN activists in this science back in Chicago in the mid-1990s, when he was a community organizer there.

So it should have been no surprise when *National Review's* **_Stanley Kurtz_** revealed in June 2012 that (1) Obama had signed a contract with the New Party pledging to support its goals, (2) the New Party worked actively to get Obama elected to the Illinois State Senate, and (3) that Obama's surrogates now vehemently deny he ever had anything to do with this radical group. Apparently, true liberals have to conceal their past to get elected.[187]

But the Kurtz expose could not be denied. He uncovered ACORN records stored at the Wisconsin Historical archives, proving beyond a doubt, that **Obama was a New Party member.** There was the contract. There was the signature. And again, no surprise, because Obama has done his best to achieve the goals of the New Party. And in so doing, **he has put small business owners and entrepreneurs at the top of his enemies list.**

A recent *Business Week* feature detailed all the ways the U.S. economy is becoming less dynamic – and moving toward a European economic model. ___**Steven Davis**___, professor at the University of Chicago's Booth School of Business laid out the similarities between the Obama economy and European economies:

> "… higher unemployment rates, longer unemployment spells, steep falls in the employment rate in the working-age population, a slower pace of worker flows, and a slower pace of job creation and destruction." [188]

And this souring business climate wallops the entrepreneur the hardest. The number of startup companies is dwindling by the year. Economists tabulate this by counting the number of new firms as a proportion of all companies, and then finding a ratio. The startup ratio in 2010 was at an all-time low of 8%, down from 11% in 2006 and 13% during the 1980s.[189]

Small businesses are taking the biggest hit from Obama's laws and regulations. A Chamber of Commerce poll in January 2012, found that three out of four small business owners blamed Obamacare for impeding job creation. Obamacare could also force as many as 80% of small businesses to change their health care plans.[190]

The Small Business and Entrepreneurship Council has warned that small business owners:

> "...remain on edge regarding the tidal wave of federal government regulations that has been advanced or proposed over the past two years. ... The pain of the harsh recession was intensified and lengthened by this hyper-regulatory environment." [191]

Strangling in Red Tape, While Bureaucrats Party Down

Obama's hyper-regulatory environment is strangling small businesses. *The Competitive Enterprise Institute* (a free market think tank) published research report in 2012 on the outrageous costs involved in complying with federal regulations. The report, *Ten Thousand Commandments* notes that: [192]

- ► Estimated regulatory costs, while "off budget," are equivalent to over 48% the level of federal spending itself.
- ► The 2011 Federal Register finished at 81,247 pages, just shy of 2010's all-time record-high 81,405 pages.
- ► Regulatory compliance costs dwarf corporate income taxes of $198 billion, and exceed individual income taxes and even pre-tax corporate profits.
- ► Agencies issued 3,807 final rules in 2011, a 6.5% increase over 3,573 in 2010.
- ► Of the 4,128 regulations in the works at year-end 2011, 2012 were "economically significant," (meaning they wield at least $100 million in economic impact).

Meanwhile, as small businesses struggle to untangle themselves from these regulations, government bean counters from the General Services Administration are off in Vegas ransacking hotel rooms, hiring hookers, badmouthing the very taxpayer who is footing the bill. And Obama says nothing about it – it's business as usual in his Washington. To them, the people out beyond the Potomac are just statistics. Lines on a chart.

Tell that to **_Michael Barrera_**, who runs the Hispanic Chamber of Commerce. He hears the stories of Hispanic business owners threatened by Obama's policies, particularly Obamacare. Barrera writes:

> "…a Hispanic small business owner who has been in business for over 20 years in Colorado and employs close to 200 employees stated that after becoming more aware of the new requirements imposed by Obamacare, he believes his business cannot afford the new mandates. He further stated it would be cheaper to just pay the fines, thereby requiring his employees to use government-run health care.

> "This is more than just a 'cold hearted' business decision as many of those who work for him are actually extended family or long term employees he is personally close to and cares about. In addition to forcing his employees to fend for themselves with the government-run health insurance, he and his immediate family will also lose the cost benefits of being part of a group insurance health plan. This will also cost him considerably more money because he, along with members of his immediate family, have pre-existing conditions who will now be forced to purchase considerably more expensive individual family health insurance. Additionally, the current economy and the pending health insurance costs have forced him to lay off some employees, including family. There are no immediate plans to hire new employees.

> "Another Hispanic business owner, who owns several restaurants throughout Texas, stated his business is currently in good shape financially and has substantial money on hand. However, due to Obamacare's impending costs to his business and the uncertainty of the law's mandates, he has halted all plans for expansion — including the opening of new restaurants. This translates into less work for potential contractors, fewer hours for his current employees and fewer new hires. These expansion plans would have allowed him to grow financially and provide economic opportunities for others."

> *"The conditions created by Obamacare are job killers. In the long run, more and more businesses will stop providing health care causing more people to use government-run health care. This leads to more government spending, further exacerbating small business' second biggest fear—the exploding national debt."[193]*

And Obamacare is in an early stage. Obama now plans to impose even more stringent regulations on small, self-insured health plans. This will make it more difficult or even impossible for small businesses to insure their employees, forcing them into Obama's Health Insurance Exchanges. There will be no escaping Obamacare. Even if you want to self-insure your employees, Obama's going to make it outrageously expensive or impossible.[194]

Small Business Owners Have Begun Speaking Up

Wayne Allyn Root is a small business owner who graduated from Columbia – alongside his classmate Barack Obama nearly 30 years ago. Root has started several businesses during the past three decades and he's been successful at it. Root is angry about what Obama is doing to small business owners like him. He writes in *Newsmax*:

> *"In the old America known by my father and grandfather, small business owners were 'preferred customers,' metaphorically wined and dined to create jobs and keep us in business. **But in Obama's bizarre world of progressives, socialists, unions, and big government, we're demonized as evil and greedy, singled out for punishment...***

> ***"The harder we work, the more we succeed, the more they want to steal our money and redistribute it to others who don't want to work as hard, or don't want to work at all. Some of these people collecting entitlements, welfare, food stamps, aid to dependent children, free meals at school, housing allowances, free medical, and free education, aren't even in the country legally.***

"At times it seems even many Republicans are in on this conspiracy. Together these D.C. establishment politicians have tried to damage or ruin our lives so many times, it's becoming quite clear it's no mistake, no coincidence.

"It's a purposeful plan to wipe out small business owners by burying us in higher taxes and adding layers of oppressive rules, regulations, laws, and lawyers, until we can no longer survive."[195]

But Obama doesn't care. Small business owners can't contribute as much as Wall Street chieftains and trust fund babies, and they can't be bought off with goodies-for-votes, so they are the ones who must be made to pay for all those goodies, make to pay as much as they can bear, and then some.

<u>Bruce Hottle</u> is a small business owner in Pennsylvania. He writes:

"I want to reiterate that we can't tolerate anymore of President Obama's hostility towards job creators. Small businesses, as everyone knows, are the engine of job growth in Pennsylvania and in our country. The free market is a fundamental part of our society and has worked for hundreds of years but President Obama just doesn't seem to understand that.

"I run a small business called Eagle Concrete Products here in Somerset County in Pennsylvania. I can tell you that our bottom line has been negatively affected by this recession. What's even more frustrating is President Obama's desire to add even more road blocks to job creation. We work with a lot of small developers, housing developments, strip malls, waterline products, sewer line products and so on. We've priced out, estimated the costs for numerous projects in Southwestern Pennsylvania and the owners of those projects put them back on the shelf every time the president comes out with one of his new programs or makes a speech where he attacks job creators and people who are willing to risk their capital to create jobs and improve our economy.

"It just becomes more difficult every day. One needs to look at the cash that American business have in reserve right now, I think its approaching $3 trillion. They're afraid to spend that cash because every time the president makes a speech, he's got some new program or some new way of getting rid of our debt that puts it all on the backs of America's small businesses and job creators.

"The president has been absolutely hostile to job creators like me. We've piled on layers and layers of new regulations and it almost makes it impossible to hire new workers. The cost of adding someone to the payroll far exceeds the cost of overtime for existing employees. When we look at projects that we bid and how many people we're going to have to hire, what's it going to take to do the job, we price it out both ways: new employees with no overtime and one with our existing employees with overtime.

"Businesses like mine rely on infrastructure and energy to sell our products. I've got five trucks that deliver my products throughout Southwestern Pennsylvania. The Obama administration's use of the EPA has created roadblocks upon roadblocks. The administration has blocked new oil exploration, natural gas and coal and other reliable forms of energy that reduce our costs and improve our productivity."[196]

Pennsylvania Congressman ***Mike Kelly***, himself a former small business owner:

"This administration has been on steroids when it comes to new regulations, at four times the rate of the Bush administration. And in the president's view, he thinks that we'd be better off if we just had political appointees or government bureaucrats and not private job creators making the critical decisions when it comes to our economy.

"The president has used all of the tools at his disposal including the EPA to prevent the development of American energy and

infrastructure. I have to tell you, that when you look at our country, we have been given gifts from God that no other country in the world has, when you talk about coal, oil and gas. And two things we don't talk about are tillable soil and potable water. This is a country that does not need to rely on anybody from outside our borders for our own success. But you can't do things like blocking the Keystone Pipeline that would have created 20,000 jobs and got those refineries back and got things going again.

"If it's really about fairness, then fair means fair to everybody. We have pitted the business owners against the workers. Not the workers and the owners themselves, but a government that picks and chooses winners and losers and tries to divide us. You can't have that.

"The president has never managed anything, other than his own personal narrative, in his entire life. This is a person who has never actually worked in the private sector the way we have. He's never created a job, he's never run a business. He really doesn't have any plans to change course. He's going to double-down on these failed policies, if given a second term and for the sake of our economy this has got to be stopped."[197]

The Job-Destroying Environmental Protection Agency

Few can or should argue with the loftiest of aims of the Environmental Protection Agency (EPA). We all want a cleaner environment, but sensible people also want a balanced approach to those environmental concerns that recognizes the competitive needs of business. Obama's EPA, run by Lisa Jackson, leaves sensible behind. Ms. Jackson is the point of the spear in destroying jobs and the hopes and dreams of millions of Americans.

In May 2011, the U.S. House Small Business Subcommittee on Oversight, Investigations and Regulations, held a hearing on the EPA's impact on small businesses. Here, it was revealed that small businesses face an annual regulatory burden of $10,585 per employee, which is 36% higher than the regulatory cost facing large firms. **Complying with environmental edicts cost small businesses 364% more than large firms.** As these Congressional hearings were being held, the EPA remained at work finalizing 30 more "significant" regulations to create even more costs and paperwork burdens on small business owners.[198]

The National Federation of Independent Businesses (NFIB) **is warning its members about the impending dangers.** One EPA regulation related to "Boiler Maximum Achievable Control Technology" is expected to affect some 200,000 boilers and potentially destroy 60,000 jobs.

EPA restrictions on coal ash will cost more than $100 billion in added costs, force 20% of coal fired plants to close, and kill more than 100,000 jobs.

EPA's Ozone Rule – which is on hold – but will be implemented if Obama gets another four years – will cost employers $1 trillion to implement and destroy millions of jobs.[199]

The American Coalition For Clean Coal Electricity released a report in September 2011 showing that EPA regulations kill at least 183,000 jobs a year! And, what's worse, the EPA has estimated that it will need another 230,000 government bureaucrats to implement their job killing policies – at a cost of $21 billion! Now, isn't that special? [200]

The Obama Administration has been wildly successful at killing private sector jobs, while expanding the numbers of mindless bureaucrats who are being hired to "regulate" everything in sight.

In fact, according to Senator Jim DeMint (R-SC), **the Obama Department of Health and Human Services has added 9,424 jobs since Obama took office! The number of bureaucrats in the Center for Medicare and Medicaid Services increased by over 800 bureaucrats. Both of these agencies are responsible for implementing the stifling new regulations for Obamacare!**

And, over the past two years**, the Obama federal government has issued a whopping 12,307 pages of regulations in the Federal**

Register![201] No wonder our economy is in ruins and small businesses are crying for relief from the avalanche of regulations upon them.

The Obama Administration is deliberately choking business owners with regulations and burdensome taxes.

I have created a special website with the entire list of names of Obama's enemies at http://www.obamasenemieslist.com. To access the list please use the login name: Patriot and the password: wewillnotbeintimidated.

At the website you can also stand with those being targeted by adding your name to the list to tell Obama he cannot punish us all.

The Punished: Pro-American Friends Abroad and our National Security
If the Lefties and Righties Hate My Defense Policy...
Did I Do Something Right?

In the 2008 campaign, Obama was the darling of the "disarm baby disarm" wing of the Democratic Party. He even posted a video on YouTube for an anti-war group and made the following promises to his anti-military buddies:

> *"I'm the only major candidate who opposed this war from the beginning. And as president I will end it. Second, I will cut tens of billions of dollars in wasteful spending...*

> *[He didn't]*

> *"I will not weaponize space...*

> *[He didn't]*

> *"I will institute an independent Defense Priorities Board to ensure that the Quadrennial Defense Review is not used to justify unnecessary spending.*

> *[He didn't]*

> *"I will set a goal of a world without nuclear weapons. To seek*
> *that goal, I will not develop new nuclear weapons; I will seek*
> *a global ban on the production of fissile material; and I will*
> *negotiate with Russia to take our ICBMs off hair-trigger alert,*
> *and to achieve deep cuts in our nuclear arsenals."* [202]

This last promise he did deliver on. In February 2012, Newsmax reported that **Obama was working to reduce up to 80% of our deployed nuclear weapons.** If this is accomplished, **it will reduce our deployed nuclear weapons from 5,100 to only 300, where we were in 1950.** The real question is, **is 300 a sufficient number in the larger context of national defense?**

There's no doubt that a unilateral reduction in nuclear weapons can only embolden hostile nations—including North Korea, China, and Iran. But does it invite recklessness or nuclear adventurism on their parts? If any man knows the nuclear scenarios inside and out, it's retired **_Lt. Colonel Robert Patterson._** He carried the nuclear codes in a briefcase for President Clinton.

In 2010 Patterson wrote *Conduct Unbecoming: How Barack Obama Is Destroying The Military And Endangering Our Security* and leveled this indictment of Obama:

> *"…we now have a commander in chief whose administration*
> *is unqualified for and incapable of addressing the threats we*
> *face as a nation. Our current administration at its core refuses*
> *to acknowledge and confront our enemies. Instead, we have a*
> *president who wants to kick the "ass" of British Petroleum, but*
> *doesn't want to kick the ass of an ideological enemy sworn to*
> *defeat us, which murders innocents and suppresses human*
> *freedoms around the globe."* [203]

Military historian **_Victor David Hanson_** also weighed in similarly in a 2009 monograph, *How The Obama Administration Threatens Our National Security:*

> *"During the first year of the Obama administration, those*
> *previously deemed hostile to the United States earned*

more attention than staunch allies. The pattern was quite remarkable." [204]

Hanson refers to **Obama's betrayal of pro-American Czechs and Poles in favor of Russia's Vladimir Putin,** when he killed off a strategic NATO missile defense system.

Obama has also snubbed Israel, our staunchest ally in the Middle East. U.S. relations with the Israelis are worse than at any time in 60 years of existence. Israel is *"an oasis of democracy in a vast desert of autocracy"* as Hanson puts is so eloquently, but that's of no concern to Obama.

As the 2012 election season geared up, Obama did attempt to mend fences with Jewish voters, but only those viscerally incapable of voting Republican returned his calls.

All over the world, Obama has made it policy to manhandle allies and mollycoddle enemies. The result of these policies in obvious and unsettling. Our enemies see no obstacle to their regional political ambitions, and our friends see no future in our democratic axis.

Obama's Worldwide Apology Tour

Obama's undermining of our national security began as soon as he took office. He hopped on Air Force One and circled the globe, giving speeches and apologizing for America's greatness. His stated goal was to "reset" America's relationship with the world – and he did this by apologizing for our greatness and our influence.

In April 2009, Obama gave one apology speech in Turkey and another in Latin America. He accused past administrations of being *"disengaged, and at times we sought to dictate our terms"* to other nations. He pledged that in the future, there would be no *"senior partner"* or *"junior partner"* in our relations with other nations.

**Obama's philosophy is in line with the Communist Manifesto, which says it desires *"to abolish countries and nationality,"* and *"the exploitation of one nation by another will also be put to an end."* **[205]

Then fresh off his pacifist apology tour, he went all macho. He escalated the war in Iraq that he'd previously opposed. He doubled down on a military solution in Afghanistan that he'd also previously opposed. He slipped into Pakistan to kill Osama bin Laden, and it was in fact an invasion of a sovereign nation. He sent troops into several African nations, with no official explanation. He kept Guantanamo open and continues to hold terrorists there, despite having once condemned that "immoral" place. He ordered drone strikes on Taliban combatants around the world, and keeps an official "kill list" which, we all dearly hope, does not overlap with his official enemies list.

These tactics are clearly at odds with his campaign promises and the global expectations for his presidency. And this contributes to a more unstable, uncertain, and unsupportive world. When U.S. intentions cannot be relied on by either friend or foe, it breeds an unhealthy insecurity. And that is *seldom* good national security policy.

Spiking in the End Zone—Unbecoming and Dangerous

I'm proud of the U.S. Military for taking out bin Laden—it was an expertly run mission, and long overdue. That President Bush could not do it after eight long years and billions in added defense spending . . . was initially why so many conservative voters soured on his presidency. But then shortly after taking out bin Laden, Obama couldn't resist. His ego got the better of him, apparently. He did what no U.S. President has done. He threw a big party and revealed national security secrets and publicly named the members of the SEAL team that carried out the mission.

He turned the soldiers into celebrities, and posted their faces for all the world to see. First to express shock at this were the SEAL officers themselves. They have a code, and it involves never saying anything. That's safest—for them, and best—for the security of our nation. But Obama apparently didn't care. He worked his media event, his moment in the end zone, his spike.

Then after even liberal supporters like Arianna Huffington editorialized against his unseemly display, Obama took it up into the stands.

He granted a Hollywood filmmaker unprecedented access to classified material and personnel for a movie on the killing of bin Laden. The company distributing the film is Sony, which held a huge fundraiser for Obama in the spring of 2012 and raised $4 million. The movie deal was orchestrated by The Glover Park Group, a Democrat-leaning outfit that is headed by a former advisor to Al Gore.

So Obama first betrayed the honor and safety of our soldiers, then he used government resources for campaign purposes.

Purposefully Subverting America's Allies

One of the hardest things for a large government to do is keep leaks under control. There are many people in government who when a decision doesn't go their way, are quick to get even on the street and in the media. Under Obama, a dangerous long-time problem with leaking of classified documents has reached unprecedented scale.

His operatives leaked details that exposed Britain's involvement in a covert mission involving the so-called underwear bomber.

They also leaked top-secret information on the expansion of CIA drone attacks in Yemen. [206]

They violated a longtime Cold War taboo by revealing how many nuclear weapons we had in our arsenal.

When PFC Bradley Manning turned traitor, and stole thousands of sensitive defense documents to hand over to Wikileaks, Obama's operatives made light of this major national security breach. Attorney General Eric Holder claimed he was going to deal with it, but gave no specifics. Secretary of State Hillary Clinton joked about it: *"I'm writing a cable about it, which I'm sure you'll find soon on your closest website."* White House Press Secretary Robert Gibbs downplayed it: *"We should never be afraid of one guy who popped down thirty-five dollars and bought a web address."* [207] Downplaying the significance of posting thousands of national security documents online is beyond irresponsible; it's dangerous.

They leaked sensitive information on our ally Israel and its plans to strike Iran before that rogue nation finishes its nuclear

weapon. Obama's operatives spilled the beans on Israel's secret dealings with the government of Azerbaijan to set up a staging ground for a possible strike against Iran. This classified information appeared in *Foreign Policy* on March 28, 2012. Four unnamed senior diplomats and military intelligence officers leaked it.

Many analysts believe Obama was personally peeved with Israel because he had failed in his personal attempts to charm the Israelis into cancelling their plans. So he upped the ante by leaking the information on Azerbaijan—in order to make it less likely that Israel can successfully complete its mission.[208]

True or not, **every Commander in Chief must be held personally responsible for the leaks in his administration.** That is the only way the chain of command can work.

Obama Undermines Our National Sovereignty

Former U.N. Ambassador *__John Bolton__* is deeply concerned that Obama is more beholden to international law, international organizations and international treaties rather than to the nation and Constitution he's sworn on oath to defend. Bolton outlined his concerns in a monograph titled *How Barack Obama Is Endangering Our National Sovereignty:*

> *"Barack Obama is our first post-American president—someone who sees his role in foreign policy less as an advocate for America's 'parochial' interests and more as a 'citizen of the world,' in his own phrase. He broadly embodies many European social democratic values, including those regarding sovereignty, so it was not surprising that an ecstatic student said after hearing him on one of his first overseas trips, 'He sounds like a European.' Indeed he does."* [209]

One of the most serious threats to our national sovereignty, says Bolton, comes from Obama's willingness to submit the United States to the rulings of the International Criminal Court (ICC). President Bush rejected the treaty that would have entangled the U.S. with the ICC, but Obama is rushing ahead to get us enslaved by this unrestrained court. **If we end up under the jurisdiction of the ICC,**

every military decision we make could come under the scrutiny of this court. In fact, it is possible that those within the CIA who have engaged in enhanced interrogation techniques could be brought before this court and tried as war criminals.

In addition, many Obama administration officials have publicly expressed support for international "human rights" norms in the conduct of war. Who gets to decide what these norms are? Russia? Iran?

As Bolton notes:

> "*Under our Constitution, we are fully capable of deciding how and when to use military force, how our warriors should conduct themselves, and how to deal with those who violate our standards. We do not need international human rights experts, prosecutors, or courts to satisfy our own high standards for American behavior.*" [210]

If Obama gets his way in his second term, our national sovereignty could wind up submerged in U.N. treaties and our future determined by the International Criminal Court.

A Summary Look at Obama's Plans to Disarm America

While Obama has been unpredictably strident and offensive in his foreign affairs, he didn't plan to be. He came into office with a complete policy agenda ready to roll. ***The Center for Security Policy*** has kept a detailed timeline of his agenda items, tracking them from idea to Executive Order. Here are a few excerpts from the timeline:

► Second day in office, he posts a notice on the White House web site that he is willing to meet with the fanatics who run Iran—without preconditions—to work toward the abolition of nuclear weapons. [They're still laughing at that in Teheran]

► The same day, he ordered the closing of CIA holding facilities for interrogating Islamic terrorists. [But didn't follow though]

► His first formal interview was not with a U.S. network, but with the Al-Arabiya TV network which is funded by Saudis to spread the Wahhabist hatred.

- In March, he forbade the use of the term "enemy combatants" to describe Islamic killers.
- In March, he also waived export controls to permit the transfer of high-tech items to China.
- In April, he cancelled an order for new F-22 Raptor fighters, against the advice of his Air Force Chief of Staff.
- Also in April, as I discussed, he gave his infamous apology speech for America's greatness while in Turkey and he released detailed confidential information on enhanced interrogation techniques—damaging our nation's credibility.
- In August, Attorney General Eric Holder said he would investigate CIA officers who may have been involved in enhanced interrogations of terrorists.
- In April 2010, the terms "Islam," and "Jihad" were banned from the National Security Strategy.
- Also in April, Obama nominated Elena Kagan to the U.S. Supreme Court—as Dean of Harvard Law School Kagan tried to ban recruitment of law school students to become JAG officers. [211]

The list goes on and on, but you get the idea.

If a Policy or Weapon System Could Benefit the United States and Our National Security, Obama Has Tried to Kill It or Rescind It

Some people say Obama's goals are evident by his deeds. He wants to make certain that our nation is vulnerable to attack from a variety of enemies around the globe—including Hugo Chavez, the America-hating, Castro-admiring tyrant in Venezuela—who is working to develop a nuclear capability. Once he gets the bomb, we're in real trouble. There's also China, North Korea, Iran, and Russia. I think Obama is driven by self; by personal ambition. So he consorts with socialists or capitalists, allies or enemies—he doesn't particularly care, as long as it advances his personal agenda.

If I'm correct, even a little correct, that's a dangerous conclusion to reach about the guy on top. History is full of egomaniacs and appeasers, and a great price has been paid for them. Nobody knows this more than our soldiers. They know it firsthand. They know the cost of nonchalance in the Oval. They know what it's like to be on an enemies list—they see it every day. They never expected it from their own Commander in Chief. ***Every soldier, sailor or Marine who is willing to die for his country; every CIA operative who is working to protect us from Islamic terrorists; every defense contractor and weapons researcher or analyst is on Obama's list.***

Obamas Enemies List is Growing Very Large.

I have created a special website with the entire list of names of Obama's enemies at http://www.obamasenemieslist.com. To access the list please use the login name: Patriot and the password: wewillnotbeintimidated.

At the website you can also stand with those being targeted by adding your name to the list to tell Obama he cannot punish us all.

SECTION III: Obama Rewards His Friends

The Rewarded: Democratic Leaders and Race Hustlers

Segregated America is Democratic Party America
Early in 2012, the Manhattan Institute released the results of an exhaustive study that should have rocked the conscience and consciousness of a nation—and certainly of every veteran of the civil rights movement and every American of African descent. That the study was ignored by the Left-stream Media and quickly forgotten was further proof that Obama and the Democratic Party are more interested in keeping jobs for themselves than for ending the terrible era of segregation and Jim Crow.

For the study proved, almost undeniably, that **the lives and livelihoods of black Americans under Obama's Democrats of the 2010s, is quite similar to how it was under the Bull Conner Democrats of the 1950s.**

Only the geography has changed.

It's no longer white Democrats putting down black people with ropes, rules and hate. It's now mixed-race Democrats putting down black people with false promises and deceit. These Democratic leaders have created an entirely new masked racism to replace the old thick-veined racism. Many of them don't even know they're doing it, from appearances sake. But Obama knows. He's way too smart to be an innocent in the new political order—which can only be called the New Jim Crow.

The proof is in the map ahead, damning enough. Look at it closely, please. Take a moment to verify the facts and figures for yourself so that you can know the truth about the modern Democratic Party. For this truth is every bit as shameful as slavery, as Dred Scott, as Bull Conner and other Democratic Party backwardness of the past.

And this truth should be shouted out every day from the base of the Martin Luther King, Jr. Memorial in Washington so that when Americans come to visit a mighty warrior, they also know how his legacy is today being betrayed by one political party, and one party only.

Segregated America is Democratic Party America: The Map

(To view an image of the map, visit: www.punishourenemies.com/ mapofsegregation)

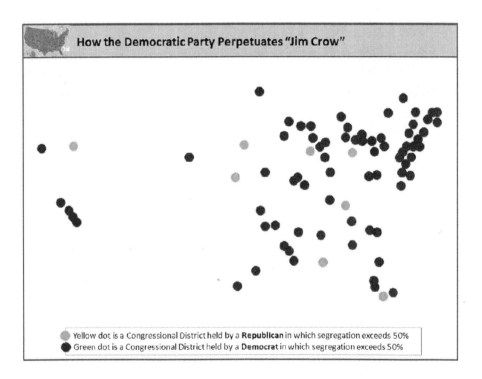

How the Democratic Party Perpetuates "Jim Crow"

Yellow dot is a Congressional District held by a **Republican** in which segregation exceeds 50%
Green dot is a Congressional District held by a **Democrat** in which segregation exceeds 50%

I began with an analysis done by ***Edward Glaeser*** of Harvard and ***Jacob Vigdor*** of Duke for the Manhattan Institute. In this analysis, titled "The End of the Segregated Century: Racial Separation in America's neighborhoods, 1890-2010" they showed that America has made great and impressive strides in ending the segregation of old. There are today only 200 areas of the country where more than 50% of the people live in segregation, high crime and poverty. So I went ahead and placed a "yellow dot" in those areas. Then I overlaid a map of the districts held by Democrats in the 112th Congress, and placed a "green dot" in the center of each of those districts. When the green circle overlaid the yellow circle, naturally, I got a blue circle.

As you can see clearly on the map, in the 200 areas of America where segregation continues to be the sad practice and legacy, all but six of those 200 are represented in Congress by a Democrat. Veritable blue states—since Segregated America is Democrat America. The rest of the country, represented almost entirely by Republicans, have long since adapted to the common sense notion that people ought to be judged by the content of their character.

Now the **Manhattan Institute** is a conservative think tank, and so liberal leaders reflexively attacked the study even before reading it. They were afraid the study might expose their methods and put them out of work. But their attacks gained little traction, because the study didn't have an agenda. It merely crunched the data from the Census Bureau and concluded:

- ▶ There has been an exodus from struggling old industrial states
- ▶ There has been an inflow to prosperous new Sunbelt states
- ▶ U.S. cities are more integrated now than at any time since 1910
- ▶ In the 1960s nearly 50% of blacks lived in ghettos, today it's only 20%

This is census data, pure and simple. It's all pretty good news and hard to argue with—no matter your politics. And as I said, the

Manhattan Institute wasn't arguing with it, just presenting it. I'm the one with an agenda—with a point to make. An important point.

This map brings into sharp focus a couple of inconvenient realities, like how eager Democratic leaders are to trade on any misfortune to keep blacks voting Democratic. For example...

If You Have to Incite a Race Riot to Keep Racial Control, Start It

Take the Trayvon Martin-George Zimmerman tragedy. The shooting of a young black man by a young Hispanic man happened in Sanford, Florida, represented, as our map shows, by Democrat Corrine Brown. It was a terrible incident, but a local incident in every way. Not something a president should enter into. But Obama did. Effortlessly he told us *"if I had a son, he'd look like Trayvon."* That was a rapier thrust and dutifully translated on the spot by Jesse Jackson who called Martin a *"martyr"* because *"blacks are under attack"* and *"targeting, arresting, convicting blacks and ultimately killing us is big business."* **Both Obama and Jackson succeeded in inflaming events, like an experienced race hustler might. And to complete the distortion of the tragedy, the media stepped up to criminally edit the 911 transcripts so as to twist the truth, and incite the race riot they so desperately desired.**

And they got what they wanted.

A Reuters/Ipsos poll came out amidst the entire furor and found that Americans were divided along racial and political lines about the shooting—even though they knew none of the facts of the case. In the poll of 1,922 Americans, which is not a large poll but certainly instructional, 91% of blacks considered Martin's death "unjust" and 35% of whites did. [212] Those numbers mirror Democrat Party affiliation. There was nobody in that party interested in justice, only in political gain.

And as a result, the police there in the hot streets of Sanford buckled. Despite no new evidence surfacing in the case, the legal establishment gave in to the mob and charged Zimmerman with murder.

For none of those issues were known at the time.

The only thing that was known was this: **It should have been a matter for local officials to decide—not the president. Because when the president does it**—from the highest office and with all the resources and assuasive power at his disposal**, he becomes a substitute for justice and an arbitrary *Punisher in Chief*** and in the end, no different from the southern Democrat lynch mobs of old.

Curious that throughout the hypermediated event, while the nation's attention was focused on law enforcement, Obama didn't once mention that his son could also look like Tyrone Woodfork. That was the boy who broke into the home of an elderly white couple, Nancy and Bob Strait, sexually assaulted and murdered Nancy, and left Bob, who was a veteran of the Normandy invasion, with severely broken bones and misery.

And no mention of the 500 other black men murdered every month, nine in ten of them by other blacks. No mention that blacks commit crimes against whites at an overwhelming rate. No mention of the truth that in black communities nationwide—almost all represented by Democrats—blacks continue to live with the cold reality that their own public outcry is their only hope of attaining justice. Because none of these mentions fit the "blame whitey" script of the New Jim Crow promulgated by Democrat politicians desperate to hold onto their jobs—at any price.

Or no mention of all the other crime that his administration has done nothing tangible to address. Columnist **_Walter Williams_** listed some major crimes of the past few years in a poignant *Human Events* article, including:

> On March 4, two black Kansas City, Mo., youths doused a 13-year-old boy in gasoline and set him on fire, telling him, "You get what you deserve, white boy." [213]

Dr. Williams is the former chairman of the economics department at George Mason University, and author of *More Liberty Means Less Government*. He does his homework. He details how the needle hasn't moved down on crime during this administration. If anything it has gone up, so much so that Chicago Mayor Rahm Emanuel was forced to shut down Chicago beaches last summer because black mobs were terrorizing white families. And what became of all of this serious crime, Williams asked:

> "None of those black-on-white atrocities made anywhere near the news that the Trayvon Martin case made, and it's deliberate. Editors for the Los Angeles Times, The New York Times and the Chicago Tribune admitted to deliberately censoring information about black crime for political reasons, in an effort to 'guard against subjecting an entire group of people to suspicion.'

> "One doesn't have to be a liberal, conservative, Democrat or Republican to see the danger posed by America's race hustlers, who are stacking up piles of combustible racial kindling and ready for a racial arsonist to set it ablaze. Recruiters for white hate groups must love President Obama's demagoguery in saying that a son of his would look like Trayvon but not saying that Melissa Coon's 13-year-old son, who was set on fire, could have looked like a son of his. After all, the president is just as much white as he is black.[214]

But this is not about the color of crime. This is not tit for tat, or this heinous crime from a deranged lefty for that heinous crime from a deranged righty. I don't want to play that game to score political points.

A Crime is a Crime, Regardless

This is about the how a tragic case turns politically noxious when a president makes a cold, political calculation to divide the nation over it. More so when angry Lefties like Jesse Jackson, Al Sharpton, Maxine Waters, Van Jones and Spike Lee pile on, terrorizing the innocent. Even more so when they all these Democratic leaders team up and give their tacit blessing to nationwide protests that can only end in rage and ruin. But that's exactly what happened, and from there on the case sloped downward from sickening tragedy to absurdist spectacle.

Everyone got involved, to get their 15 minutes of higher ratings. Amid the ugliness were Black Panthers putting a $10,000 'dead or alive' reward on Zimmerman; neo-Nazis on goose-stepping armed patrol or drunk in an alley—depending on which stupid media account you caught; hyperventilating blather from fame-crazed media types like Geraldo Rivera; doctored 911 call tapes—with every media outlet doctoring them differently; hacking of Trayvon Martin's Twitter account; filmmaker Spike Lee instructing thousands to attack an uninvolved elderly couple—continuing his storied history of feckless attacks on the Man; and on and on. It was a bounty of race-crazed ugliness, and all abetted by Obama.

Blessing a Million Hoodie March

Obama didn't march at the "Million Hoodie March" in New York, but given the tacit support of the demonstration that he had given, he should have. Demonstrators in New York and around the country had no real agenda, except to whip up blacks and distract them from the number one topic at that point: how few jobs and real opportunity had come out of the Obama administration. Better to keep them marching, and shouting clever slogans, then to turn against the man—oops, this administration.

It was a poignant march, and when Trayvon Martin's father shouted over a megaphone that *"Trayvon Martin was you, Trayvon Martin did matter,"* we all felt the depth of his sadness, and shared it. But when the demonstrators reacted with cries of *"Shame! Shame!"* and *"We want arrests!"* when not a single one of them knew the full facts of the case, the hooded throng had clearly degenerated into a "lynch mob" stoked by their president. A student originally from Nigeria was so moved, he told reporters *"I feel explosive – I feel betrayed by my country. I feel like history is repeating itself."* How an isolated shooting of a young black man, one of 50 a month who are shot down—mostly by other black men—could lead a young student to "feel explosive" and "betrayed" is hard to grasp on any intellectual level. Perhaps this was just one emotionally worked-up guy. Or perhaps he was unaware that he was inadvertently agreeing with Trayvon Martin's mother who said that *"this is not about a black or a white thing, this is about a right or wrong thing"* and that everyone on that New York Street and in the White House was doing the terribly wrong thing.[215]

Good people can argue about Florida's 2005 law known as "Stand Your Ground" which allows people to respond with deadly force if being attacked. Supporters of the law say that it empowers potential victims, opponents say it triggers vigilantism. Either way, it is the law in Florida, and we are a nation of laws. Don't like the law—seek to change it. But do it honestly. Talk about who is doing most of the shootings in America, and who is getting shot at most.

In the end, **George Zimmerman** was arrested and charged with second-degree murder but not because the authorities had any new or overwhelming evidence. Special prosecutor Angela Corey was pained to state publicly that Zimmerman's arrest was not "in response to public demand."[216] But coming 46 days after the shooting suggests otherwise. Sanford police arrested Zimmerman because they knew locals would riot, and tear apart the city, if they didn't arrest him. And it was a legitimate fear—such a riot had, of course, been OK'd at the highest levels.

And what will Obama's nation-dividing course give us next in the trial of George Zimmerman? We got a clue from Alan Dershowitz, the renowned law professor at Harvard. His analysis of the court case ahead is telling:

> *"Most affidavits of probable cause are very thin. This is so thin that it won't make it past a judge on a second degree murder charge…. There's simply nothing in there that would justify second degree murder."* [217]

So if the jury finds Zimmerman innocent of charges, will Obama then wink to Sharpton who will lead a nation-bashing riot? I've seen nothing to suggest otherwise.

Few People Willing to Speak the Truth on Race

Few people are willing to speak the truth on race in America today—Rush Limbaugh is one of those few. Limbaugh is a firebrand, effectively so. He totally infuriates liberals. But how could any liberal with any conscience not look upon Obama's actions during the Martin-Zimmerman tragedy with disdain. Obama's actions were clearly intended to boost his reelection chances by linking the tragedy somehow to conservatives:

> *"If in the White House they wanted to cool this down, which they should do, they could do it. All it would take . . . would be Obama addressing the nation to calm this down, and then speaking about it in genuine American terms, not racial terms. If they wanted to do that, they could. Other presidents have. It's not happening here…*

> *"… they believe that they can tie all of this to the existence of Republicans and conservatives, that the racial problems exist because of never-ending racism of the right, never-ending racism of Republicans…*

> *"…there are people in the race industry who became excited that this event took place because it allowed them to carry forward with their template, that we still are a nation, essentially, with slaves."[218]*

Another Honest Voice, This One From the Left

For most of his life the renowned playwright David Mamet towed the liberal line, because that line once made sense. But as he saw the line devolve, he started questioning his own politics and wrote about it in *The Secret Knowledge.* This book should be required reading by everyone who voted for Obama in 2008, because Mamet does such a wonderful job of framing the prickly issue of race with a dramatist's insight:

> *"Perhaps there is another view of the world, in which every transaction need not be reduced to victim and oppressor.*

What would such a worldview be? What skills might one need to see the world thus, as a flea market rather than a slave market? Identity politics reduce the world to victims and oppressors. But is there another way of looking at the world?'[219]

Still Another Honest Voice, and Persecuted For It

Another American willing to speak the truth on race, even at great personal harm to her family, is **_Deneen Borelli._** She's an accomplished American of African descent and in recently authoring *Blacklash,* she brought a uniquely valuable perspective to the race war that Obama has ignited.[220] It gives me great pleasure to offer several excerpts from her book, and a plea that you buy a copy and devour the entire thing.

Obama Should Have Changed Things-but He Didn't

Here are insights from Mrs. Borelli for us all:

"The naysayer will tell you that black Americans are kept down, but from my standpoint, the very fact that Obama was elected demonstrates how far we have risen above the racism that plagued us decades ago. Obama's election should have put the race card to bed, but it didn't. It should have ended affirmative action, but it didn't. It should have been the end of the Al Sharptons and Jesse Jacksons as the voice of the black community, but that never happened either. All in all, the election of Barack Obama to the office of president should have changed this country's view of race. But it didn't..."[221]

Come A Long Ways Since the 1950s

"During the 1950s and 1960s, the black community fought and died for equality in housing, jobs, and education. It was a horrible era and as a people, we fought hard for equality. Today, however, I believe strongly that if you are black in this country and you haven't yet achieved equality—it's not society that is the problem, it's you. You're not working hard enough or striving for what you want. Before blaming society or looking to government to be responsible for you and your family: look

in the mirror. What choices did you make? Drop out of school? Hang out with the wrong crowd? Get involved in drugs or gangs? Is teen pregnancy the government's fault? No, young people should avoid engaging in risky sexual behavior. [222]

Old Civil Rights Guard—Step Aside

"I have two words for the old civil rights guard: step aside. Your time has passed and your message is dated. These days you are doing more to hurt the black community than you are helping it. And in the process, you are dismantling the greatness of the American nation. You aren't just hurting blacks with your backward tactics, but the country itself.... Let me be clear—we appreciated what you did, but now your old guard message needs to be modernized because hanging on to it only benefits you and hurts everyone else." [223]

Getting Worse for Blacks, But Why?

"Why aren't black kids improving and growing at the same rate as their peers? My opinion: It's all in the message from the career black politicians who promote big government solutions that result in stagnation and government dependence. They are playing the blame game and using the race card as their ace in the hole to avoid accountability. Hey, blame your problems on race and don't take responsibility for your life, even when you mess it up. That's easier than providing solutions. And let's face it: it keeps these guys in business." [224]

Sorry Legacy of Oppression

"Yes, he will have been the first black president elected in the United States, but his story, long after he has left office, will be about how he created oppression in America through the failure of his progressive policies. The black community will be the net losers, not winners, of the first black president in American history. The irony of his presidency will be based on his misguided notions expressed through his policies..." [225]

Sending a Message of Malaise

*"Obama's rise to the office of president of the United States
from a single-parent household should have made life easier
for struggling Americans. Instead his policies will make it more
challenging, if not impossible for the less fortunate to gain
upward mobility. He's bankrupting the country and its people,
he's expanding and entrenching the bureaucracy and he's
drawing a roadmap for Americans to live a life of government
dependency. The Obama welcome mat for working-class
Americans should read: Welcome to a country that discourages
advancement, entrepreneurialism, and self-fulfilled
achievement. Welcome to a country that, in essence, wants you
and your family on a government run plantation for decades to
come."* [226]

If Obama Can't Win on His Record,
He'll be the Racist in Chief

As Ms. Borelli articulated so well from the point of view of a black woman, the election of Barack Obama proves how far we've come as a nation, and it should have turned a page for us all. It should have left race hustlers like Al Sharpton and Jesse Jackson behind. It should have advanced and even completed Dr. King's dream. But this didn't happen, ironically, because of Obama himself.

Simply put, we've never had such a divisive—and you can even argue, racist—president. Obama has divided our nation with a bitter anger that calls to mind the old Jim Crow era. And, as he clumsily revealed on an open mic with Russian President Dmitry Medvedev, he's only getting warmed up.

America wanted a leader—they got a community organizer. And what do community organizers do? They make demands. They threaten. They extract. That's what they do. They treat people different based on race. Obama and the leadership of today's Democratic Party are fundamentally racist in their actions, if not in their own minds. They see their job as meting out rewards and punishments based on race. That is, was, and will always be, racist.

Apologists for this radical liberalism claim it's not racism at all; it's reverse racism, they say. And it's needed to right so many past wrongs, they say. There was a time when I agreed with them; that time was in the 1960s and 1970s when the fight for basic human rights was being waged at a terrible cost to individual lives and in a wending of the national fabric. It was a war led by Republicans, until the Democrats stole the issue fair and square. But today that fight for civil rights has devolved into an uncivil affront. The so-called civil rights leaders in a transparent effort to stay relevant have built massive levers that they use to divide, to pit one group against another, so they can show up in time to save the day. It's a tired, worn-out script now. And it must stop.

When Historians Look Back on this Time

Long after today's political combatants have left the scene, and the historians are trying to sort out Obama's presidency, they will surely call it a momentous victory in America's struggle against racism. They will be right in doing so. They will talk about the Africans struggle in America like a good three act play.

1. The arrival of "20 and odd" blacks in late August of 1619 aboard a Dutch man of war to be sold into servitude for supplies.
2. A civil war that pitted brother against brother over what kind of nation we would be, with narrow definitions of "freedom" losing out to a genuine definition.
3. Then a long healing process allows a majority of the country to select a half white, half black man to the presidency. Half of each; somehow very fitting; somehow less than. But a proud moment for all but fringe haters—and they don't matter.

Yes, a good storyline, nicely bookended. But the story is not over, of course. And so we wonder how those with a broader view of history will view the presidency of Barack Obama?

Clearly the young senator from Illinois overcame the Clinton machine in the primaries and then the Republican machine in

November 2008 based, in large part, because he is black. This is well known, no mystery to it.

Almost every single black American voted for him—even if they didn't know anything about him, which party he was in, if he was blind, married, or diseased. Racial pride can be a powerful motivator. I understand this.

Many whites wrestle with guilt over the sins of our forefathers, and voting for Obama was a way to atone. It was a way of proclaiming loud and clear, *"I am no racist."* Voting for a candidate based on the color of his skin, and not the depth of his talents, is not a rational approach to an important decision—but people are seldom rational in their voting. I understand this.

And many whites voted for Obama because they felt he was the most qualified man for the job—and his mixed ethnicity had nothing to do with their decision. I understand this, as well.

But I talk to a lot of people who voted for Obama in 2008 because of a guilty sense of obligation, and yet now they feel guilty of racial bias. They know they discriminated in their voting—on the basis of race. They know that that is in itself racism, pure and simple. Many were likely guilty of this racism again in 2012.

The Rewarded: Hollywood, Lobbyists, Rich Liberal Donors
If You're Rich and Gorgeous, Let Me Show You the Love

When Obama looks back on this last election, his fondest memory no doubt will be the evening of May 10 that he spent with his pal George, and a few dozen bazillionares. The Pal was movie star George Clooney, and the bazillionares were Hollywood's finest. All showed up to mug with Obama, and raise $15 million to keep him in a job. Nobody knows how to care for their own better than Hollywood.

In coverage for the *Los Angeles Times*, Steve Lopez pointed out the glaring hypocrisy of those in attendance at George Clooney's house in Studio City:

> *"...his house will be full of that particularly unctuous strain of liberals who live for events like this that make them feel good*

about themselves but don't really give a toss for their own community. Los Angeles could end up declaring bankruptcy and these posers will be telling friends about their big night at George's house."[227]

While Clooney and other Angelenos were busy posing with the president and waxing fretful about the terrible situation in Sudan, the city of Los Angeles was equally busy shuttering school libraries, laying off teachers and shutting down fire houses. The things these beautiful Hollywood types profess to deeply care about.

Of course if they did truly care, and they had any interest in demonstrating that their beauty is more than skin deep, they would instead shell out $40,000 a head to raise money for teachers who don't make that much in a year. They would insist on a Hollywood soiree to save a library or a park. They would even cut an album on behalf of campaign finance reform—so hypocrisy like theirs could be 'cured' – or whatever the proper solution might be.

One big celebrity who was not there was **_Jon Lovitz_**. The comedian actor didn't get any laughs at the White House when he slammed Obama, who he had supported first term. In a recent podcast, Lovitz had some choice words for a president who would try to punish those who work hard and achieve success:

> *"He's amazing. He had nothing . . . and the guy ends up being at Harvard. He's the president of the United States. And now he's like, @#$% me and everyone who made it like me."* [228]

But 150 other of the brightest Hollywood luminaries were on hand at Clooney's party. Here's just a few of those who can count on plenty of screenings in the White House private theater in a second Obama term include (more or less in the order of love Obama heaps on them rather than on real problem cases):

Actress Barbra Streisand, producer Jeffrey Katzenberg, acting couple Brad Pitt and Angelina Jolie, actress Scarlett Johansson, comedienne Ellen Degeneres, no-longer-bestest-pal Oprah Winfrey, producer Harvey Weinstein, actor Matt Damon, singer-songwriter-activist Melissa

Etheridge, actor Robert Downey Jr., actor Tobey Maguire, actor Leonardo DiCaprio, caterer Wolfgang Puck, actor James Brolin, producer Steven Spielberg, actor J.J. Abrams, agent Bryan Lourd, agent Chris Silbermann, actress Halle Berry, actress Reese Witherspoon, actress Teri Hatcher. All gorgeous to look at, all very talented, but…

Actually, I do not hail from the "shut up and sing" school. I believe everyone, regardless of their day job, should speak out for what they believe in … and be just as hypocritical as they so desire. And I believe likewise that if Obama wants to call big starry-eyed attention to his show business ties even while thoughtful critics are dishing up mixed reviews, calling him "more pop culture hotshot than effective statesman," then that's his right, as well.[229]

But then Obama has got to "zip it" when conservative PACs like American Crossroads mock him as a "celebrity president," and juxtapose clips of Obama on *Late Night With Jimmy Fallon* and Obama singing Al Green's *Let's Stay Together,* with Obama's real failures; spurring employment for those who have plenty of time to watch Fallon's show, and feel their lives falling apart.

And then Obama has to deal with the larger problem he faces. This race, media strategist Fred Davis was able to prove, with hard stats to back him up, that **however much people adore Hollywood's beautiful people, they know the economy is 'coyote ugly' and we need real solutions.** *230* We don't need a president who had already held 133 re-election fundraisers even before the Clooney shindig (yes; that is far more than any of his predecessors). We need a president focused on the job, not on Scarlett Johansson.

No Lobbyist Gets through My Door (Unless Accompanied by a Donor)

Obama who has done for 'audacity' what Clinton did for marital vows, sunk to a new low in November 2011 at the home of pal Antoinette Bush. At the party, according to reliably supportive writers at the *New York Times*, Obama complained that the nation's capital should be more *"responsive to the needs of people, not the needs of special interests." 231*

Credit goes to the *New York Times* for also pointing out that Ms. Bush is a talented lawyer with top firm Skadden Arps; she's the cousin of Obama's longtime confidant Valerie B. Jarrett; she's visited the White House at least nine times during his term; and she's let lobbyists tag along on several of those visits. Oops.

Obama made a big point in his campaign, and then in the White House, that he would not under any circumstances accept contributions from registered lobbyists or grant them any favors. But the *New York Times* writers did some legwork, and cross-referenced campaign donations to White House visitor logs. What they found was:

> *"Special interests have had little trouble making themselves heard. Many of the president's biggest donors, while not lobbyists, took lobbyists with them to the White House, while others performed essentially the same function on their visits...*

> *"The regular appearance of big donors inside the White House underscores how political contributions continue to lubricate many of the interactions between officials and their guests..."* [232]

Obama and a long line of administration officials have tripped over themselves rushing into the White House press room to express their shock that there's lobbying going on, and to further insist that campaign donations have no bearing on White House visits, and to even further tell how they've tried to curb the influence of money in politics by banning executive branch employees from taking 'gifts' from lobbyists. Banned!

So why then did Patrick J. Kennedy, he with the good family name, donate $35,800 to Obama's Victory Fund just before seeking administration support for a pet project of his?

Kennedy had no problem being honest: contributions, he said, are simply a part of *"how this business works"* and *"it won't hurt when I ask them for a favor."* [233]

And so why did Antoinette Bush make a contribution as a Democratic fundraiser last May—on the same day she was visiting the White House?

Bush actually has no problem being honest either. She admitted that she *"had the same clients in the Bush administration as well as the Obama administration."*

Right.

But Obama was the one who would end business as usual. It was core to his 2008 campaign promise, and he acted on it in the White House, supposedly.

And for any doubters who might still be tempted to buy the Obama line that he runs a clean administration, and lobbyists have been shown the back door, there was an interesting study done by Ran Duchin and Denis Sosyura of the Ross School of Business at the University of Michigan. These guys don't work for either party. They're academics in the old-school sense. They studied how Obama spent the stimulus funds, and whether there was any crony favoritism displayed. They then published their findings in Science Direct website in May 2012. Here's the key conclusion from their Abstract:

> *Using hand-collected data on firm applications for capital under the Troubled Asset Relief Program (TARP), we find that politically connected firms are more likely to be funded, controlling for other characteristics. Yet investments in politically connected firms underperform those in unconnected firms.*[234]

Apparently there is a positive correlation, as the researchers say, between being an Obama crony and being a slack—er, underperformer.

Our Bad Apples are Better Than their Bad Apples

One of Obama's big bundlers, the people who deliver suitcases full of cash to the campaign headquarters, also spends her time opening up offshore tax avoidance schemes for convicted criminals. Yes, the very schemes that Obama rails against in his speeches.

One bundler, Marjorie Rawls Roberts, will raise as much as $200,000 for Obama, and he will do nothing to stop her. Nothing, even though she recently helped convicted $7 billion Ponzi schemer R. Allen Stanford to hide tons of cash in the U.S. Virgin Islands. Stanford was convicted of defrauding 30,000 of his investors, and he owes $212 million in back taxes.[235] Yet through his support of bundler Roberts, Obama is sending a message that raising $200,000 for his re-election campaign is more important than doing the right thing: shaking every single penny out of Stanford and trying to repay defrauded investors.

As for Ms. Roberts, Stanford is only one of her clients. She has plenty more convicted felons and scurrilous characters she represents, and, we can only presume, hit them up for big contributions to Obama's re-election. **If playing dirty is part of the Obama campaign book, shouldn't he at least stop insisting that he came to Washington to put an end to business as usual?** Or, having fallen quite short of that goal first term, shouldn't he stop pretending that he'll complete the job in a second term?

I doubt that Ms. Roberts would disagree with me that she's small potatoes to another Obama bundler, former governor of New Jersey, and thief Jon Corzine.

When Corzine isn't busy telling Senate investigators that he "simply doesn't know" where $1.2 billion in MF Global customer funds disappeared to, he raised $500,000 for the president's re-election.[236] He has also personally contributed more than $275,000 to Democratic causes since 2007. Maybe that's why Obama and the Senate Democrats don't hand Corzine over to Jack Bauer to beat the truth out of him.

Here we have a high-powered Democrat stealing over a billion dollars from investors, and nobody is holding him accountable. The man should be in stockades; instead he's keynoting Democratic Party fundraisers. Why is the Obama Justice department letting him off? How do they rationalize that? I don't know. I'm not that creative. The only thing I can figure is, Obama and Holder got together and decided that our bad apples are better than their bad apples.

The Rewarded: Union Bosses, SEIU, UAW, Teamsters, et al
Union Bosses got Me Elected—I Owe Them Everything

Union leaders merrily threw millions in union dues into Obama's coffers to get him reelected. They know Obama is a good investment;

they have years of proof. Unions had been all but marginalized in America—having long outlived their usefulness—until Obama came along to forestall their demise.

Unions, along with George Soros, spent a record one billion in cash and kind in the 2008 election—a point that the Left-stream Media conveniently forgets when attacking the Citizen's United Supreme Court decision that now allows businesses to compete on equal footing with unions in the electoral process. Fair is fair, but I digress. Too much money is spent overall in elections, but I digress some more. Because this section of the book is about the rewards that unions have received in Obama's first term, and the rewards they'll receive in a second—all at great expensive to businesses in a global marketplace.

Obama's biggest union supporter is Service Employees International Union (SEIU), a 2.2 million member organization operating in three service sectors: health care, public services (schools, bus drivers, childcare providers, etc.) and property services (security and janitorial for commercial and residential properties).

SEIU Has What It Calls "Muscle for Money"

Muscle for Money is not a program to build the health or welfare of its members, like the name might suggest. It's a program crafted for the sole purpose of discrediting and intimidating opponents into supporting its unionization efforts. **Muscle for Money spends million actively smearing social and religious groups as well as companies big and small that resist the union's advances.** One of the newest tactics of SEIU is to picket the homes of corporate CEOs—an activity that drives a wedge between union workers and management, hurting both, but SEIU doesn't care. [237]

They have bigger problems.

They fear being exposed for being almost totally irrelevant in modern America, and so they adopt the tactics of desperate people at the end of their rope. SEIU is run currently by Mary Kay Henry who previously created SEIU's gay and lesbian "Lavender Caucus" and sits on the board of FamiliesUSA, an organization dedicated to promoting

Obamacare. I mention these efforts of hers because neither of them helps SEIU's members in any significant way. But they sure advance the personal ideologies of the union bosses. **And I suspect that less than one in four union members knows how their hefty union dues are really being used.**

But they do know how indebted Obama feels to them. Obama told them in 2007:

> *"We have stood side by side.... We have worked together. And you have seen that I was willing to stand by your side even when it wasn't politically convenient. Your agenda has been my agenda in the United States Senate. Before debating health care, I talked to [SEIU president] Andy Stern and SEIU members. Before immigration debates took place in Washington, I talked to [SEIU International Secretary-Treasurer] Eliseo Medina and SEIU members. Before the EFCA [Employee Free Choice Act, the "card check" bill for organized labor], I talked to SEIU. So we've worked together..."[238]*

Yes they have. In her investigations of this cozy relationship, conservative columnist Michelle Malkin found:

> *"The SEIU political action committee poured an estimated $80 million worth of independent expenditures into the campaign coffers of Democratic candidates in 2008 — more than $27 million of which went to Barack Obama. The union proudly claimed that its members 'knocked on 1.87 million doors, made 4.4 million phone calls, registered 85,914 voters and sent more than 2.5 million pieces of mail in support of Obama,' in addition to sending SEIU leaders to seven states in the final weekend before the election to get out the vote for Obama and other candidates."[239]*

And what did Obama do to return the favor?

He peppered his administration with SEIU operatives and gave SEIU's former leader Andy Stern unprecedented access to the Oval Office. Stern was given a seat on Obama's "Fiscal Responsibility Summit" in 2009. SEIU secretary-treasurer Anna Burger and Dennis Rivera,

SEIU health care chair were given roles in Obama's health care summit. Former SEIU political director Patrick Gaspard was made White House political director. Craig Becker, an SEIU lawyer, was put on the National Labor Relations Board where he ran point on **the "card check" program, which with Obama's blessing, aims to craftily coerce workers into joining unions even when they don't wish to.**[240]

United Auto Workers Get Sweetheart Deal, Bondholders Get Shafted

Obama also took tens of millions in donations from the United Auto Workers over the years. And he's happily repaid UAW activists for their support—by seizing control of General Motors and manipulating the "bailout" to give the UAW an eye-poppingly generous stake in GM. **Obama did it by shafting the people who were bondholders, many of whom were counting on their investment in GM to help fund their retirement. Now there they are left hanging high and dry.** Typically, bondholders are naturally the first to be paid off in a corporate reorganization.

GM's creditors at the time were owed $27 billion. GM also owed $20 billion to a UAW trust fund—the Voluntary Employee Benefit Association. Despite this, Obama gave the UAW a 17.5% interest in the "New GM" and he gave bondholders only 10% interest.[241] As of February 2012, thanks to Obama, the UAW owns 10.3% of GM and a whopping 41.5% of Chrysler. Nice payoff. If you can get it.[242]

And the payoffs just keep coming for the UAW. Last year, investigators on the House Energy and Commerce Committee discovered a little-known provision in Obamacare that hands out nearly $2 billion in taxpayer dollars to unions, state public employee systems and big corporations to subsidize the health coverage of early retirees. No such "payola" made its way to businesses, only to Obama's pals. The United Auto Workers came away with $207 million from ObamaCare. According to Byron York, writing in *The Washington Examiner*:

> "...payments to individual states were dwarfed by the payout to the auto workers union, which received more than the states of New York, California, and Texas combined. Other unions also received

government funds, including the United Food and Commercial Workers, the United Mine Workers, and the Teamsters." [243]

The Teamsters and Obama, a Love Story

Jimmy Hoffa, Jr., is a chip off the old block of his hoodlum father who brought the Teamsters national infamy. Jimmy Sr. disappeared in 1975, and Jimmy Jr. has been in the Obama camp from Day 1. He threw his considerable weight behind Obama in 2012 because he has a good memory. He knows that his wrestling the once politically centrist union into backing Obama in 2008 netted a bounty of political payoffs, including:

▶ A Justice Department that loses the paperwork on past federal probes into the Teamster's mob racketeering.
▶ A Treasury Department tax exemption from some of the more burdensome restrictions in Obamacare.
▶ A White House Executive Order requiring large-scale public construction projects worth $25 million or more to be unionized.

Jimmy Hoffa was the warm-up act at an Obama rally in Detroit in the fall of 2011. He ranted against Tea Party activists and told his followers:

▶ *"Let's take these son of a bitches out and give America back to an America where we belong."* [244]

There's no mention of Obama coming to the podium and condemning his remarks. Clearly, the two men are uniters, simpatico in pursuing the best interests of the nation. Not unlike the other powerful union Obama is running favors for…

The Rewarded: The National Teachers Union (Oops) Association
It's Not Really Child Abuse If Our Teachers Do It
If Obama cared one whit about poor black children in Washington, D.C. schools, why has he zeroed out funding for the D.C. Opportunity Scholarship Program? And zeroed it out not once, but several times?

This is a small program, but an important one that provides scholarships to 1,600 low-income students to attend private or parochial schools. Since 2004, more than 10,000 families have participated in this program. It boasts a 91% graduation rate – 30% higher than D.C. public school students. Children here are given a chance to attend quality schools in a city that is known for its lousy and violent public schools.

Attending a public school in D.C. is like going to Juvy. More than 60% of 4th graders can't read at grade level and only 14% of 8th graders are proficient in reading. On an average day, police receive almost twenty alarm calls from D.C.'s public schools, five of them for violent incidents.[245] But Obama has repeatedly tried to zero out funding for this program. In his 2013 budget, he hiked funding for the Department of Education by $70 billion but couldn't rub two dimes together for this local scholarship program. At the last minute, Speaker of the House John Boehner blocked Obama and saved the program.

It appears that Obama would rather have black children from low-income homes trapped in crime-filled schools than attend private or parochial schools where they're safe and are actually getting an education. But that's not the case, of course.

Obama is simply caving to the outrageous demands of the one organization in America that has license to abuse children with impunity. **Of all the dysfunctional, inbred, self-serving, culture-destroying unions in America, none is more despicable than the National Education Association (NEA). B**y choice, the NEA must support radical left candidates. No self-respecting candidate would be caught dead with their endorsement, as we will see.

But the NEA did endorse Obama in the summer of 2011 for a second term, even before a Republican candidate was picked. The NEA doesn't pretend to care about the electoral process, or even about the children whose lives they shape, or even about teachers. The NEA exists to keep union bosses in power. **They spent over $60 million to get Obama re-elected, and they recruited 10,000 teachers to work for him!**[246]

The NEA is a Radical Labor Union with a Stranglehold on Our Nation's Children.

They are a consistent supporter of Big Government and central-ized control, like Marxists, of what's taught our kids. And, every year like clockwork at its national convention, the NEA cranks out dozens of "resolutions" that are meant to push the radical goals of the union.

Out to Rewrite the Past, and Thus Control the Future

This year, the 2012 NEA resolutions run 108 pages long with several amendments that would shock an independent-minded voter. For example, Amendment I-53 calls for reparations for slavery! It says:

> "...the descendants of those subjected to slavery in the U.S. have the right to seek redress for the injustices inflicted upon their ancestors."

One NEA resolution calls for free public education to *"undocumented immigrants"* and opposes allowing Immigration officials to enter school property. It wants access to college for these *"undocumented workers"* – including the payment in-state tuition.

Another NEA resolution is intended to *"reduce racism, homophobia, ethnic and all other forms of prejudice"* which is wonderful at face value. But the programs the NEA devises to accomplish these goals involve degrading, discriminating against, and even defaming white people. Kind of defeats the point, and actually increases divisiveness. They don't care.

The organization also insists on promoting the claim that "global warming" is destroying the planet, when nobody knows for certain. Obama has said that "the science is decided" on this, joining all these educators and enlightening radicals in forgetting the condemnation of Copernicus for suggesting that science wasn't decided back then, either.

Resolution B-51 calls for the teaching of birth control methods, sexual orientation, gender identification, and about homophobia. In short, this is where teachers freely promote the gay political agenda – including the normalization of trans-sexuality and the marginalization of traditional Christian values.

Resolution B-60 calls for teaching children about the United Nations, disarmament, economic disparities, resource distribution. This is where teachers get to promote the destruction of our national sovereignty under the U.N., socialism, income redistribution and anti-capitalist claptrap.[247]

The list goes on and on. Obama may not agree with all the wacky stands the NEA takes. But again, why should he care? As long as their $60 million is spent on him, and their 10,000 teachers are dispatched to walk people to the polls, he is happy to give their agenda top priority. Besides, it fits with his larger plan…

Obama's Plan for Centralized Control of Education

Obama can't seem to control his totalitarian impulses. No matter what the issue, he sees the centralization of power in his hands as the only solution. The education of our children is no exception. He wants to make sure that the federal government is the final authority on what gets taught in our nation's public schools. His goal is to subvert local, state or parental authority over education.

But Obama's radical Marxist ideology and goals are nothing new; they follow the **Communist Manifesto** which states they want *"to stop the exploitation of children by their parent"* and *"replace home education by social."*

And Marx's feelings about traditional families? *"The bourgeois clap-trap about the family and education, about the hallowed co-relation of parents and child, becomes all the more disgusting…"* The Marxist solution to taking over the "old social order" is: *"Free education for all children in public schools."* Of course, their goal is to start indoctrinating children in Socialism as early as possible, when they say: *"All children will be educated in state establish-ments from the time when they can do without the first maternal care."*

Obama wants centralized power of education for himself. His plan will likely succeed now that he gets four more years in the White House.

The Pioneer Institute published a lengthy paper on Obama's plans for education, tapping the insider perspective of former Department of Education lawyers ***Robert Eitel*** and ***Kent Talbert***. They wrote:

> *"Actions taken by the Obama administration signal an important policy shift in the nation's education policy, with the department placing the nation on the road to federal direction over elementary and secondary school curriculum and instruction.*

> *"Obama is using the carrot of waivers and millions in grants to entice states to give up their responsibility over education and hand it over to federal bureaucrats. That move will result in the loss of parental input into what's being taught in local schools. All decisions will be made by Obama-approved faceless, un-elected bureaucrats in the Department of Education.*

> *"Obama is moving ahead to centralize power even though federal law specifically prohibits such actions. The law bans any federal intrusion into any direction, supervision, or control over the curriculum, program of instruction, administration, or personnel of any educational institute, school, or school system, or over the selection of library resources, textbooks, or other printed or published instructional materials..."*[248]

Lance Izumi, an education expert with the Pacific Research Institute has issued a warning about Obama's takeover of education. In *Obama's Education Takeover,* he writes:

> *"As seen so far, the national standards are costly, academically questionable, and deficient, contra-legal, and contra-constitutional. There is more than enough reason for the public, especially parents, to want change. Yet they are unlikely to get it given the byzantine centralized nationalization process created by the Obama Administration.... [The] Constitution omits any mention of public education, thus leaving that responsibility to the states, respectively, or to the people under the 10th Amendment, which says that any power not enumerated in the Constitution and not prohibited by it is the province of the states and the public."*[249]

But, of course, laws and the Constitution haven't stopped Obama in the past, nor will they in the future.

They're just speed bumps along the road to centralized control. The Heritage Foundation report on Obama's plan for nationalizing education states:

> *"For four and a half decades, the federal role in education has been growing. Costly in terms of taxpayer dollars spent and local control of education lost, this expanding federal control has failed to improve outcomes for America's children.... Constitutional authority for education rests with states and localities, and ultimately with parents—not the federal government. The federal government has crossed this line in the past, but dictating curriculum content is a major new breach that represents a critical level of centralization and a major setback for parental rights."[250]*

Of course, the NEA is playing a lead role in creating Obama's centralized program. The NEA believes that their involvement "provides teachers with far more manageable curriculum" as they "exercise professional judgment" in deciding what's best for students.[251] What a political payoff! The NEA spends $60 million and have 10,000 teachers lobbying to get Obama re-elected and they get rewarded with exactly what the union bosses want: shared control with Obama over the choices in curriculum and teaching materials in all 50 states. They can bypass parental and local authorities at every public school. They can ram their claptrap right down students' throats—and there is no recourse for parents.

Meet the Kind of Teachers the NEA Gives Us

In a real educational system, as opposed to what the NEA and Obama are giving us, the good teachers would rise to the top and the bad teachers would be weeded out. But what we'll have instead is the tyranny of the mediocre and downright scary. To illustrate what I mean by this, let's look in on a Twitter conversation that ***Kyle Olson*** recently had. Olson is the author of *Indoctrination: How 'Useful Idiots' Are Using Our*

Schools to Subvert American Exceptionalism. So he knows a little something about his subject, and he clearly comes to the conversation with earned bias. He got in a heated row with an anonymous (of course) teacher who calls himself "Frustrated Teacher." Here's a transcript and faithful rendering of the exchange:

> **Frustrated Teacher**: *"Teachers often combat the nonsense parents instill in their kids. That surely bothers U cuz misinforming yr kids is impt 2 U."*

> **Kyle Olson**: So parents sometimes screw up their kids, and it's the job of teachers to 'unscrew' them by teaching them to freely engage in premarital and homosexual sex; to hate the free enterprise system and national sovereignty; to blindly believe in 'global warming,' and to accept the foolish idea that the American taxpayer should pay reparations to blacks for slavery – an institution that was abolished in 1865. Americans did pay for slavery. It was called the Civil War and hundreds of thousands of white soldiers died so blacks could be free.

> **Frustrated Teacher**: "You have NO standing to discuss education anyway. You're a nobody who knows little about schools, education, children or policy."

> **Kyle Olson**: It would be good to remind you that your salary is paid by taxpayers…

> **Frustrated Teacher**: "Pay & mind ur business. Once U understand education, then U cn make it ur business. I C no evdnce u have."

> **Kyle Olson**: Perhaps taxpayers confronted with this display will want to opt out of the system and take their tax dollars with him.

> **Frustrated Teacher**: "If you don't like American schools, take your kids out and put them in private schools and STFU."[252]

What an inspiring example of a progressive teacher! I doubt that this teacher is in any way representative of most teachers; instead I suspect he's a union rep and doing his NEA duty to engage with those who might dare criticize the federalized standards Obama will be delivering unto our children in the years ahead.

While he is clearly not representative, Mr. Frustration is not so different from the multitude of teachers who proudly call themselves progressive thinkers—that is, only one opinion counts, theirs. A perfect example of that happened in a North Carolina school recently. A political discussion was underway. A student had the audacity to criticize Obama, and the teacher started yelling at the student. In the audio clip played on Fox News, the teacher yelled, *"That's disrespect!"* The student responded, *"You're disrespecting Romney!"* And on and on it went. The student, Hunter Rogers explained:

> *"I've been told in my life that you'd have to threaten the president to get arrested, and she kept telling me over and over again people were arrested for disrespecting and slandering the president. At the time, I wanted to laugh."*[253]

It is high time that America gets leadership willing to take on the teacher's union and reverse our nation's slide into academic mediocrity. We have a huge problem, and it didn't start with Obama. Previous administrations tried to address the problem. George Bush's No Child Left Behind Act of 2001 hardly moved the needle. That's partly because federal programs never seem to gain traction. That's well known, but lost on most in Washington. And lost in spades on Obama who recently authorized $100 million in grants to research why teachers can't get through to their students and improve reading skills. Yes, one hundred large to study why teachers are failing America.

It's how Obama pretends to be on the job. Throw money, lots of money, at the problem and they you can say you're "doing big things" even if the needle doesn't move.

Clearly there is blame aplenty for our failing education system. Obama inherited a mess. But as a community activist in Chicago, as a guy on the street, he should have had a better perspective. As Deneen Borelli writes in her excellent new book, *Blacklash*:

> "He should have been personally aware of the failed consequences of big government policies to solve the multitude of problems facing inner-city blacks. His efforts are only going to perpetuate the ongoing tragedy. **Why work hard in school? The government will take care of you, feed you through food stamps, and give you free health care. Instead of promoting policies to encourage personal responsibility and independence, Obama's policies will sadly drive more Americans to the government plantation.**" [254]

The Rewarded: The Greedy Takers, The Irresponsible, Big Government Lovers & Government Plantation Dwellers
The Bigger the Government, the More Votes I Get…
What's Not to Like?

Obama loves Big Government as much as he loves himself, because it gives him an easy way to capture unthinking voters and take more control over our daily lives. It's a twofer for an unprincipled man like Obama. Not only is he increasing the numbers of bureaucrats who control our lives, he's putting into place aerial surveillance systems to make sure we do his bidding…

Bloating the Federal Government with Binge Spending

Since Obama took office, the private sector work force has shrunk by 2.6% — shedding 2.9 million jobs. The federal work force, however, has grown by 7% — adding 144,000 jobs!

But, that's not enough for Obama. He wants a lot more. In his 2012 budget, he proposed adding 15,000 more jobs to taxpayer supported positions—including 4,182 Internal Revenue Service workers and 1,054 more just to handle the growing overreach of Obamacare.

Of course, each of these federal jobs comes at the expense of private sector jobs. **_James Sherk_** and **_Rea Hederman_** of the Heritage Foundation explain how:

> *"Government spending substitutes for private-sector investment; it does not supplement it. Increased government spending further reduces private-sector investment, making the problem of low job creation worse...*
>
> *"Moreover, government spending misdirects economic resources. Political priorities, not economic return, drive government spending. The desires of influential Members of Congress and political fads determine where government appropriations are allocated. This often differs greatly from the use that creates the most wealth and jobs."*[255]

It's not just unbridled federal spending and hiring that's troubling. It's the things we taxpayers are getting for that spending and hiring. **We're getting an unsubtle shift from a nation that has a government, as Lincoln and Reagan warned, to a government that has a nation.** Other names for such a government are fascism, totalitarianism, and police state. We have not yet arrived at these distressing destinations, but the train has left the station under the last several presidents. And Obama, despite his public condemnations of coal, is stoking the engines.

Nowhere in government is Obama's objective more apparent than at the Environmental Protection Agency (EPA).

Spending $21 Billion a Year to Kill Business

In 2011, the EPA said it needed to hire *an additional* 230,000 bureaucrats at an outrageous eye-popping cost of $21 billion for the sole purpose of monitoring "greenhouse gas" emissions, and dealing with the deadly problem. Believing that "global warming" is real, and dangerous to boot, and because they genuinely do care about the planet but have little understanding of how the planet's physical properties actually work, the bureaucrats at EPA have been dispatched to punish profit-making companies that emit too much carbon dioxide. **As a result, they send those companies and their jobs packing overseas.**[256]

But that's OK, say Obama spokesmen, those who lose their jobs can always apply for positions at the EPA. **Only a community**

organizer and professor with zero business experience could concoct such a flawed logic path. Not just flawed, but faulty. Carbon dioxide, as we all learn in grade school, is one of the building blocks of life on this planet. Plants need it for photosynthesis. Humans breathe it out. Life on earth would cease to exist without it. But somehow the geniuses at EPA decided they know precisely how much of it we should have. And to keep that impressive logic of theirs going, they labeled it a "pollutant" and then went berserk trying to punish carbon dioxide polluters.

EPA Spying on Farmers

It happened in early summer 2012. Reports were whisking across the plains states that the EPA had enlisted drone aircraft to spy on Nebraska and Iowa farmers!

Yes, these drones were making sure that farmers were obeying the EPA's Concentrated Animal Feeding Operations (CAFO) which details how much cows would be allowed to poo, and then what to do with the poo. Serious business. And the EPA was on the job, with unmanned aerial flyovers. Before long, the EPA took to the microphones to deny any use of unmanned drones, but did admit to using manned aircraft to spy on farmers.

Since 2010, there have been at least eighteen documented flyovers in Nebraska and Iowa – and eight U.S. farmers have been hit with punitive fines from the EPA.[257]

The EPA is also Obama's weapon of choice for destroying the energy industry in America. When he failed to force his cap-and-trade folly through Congress, he decided to use the EPA instead to implement his anti-energy agenda. His goal is to destroy the oil, natural gas and coal industries and force Americans to use alternative energy sources like wind and solar power. The EPA has become judge, jury, law enforcement and executioner on all things environmental. And it is using extra-legal methods to enforce its claims over every stream, lake, river, mountain, farm, endangered bug, plant and animal species, etc. in America.

Take the case of **_Chantel and Michael Sackett_** of Idaho. They had purchased a lake-front property in a small town and were planning to build a modest home. They prepared the land and were ready to lay the foundation when EPA zealots descended upon them and advised them of their egregious offenses—they were, it turned out, building on protected "wetlands." They were ordered to stop building, and to restore the land to its original condition or go pay a steep fine. They couldn't build on property they had lawfully acquired. And they had to spend more money to "restore" the land, with no financial aid from EPA, costing them more than they originally paid.

Not only that, but the Sackett's faced fines of $35,000 a day for non-compliance. Most people would have caved at that point, but not the Sackett's. They got free legal help and challenged the EPA bully. [258]

Their case went all the way to the U.S. Supreme Court, as it should have. The high court told the EPA to pound gravel. It was a victory for common sense, property rights, and the U.S. Constitution. But it didn't stop the EPA from continuing to harass other landowners, with the explicit blessing of their top boss in the Oval Office.

We're Being Ruled By "Czars" and We're OK with That?

At last count, Obama had appointed 46 un-elected and unconfirmed "czars" to report directly to him. He's entitled to his choice of staff, of course. But many of these individuals are so far out of the mainstream; they could *not* have been confirmed by even the Democrat-controlled Senate. **These czars are Obama's shadow government, and function freely without any cabinet level accountability. They have immense power over our lives in ways we don't even know...**

Chief among them is Cass Sunstein, the Regulatory Czar. Sunstein believes that free speech must be limited for the "common good." He believes that the Constitution is "living" and "evolving." In short, he rejects the Constitution as it is written. He also thinks the government should force broadcasters to air "diversity" ads over the airwaves. Sunstein actually believes that wild animals have "rights" and should be permitted to file lawsuits! He thinks our rights as citizens only exist by permission of the federal government!

Then there's John Holdren, Obama's Science Czar. Holdren believes that capitalism is inherently harmful to the environment and so capitalism surely must be halted for good. He opposes nuclear power and refuses to compromise. He says forced sterilization of U.S. citizens may be just the trick for solving the "population explosion." He wants to reduce the standard of living of everyone but the poor, because that will, in his view, help the poor.

Joshua DuBois is Obama's Faith-Based Czar. This guy has a college degree in "black nationalism" and interned for Rep. Charles Rangel (D-NY).

Jeffrey Crowley is Obama's AIDS Czar. He's a gay activist who thinks homosexuals alone should have free health care (not fine)!

Ashton Carter is Obama's Weapons Czar. He wants all private weapons in the United States destroyed and supports the U.N.'s plan to ban all firearms ownership in America.

Ron Bloom was Obama's first "Car Czar" He is a former SIEU operative, thinks the free market is nonsense and has written in support of Chairman Mao's contention that political power must come from the barrel of a gun.

And on it goes. Again, nobody should begrudge a president for surrounding himself with people who agree with him, who can carry out his agenda—like it or not. But when these kinds of people are the surrounders, how do we trust the surrounded?[259]

Obama Uses and Abuses the Constitution

In January 2012, Obama signed a bill permitting him to hold Americans in military custody without convicting them of anything. He did pledge to never use this power, but then, why sign the bill?

In addition, Obama ordered a drone strike on Muslim radical Anwar al-Awlaki, an American citizen. Awlaki deserved to die a thousand deaths, but **U.S. presidents do not order the executions of**

American citizens without due process. U.S. presidents do not keep "kill lists," in addition to enemies lists, that are openly published. That is not how we operate.

Obama is also waging wars around the world without Constitutional authority. He launched military attacks against Libya without congressional approval, which he is required by law to seek. This makes him no different from every modern president, but it sure ought to have his liberal supporters up in arms.[260]

When Congress rejected the stealth amnesty program called the "DREAM Act**," Obama skirted around it and just told his Department of Homeland Security to adopt enforcement policies that bring about the same political ends as the DREAM Act.**

Instead of pushing Congress to repeal federal laws against the use of marijuana, the Department of Justice just decided to stop enforcing the laws. **The DOJ stopped upholding the Defense of Marriage Act, too.**[261]

Obama's new mantra is "We Can't Wait" – not for Congress or for any other legal authority to justify his policies. He just imposes his policies on us – just as any banana republic dictator might.

A person who rules without authority is known as a tyrant, and that has become an all too appropriate description for Barack Obama.

Free Speech is Beautiful, as Long as it Freely Praises Obama

Obama has moved to tighten the government control over what is said and done over the nation's airwaves and Internet. He knows this scheme of his won't fly if examined in any detail, so he cloaked it in the innocuous-sounding "Consumer Privacy Bill."[262]

Read the fine print of this so-called consumer protection bill, and you see that the Federal Trade Commission (FCC) is given authority to tell companies like Google and Facebook how to run their business. That is how it begins.

Dig deeper and you'll see that **Obama's FCC has been empowered to "judge content" on conservative radio stations.** Running point on this for Obama is Mark Lloyd at the FCC who says he wants to **"regulate much of the programming on these stations to make sure they focus on 'diverse views' and government activities,"** according to authors Aaron Klein and Brenda Elliott writing in *The Manchurian President.*[263] When Nazi and Hitler propaganda film maker, Leni Riefenstahl helped shape German public opinion, a world labeled her efforts fascist; what do Obama's supporters call Mr. Lloyd's dictates to talk radio?

Mark Lloyd is in a key position to wipe out competing points of view on the radio now that Obama gets four more years in the White House. Now we're really in trouble.

Once again, Obama's attempts to control of the airwaves and internet harken back to the Communist Manifesto, which says Communists want **"Centralisation of the means of communication and transport in the hands of the State."** [264]

The Rewarded: Fascists, Socialists, and Marxists
Fascist Model Fits Obama Hand in Glove

In June 2012, Obama decided that young illegal immigrants get to stay permanently in America. He ordered Homeland Security to stop deporting them. Although he made it clear that he was *not* offering them "amnesty." It was instead…uh, well, yes… it was amnesty.

Obama knows that he can't force Congress to change the nation's immigration laws this late in his term. And he can't wait for judges to rule in his favor. **So he just issued an edict, aka, an Executive Order, exempting nearly a million illegal aliens from the law.** This kind of "lawless authority" caused a kind of derangement syndrome in liberals when President Bush practiced it, but they are strangely compliant now. Why, you might wonder? **Because this is not about principles and ethics and codes of conduct. This is about the Democrats crunching the electoral numbers, and poring over all the polling data, and discovering that Obama wasn't likely to win legally in November.** So why not bring in a million ringers to put Obama over the top? It's how they rolled in Chicago all these years; why not nationally?

Especially galling is the way Obama effortlessly contradicted his own previous position on immigration. In a 2011 interview with the Spanish-language Univision network, Obama said:

> *"With respect to the notion that I can just suspend deportations through executive order – that's just not the case."* [265]

Right after that interview in which Obama was being reasonable and forthright, I imagine that campaign chief David Axelrod marched into the Oval, threw his arms up in the air and belched in exasperation, "there goes a second term." Then he probably reminded his boss that after choosing to support gay marriage, and forcing Catholic hospitals to perform abortions, he needed to pander to those who call themselves Hispanic leaders or else kiss his re-election hopes goodbye. So of course he pandered.

The amnesty edict was a cynical political move to buy votes – from a voting bloc that may be slipping away from his grasp. And if the cost of these illegals would be tens of billions, with crime and poverty both setting in deeper in the border towns, constantly threatening good taxpaying Americans, oh well. There was an election to buy!

Can Obama Get Away with This?

Probably. **Obama chooses which laws to enforce and which to break.** There is no legal or Constitutional authority for his actions, but he clearly doesn't care. **He considers himself above the law.** Who will stop him? Certainly not Attorney General Eric Holder, or the Congress, or the Left-stream Media, or the Supreme Court unless an action is brought before them.

With Obama in power; gone are the days of separation of powers, checks, and balances.

This illegal alien outrage is what happens in a nation that is ruled by a fascist in training. And I don't use the word "fascist" lightly. Conservative author ***Thomas Sowell*** explained in a June 2012 column how Obama began developing fascist tendencies and probably isn't even aware of it:

> *"[Obama] certainly is an enemy of the free market, and wants politicians and bureaucrats to make the fundamental decisions about the economy. But that does not mean that he wants government ownership of the means of production, which has long been a standard definition of Socialism."*

> *"[What Obama wants is] more insidious: government control of the economy, while leaving ownership in private hands."* [266]

This is the classic definition of totalitarian fascism (as difficult as it is for most Americans to hear it used in an "American" context). **Sowell thinks the Fascist model fits Obama hand in glove because it allows him to push his centralized control theories on businesses, and if those theories fail, he can always attack the employers for their "greed."** And, he can then **demand more government bailouts (with higher taxes and borrowing) plus additional centralized control.** It's another win-win for him.

What Obama wants is the standard definition of fascism: The government controls, but does not outright own the factories or businesses. The government makes key economic decisions and businesses must suffer the consequences of bureaucratic action—good, bad or otherwise.

Sowell describes the commonality between socialism, fascism and other ideologies of the left including communism. They all operate from the assumption that:

> *"…some very wise people – like themselves – need to take decisions out of the hands of lesser people, like the rest of us, and impose those decisions by government fiat…*

> *"The self-flattery of the vision of the left also gives its true believers a huge ego stake in that vision, which means that mere facts are unlikely to make them reconsider, regardless of what evidence piles up against the vision of the left, and regardless of its disastrous consequences."*

This explains why Obama can keep on urging higher taxes and more "stimulus" and "jobs" programs in spite of the fact that his previous attempts have not been successful.

The socialist/fascist economic model of central control has always failed, and it always will. But, as Sowell said, facts don't matter. **It is only the ideology and the power of controlling millions of people that motivates the socialist/fascist.** If citizens are made to suffer under these unworkable economic theories, so be it.

What is This Liberal Fascination with European Failure?

Just reading the headlines about the economic chaos in Europe should be enough to awaken Americans to what's we're soon facing. The mess in Europe is the direct result of its leaders creating socialist/fascist systems that destroy creativity, innovation and economic growth.

The French citizens pay income taxes at an average rate of 42% and the government has grown to be 55% of all spending. And how has that worked out? Nobody really wants to work, and few do. France's debt stands at 80% of their GDP and the country hasn't balanced its budget since 1974. The food is good, though. And the girls pretty.

The U.S. is headed there under Obama. According to the **_Heritage Foundation_**, America's debt stood at 67% of GDP in 2011. It will hit 187% of GDP by 2035, unless we change direction immediately. Heritage warns:

> *"The world has seen what lies at the end of this road to perdition. Though France is a prime example of a country that is spending itself into crisis, Greece has already gone beyond that tipping point. The country's debt has exploded, 21.8% of its people are unemployed, and among the youth, more are out of work than have jobs. In the face of belt-tightening measures that came as a condition of an EU/IMF bailout — which include public sector pay cuts and pension reductions — the country turned to open political revolt with violent riots in the streets. In elections this week, Greek voters rejected the political parties that support fiscal responsibility and instead turned toward the Radical Left."[267]*

Both France and Greece are self-destructing by not embracing free market policies. So why do they continue to destruct? One possible explanation is they don't know any better. The same might be said of Obama—he is well-read and traveled, but he might not truly understand any other way. Why would he?

Obama Bathed in Marxist Philosophy His Entire Life

He was brought up in a home with a Marxist/atheist mother. He was mentored by a black nationalist Communist in Hawaii named Frank Marshall Davis. He was trained as community organizer to employ the Marxist tactics of Saul Alinsky. He attended a church for 20 years headed by a black nationalist who despises capitalism and western civilization. He got into good school after good school based not on merit, but on racial set-asides. He was a member the "New Party" when he ran for the state senate in Illinois back in the mid-1990s. He denies this, but there are photos. The New Party was a group of leftists dedicated to destroying the free enterprise system and converting our country into a European Socialist welfare state.

And with all of these life experienced and choices, the thing Obama has absolutely no experience in is . . . business. He doesn't understand business, doesn't trust it, and being socialist-minded, he seeks to control it (doubly so, as I've noted, to exact tribute).

A Warning from a European to America

Daniel Hannan a member of the European Parliament has issued a warning to America, urging us to *not* follow the path that Europe is taking, or else suffer the same consequences. According to Hannan:

"President Obama wants to Europeanize America. All right, he wouldn't put it in those terms, partly because the electorate wouldn't want it and partly because he sees himself as less Eurocentric than any of his 43 predecessors. My guess is that if anything, Obama would verbalize his ideology using the same vocabulary that Eurocrats do. He would say he wants a fairer America, a more tolerant America, a less arrogant America, a more engaged America. When you chisel away the cliché, what's underlying these phrases are higher taxes, less patriotism, a bigger role for state bureaucracies, and a transfer of sovereignty to global institutions. In other words, President Obama wants to make the U.S. more like the EU."[268]

According to Hannan, **making America more like Europe will result in more laziness, less productivity, more of a welfare mentality, less national sovereignty, the destruction of patriotism and personal charity, an inefficient health care system, and a lowered standard of living.**

A harsh and painful assessment.

SECTION IV: How Obama Stole the Election

S o there you have it. We've seen how Obama, in an effort to hold onto a job he was never qualified to hold, has **resorted to the most base of tactics: demonizing anyone who opposes him, keeping paranoid enemies lists, and seeking to divide a nation to conquer it.**

That is the fairest indictment of Obama as he prepares for a second term. But he is the president, an office I honor, and so in this book I have sought to explain in clear factual terms how Obama debased that office like none other, before him. And now I talk about how Obama stole the election. An Election I believe Mitt Romney actually won.

Obama Should Have Lost Because He Failed to Deliver on His Promises

In a recent article by ***Michael Medved*** in *The Daily Beast,* he points out that *"in the last 100 years, every U.S. president who lost his bid for a second term did so because he abandoned his principal promise to the American people."*[269] Medved ran through a hundred years of history to confirm as much:

In 1928, Herbert Hoover ran on "a chicken in every pot, a car in every garage" and most of the country had neither…

In 1980, Jimmy Carter offered a "government as good as its people" and the people thought more of themselves than of his government…

In 1988, George Bush said "Read my lips…no new taxes!" and then began raising taxes…

And in 2008, Barack Obama pledged to unify the nation and then drove us further apart…

Like Hoover, Carter, and Bush before him, Obama has failed to live up to his basic promise and that, Medved concludes, has become sadly apparent.

In his speech to the Democratic National Convention in 2004, Obama said "we are one people, all of us pledging allegiance to the stars and stripes, all of us defending the United States of America." In his January 2009 inaugural address, Obama again sought to unify and "proclaim an end to the petty grievances and false promises, the recriminations and worn-out dogmas that for far too long have strangled our politics."

Today even the most unquestioning Obama supporter has to admit that something short-circuited and that the only vaguely justifiable reason to vote for Obama again was, *"He's a Democrat."*

To some people, that's enough. But it's not to most Americans.

If Obama has any defense, it is that Washington is so hopelessly polarized now that nobody could fix it. Not even him. He can try to blame conservatives for playing games, being small-minded, and refusing to compromise. But that only calls attention to his own Chicago-style politicking, mean-spirited attacks on his opponents, and unwillingness to fight for what he believes in—preferring instead to regroup on the golf course. This is not what we pay our president to do. We pay him to lead.

"A leader is one who knows the way, goes the way and shows the way," reminds John C. Maxwell, the Christian leadership guru and author of 60 books. **A leader is not someone who uses his taxpayer-funded time and energy to compile enemies list.** When Nixon did it, good people in both parties called it what it was: unacceptable. We must do so again with Obama.

Like Nixon before him, there came a time when Obama was tested, and his worst impulses won out. His A-game hadn't worked out like he had hoped. So rather than shift the line-up, make some good trades or go back to the drawing board like good presidents have always done, Obama started paying bounties for his opponents.

And being from Chicago, with its long history of rewarding friends and punishing enemies, Obama kept a straight face through it all. No trace of embarrassment or shame as he strides athletically across the global stage. If he has any remorse, he masks it. But unlike when he first delivered his moving speeches four and eight years ago, he is no longer an unknown.

A wonderful political observer, **_Peggy Noonan_**, once wrote that Obama's early success came from being a "Rorschach blot" with his every move "carefully scrubbed and scripted" and speeches that "sounded great but contained no substance" for he was "a master in allowing you to believe whatever was most important to you."[270] But now Obama's greatest attribute, his freshness, has been spoiled. He is, Noonan concludes, "inconvenienced by reality." He has a track record upon which he can and should be judged.

Here is a Summary of Obama's Record of Four Years at the Helm

- ► Despite spending trillions to stimulate the economy and create jobs, both are stuck in first gear. And it's precisely the top-down puppeteering that is stifling the recovery. Harsh new regulations, massive government borrowing, and uncertainty about Obama's next attack on business keeps capital and talent looking for ways to flee the country.
- ► Despite slipping tens of billions of taxpayer money to corrupt cronies in "green energy" companies, no good alternative to fossil fuels has come forth and isn't expected to for decades. Meanwhile the president's policies have shot up gas prices; coal is being attacked; oil exploration and needed pipelines are restricted; power plants are closing; good solid energy sector jobs are going away by the thousands but on

a positive front, all of Obama's beautiful supporters in Hollywood will have slightly cleaner air to breath.

▶ Despite professing to be a Christian, Obama has attacked the teachings of the Catholic Church and trampled all over the religious liberties that all churches in America have rightly enjoyed since our early days as a nation. He has sought to pit one set of morals against the other, and has worked actively to debase the traditions of a Christian nation in hopes of winning over a few narrow interests who contribute mightily to Democratic Party election campaigns.

▶ Despite upending one-seventh of the U.S. economy, Obamacare remains wildly unpopular with a majority of the country and may even be ruled unconstitutional. Either way, it is wildly expensive and threatens to bankrupt the nation.

▶ Despite a legitimate success in finally eliminating bin Laden, Obama's almost naïve ivory tower view of the real world allowed Russian and China to grow more bellicose toward America; Iran to openly mock us and soon obtain offensive nuclear weapons; the Middle East to install all new tyrants who hate America even more and daily speak of the elimination of Israel.

▶ Despite the deep divisions that existed in our country before Obama, he had an opportunity like no other—a truly historic opportunity—to heal and mend those divisions. But he only deepened them. He could have brought people together and enabled the better spirits of us all. Instead, he fanned a spark into a wildfire, and whenever given the choice, he played the race card and cheapened us all.

That is the record Obama ran on, in summary.

I know Obama reads the polls—all politicians read the polls. So I know he was nervous about his ability to win a second term. **I therefore believe that the same dark impulse that led him to create an enemies list, also gave the nod to massive voter fraud.**

Before the Vote, Obama's Hackers Prepared to Commit Fraud

As Michelle Malkin reported, there are gaping holes in the security of the voting booths across the country—especially with the online ballots. She reports,

> "In October 2010, the D.C. Board of Elections and Ethics encouraged outside parties to try to find security holes in their online balloting infrastructure operated by Scytl. A group of University of Michigan students successfully hacked into the system, commandeered passwords, doctored ballots and programmed audio of the school's fight song to play whenever an e-ballot was submitted." [271]

Obama immediately hired these students. Joking, but not funny. Obama *may* have hired them. Based on his other activities and desire to win, as well as his Chicago background where ballot tampering is routine.

The hackers had many ways to stuff the ballot box for Obama— and as I write this, it is clear they got away with it. **The software programs used by the elections commissions are not fail-safe, and there are many ways to manipulate the outcome and escape undetected.**

Relevance Magazine editor Dr. Phillip M. O'Halloran recently stated, "the computer voting system in this country is a veritable can of worms, so open to tampering that if there is no organized election fraud going on, the criminals are falling down on the job… computer vote fraud is not only feasible but, by its very nature, undetectable… it is hard to conceive of an organized criminal enterprise with such a favorable combination of high profit potential and low risk."

Common Cause, in a 2006 report entitled, *Malfunction and Malfeasance: A Report on the Electronic Voting Machine Debacle*, reported on four major studies that all concluded that voting machines were vulnerable to hacking and reprogramming. "Each report concluded DRE machines to be vulnerable to malfunction and also to tampering in which a computer-savvy hacker with minimal access to the machine could introduce malicious code to the DRE software and change the results of an election. Such manipulation could be unde-tectable. In machines equipped with a modem, it could even be done from a remote location." One example is given of a machine in a previ-ous election that was proven to have erroneously cast 100 thousand non-legitimate votes for a candidate. And, by the way, all our voting machines have modems.

Also before the election, Democrats filed lawsuits all over the country effectively seeking permission to commit voter fraud. The suits asked judges to repeal any voter identification laws. Well, now we know why they filed them. **They needed to steal the vote in certain key states so that Obama could be re-elected.**

The Military Vote Suppressed

The Military Voter Protection Project found that **absentee ballot requests by the military families have dropped significantly since 2008.** This included a large drop in big swing states. As of Sept. 22, 2012 requests for ballots were down 46 percent in Florida, 70 percent in Virginia, and 70 percent in Ohio.

"These are lowest numbers we've seen in the last decade," according to **_Eric Eversole_**, founder and executive director of the project. **"There are a number of factors that go into this, but if the Pentagon was doing what it was supposed to be, this would be a non-issue."**

Eversole is talking about the Pentagon's **Federal Voting Assis-tance Program (FVAP), which is tasked with helping military members vote.**

Under the Military and Overseas Voter Empowerment Act (or MOVE Act), which was signed into law in 2009, the FVAP is supposed to assist service members with voting on military installations. This includes pro-viding military members with voter information forms when they check in to a duty station, similar to the "motor voter" programs civilians see at DMV offices.

But a U.S. Department of Defense Inspector General report released in August 2012 found that FVAP hadn't set up those voter

assistance offices—in part because of funding problems, but also because of resistance from the Department of Defense. After the report came out, Republican Texas Sen. John Cornyn wrote a letter to Secretary of Defense Leon Panetta demanding better voter assistance for the troops.

But Eversole says **"cultural hurdles" are also a factor in the missing military vote.**

"There is this idea that service members should stay out of the political process or America will not trust you," he says.

In June, Chairman of the Joint Chiefs of Staff Gen. Martin Dempsey wrote on his blog that he believed it was important to have an apolitical military. "We must understand why our military as a profession embraces political neutrality as a core value," he wrote, saying neutrality was essential to keeping the trust of the American people.

Cornyn had something to say about this, too, writing a letter to Dempsey that questioned his comments and urged him to issue a public statement encouraging the military to vote.

"I shook my head at this," says Eversole of Dempsey's comments. **"Service members must participate in the democratic process they work to defend."**

I believe something even more sinister is at work. **This is part of a coordinated effort to suppress the Military vote by the Obama administration. Obama has been outspoken about his desire to cut Defense Department spending, and Obama knew polling data shows a majority of the US Military supported Romney in the election.**

This is **why barriers to voting were in place as opposed to the encouragement to vote mandated by the MOVE Act.**

My Pre-Election Prediction

It breaks my heart that a pre-election prediction I made in my nationally syndicated column came true. Here is what I wrote:

"America used to have the most democratic elections in the world. It doesn't anymore. Antiquated technology, along with the

failure to clean dirty voter rolls of dead and moved voters, plus gridlock blocking efforts to fix the problems have left our system in shambles."

The highly respected Pew Center reported that 1.8 million dead people were still on the voting rolls in 2012. And with an electorate so closely divided, **vote fraud easily determined Barack Obama will sit in the Oval Office in January 2013 and beyond.**

And to clear the way for election fraud, Obama and his allies blocked a quality proposal called the Federal Election Integrity Act.

Rep. _**Joe Walsh**_ introduced this bill. It would simply mandate that citizens present a government-issued photo ID to vote in federal elections.   To ensure that no eligible voter is denied, the bill provides money to states in order to cover the cost of making IDs for those who cannot afford them.

Rep. Walsh knows the problems; he was elected in Illinois, a state with a history of voter fraud and stolen elections. Walsh said in his statement about the bill, "I want to be clear on something. I want to make sure every American eligible to vote has the opportunity to do so, and more importantly, I want to ensure that everyone who does vote has their vote counted. However, **every fraudulent vote cast cancels out any cast by honest Americans** — and that is what I am opposed to."

Successful Efforts to Block Voter ID Laws Helped Obama

Barack Obama lost in every state that requires a photo ID to be produced before voting. In contrast, those states on a list of highly contested swing states with no voter ID requirements were carried by Obama. The list includes: Minnesota, Iowa, Wisconsin, Nevada, Colorado, New Mexico and Pennsylvania. These states alone total 66 Electoral College votes. When added to Romney's total of 205 Electoral College votes, these states alone would have given Romney the 271 Electoral College votes needed to win even without Ohio or Florida.

Romney also likely had the states of Florida and Ohio stolen from him. These states don't require photo IDs. Ohio requires a non-photo ID, such as a library card. Florida "requests" a photo ID, but doesn't require it.

With the election results so close, the simple requirement of proving your identity is neither intrusive nor overly time consuming at the polls. It is a simple measure which would greatly improve the faith all Americans of any stripe have in the outcome.

Does it surprise you that Obama didn't win any states with photo ID laws for voting, but he won all the swing states which require no voter ID? It didn't surprise me. I predicted it.

The Evidence of a Stolen Election

Soon after the election, another member of the Obama's Enemies List fraternity penned an article which captures the reasons why the election was stolen. The author was Joseph Farah, the CEO of WND. com. His words frighten, but do not surprise me:

> "*I also know that the reigning ethos of this movement represented so ably today by Obama is this: "By any means necessary."* It was first articulated by Jean Paul Sartre in his play, "Dirty Hands." But it became popularized as a slogan of the revolutionary left by Malcolm X. What it means, in short, is that **the ends justify the means. It means violence is fine in achieving a worthwhile objective. It means lying, stealing, cheating and all those other bourgeoisie "sins" are appropriate means of furthering the cause.** Is there any doubt in your mind today that this is now the reigning ethos of the Democratic Party and its various tentacles and allies? There is no doubt in my mind."

> In September, the Columbus Dispatch in Ohio reported this sad and ugly news: "More than one out of every five registered Ohio voters is probably ineligible to vote. In two counties, the number of registered voters actually exceeds the voting-age population: Northwestern Ohio's Wood County shows 109 registered voters

for every 100 eligible, while in Lawrence County along the Ohio River it's a mere 104 registered per 100 eligible. Another 31 counties show registrations at more than 90 percent of those eligible, a rate regarded as unrealistic by most voting experts. The national average is a little more than 70 percent. In a close presidential election where every vote might count, which ones to count might become paramount on Election Day – and in possible legal battles afterward."

The Dispatch asked Ohio's chief elections official, Secretary of State Jon Husted, what could be done about this problem. His answer? Not enough. Nine months ago, he asked U.S. Attorney General Eric Holder for a personal meeting to discuss how to balance seemingly conflicting federal laws so he could pare Ohio's dirty voter list without removing truly eligible voters. Holder's office never even bothered to reply – to either Husted or the newspaper. **What does that tell you? It tells me voter fraud is and was an important tactic in re-electing Holder's boss and Democrats throughout the country.** Anyway, we all know how Ohio voted.

How about Michigan – Romney's home state? How did Obama win such a resounding victory when the polls showed the two candidates in a virtual tie? And how is it that Obama won by 9 points while Democrats suffered a string of defeats down the entire state ballot? For instance, Republicans maintained control of both the state House and the Supreme Court, while Democrats lost three ballot propositions.

Then, of course, there is the fine work of James O'Keefe and Project Veritas, which demonstrated, over and over again on camera, the willingness and ability of Democratic operatives to cheat and commit fraud to win elections.

How about WND.com's investigation in which it demonstrated conclusively that **the Obama campaign welcomed foreign contributions by intentionally leaving vulnerabilities in** *its web donation page* that allowed even those using bogus names, disposable credit cards and foreign IP addresses to donate cash? The classic example was when WND staffers did just this using the name Osama bin Laden, listing his occupation as "deceased terrorist" and employer as "al-Qaida." The contributions were accepted by the Team Obama, just as it accepted foreign contributions from the Palestinian Authority in 2008, as WND's Aaron Klein demonstrated.

Add to all this, electronic voting machine anomalies.

"I don't know if it happened to anybody else or not, but this is the first time in all the years that we voted that this has ever happened to me," said Marion, Ohio, voter **_Joan Stevens_** to Fox News. Stevens said that when she voted, it took her three tries before the machine accepted her choice to vote for Romney. "I went to vote and I got right in the middle of Romney's name," Stevens said that she was certain to put her finger directly on her choice for the White House.

She said that the first time she pushed "Romney," the machine marked "Obama." So she pushed Romney again. Obama came up again. Then it happened a third time. "Maybe you make a mistake once, but not three times," she told Fox News.

But of course **this was not just happening in Ohio. There were also eyewitness accounts of these machine malfunctions occurring in a number of other states including Nevada, Kansas, North Carolina, Missouri and Colorado.**

Officials assured us that the voting machines would be "recalibrated" and that we would not have these kinds of problems on Election Day.

Unfortunately, it turned out that there were a multitude of reports of voting machines turning Romney votes into Obama votes on Election Day.

An article from TheBlaze.com reports: *"Last week, TheBlaze brought you a story from a North Carolina voting precinct using electronic voting machines that was already experiencing issues where votes for GOP candidate Mitt Romney were being changed to Democratic candidate Barack*

Obama. Now, it's allegedly happening again, this time in both Kansas and Ohio."

Granted, reports such as these are anecdotal, but given the sheer number of stories reporting voting machine problems, it is alarming. **Coupled with dead voters and ID fraud voting, these electronic voting machine problems are significant.**

According to the Election Protection Coalition, American voters reported more than 70,000 voting problems by 5 PM Eastern Time on Election Day. With each election cycle the reports of election fraud just continue to get worse, but once each election is over we never hear about anyone getting into any trouble. Nobody even follows up on these complaints.

There were eyewitness accounts of voting machines all over the nation turning Romney votes into Obama votes. Is anything being done about this? No. Concerned voters are told to sit down, shut up and blindly have faith in the results that the voting machines are giving us even though there is solid proof that there are very serious problems with automated voting machines.

Voting Patterns in Key States Don't Make Sense
Key voting patterns were too bizarre to be legitimate.

These problem voting patterns were particularly acute in **Pennsylvania** and **Ohio.**

Pundit Press reports: *"Across Philadelphia, GOP poll inspectors were forcibly (and illegally) removed from polling locations. Audio has emerged of one incident in question. Coincidentally (or not), Mr. Obama received 'astronomical' numbers in those very same regions, including locations where he received 'over 99%' of the vote. Ward 4, which also had a poll watcher dressed in Obama attire, went massively for Obama. Mr. Obama received 99.5% of the vote, defeating Mr. Romney 9,955 to 55."*

Accordingly, **_Kris Zane_** of the Western Center for Journalism asks pointedly, **"With Philadelphia's record unemployment, record homicide rate, and an Obama-induced economy that has literally**

bankrupted the city, could Obama have won 99% of the vote? Show us the ballots, Mr. President!"

Barack Obama received more than 99% of the vote in more than 100 precincts in Cuyahoga County, Ohio on Election Day.

There were a substantial number of precincts where Mitt Romney got hardly any votes.

Third world dictators don't even get 99% of the vote. Overall, Mitt Romney received 30.12% of the vote in Cuyahoga County. There were even a bunch of precincts in Cuyahoga County that Romney actually won. But everyone certainly expected that Cuyahoga County would be Obama territory. And in most of the precincts that is exactly what we saw – large numbers of votes for both candidates but a definite edge for Obama.

However, there are more than 100 precincts in Cuyahoga County where the voting results can only be described as truly bizarre. **Yes, we always knew that urban areas would lean very heavily toward Obama, but are we actually expected to believe that Obama got over 99% of the votes in those areas?**

In more than 50 different precincts, Romney received 2 votes or less. Considering how important the swing state of Ohio was to the national election, one would think that such improbable results would get attention. Punditpress.com analyzed the vote this way:

> "In Cleveland's Fifth Ward, Obama won districts E, F, and G 1,337 to Mitt Romney's... 0. Well, maybe that's just a fluke. In the Ninth Ward, Mr. Obama won districts D-G with a paltry total of 1,740 to... 3. Hey, at least Romney got .2% of the vote! Okay, what if we look at the entire First Ward? Obama won that one 12,857 to... 94. This time Romney got .7% of the vote."

> "In total, there are 21 districts in Cleveland where Mr. Romney received precisely 0 votes. In 23 districts, he received precisely 1 vote. And naturally, in one of the districts where Obama won 100% of the vote, there was 100% turnout. What a coincidence!"

"By the way, in case you are thinking that Romney did so poorly because maybe those districts were not very populated: Nope. In those 44 districts, Mr. Obama won 14,686 to 23. That's .16% of the vote for Romney."

Finally **Colorado shows prima facie evidence of voter fraud.** According to a report in RedState.com: ***"A review of voter registration data for ten counties in Colorado details a pattern of voter bloat inflating registration rolls to numbers larger than the total voting age population.*** *By comparing publicly available voter data to U.S. Census records, it reveals **ten counties having a total registration ranging between 104 to 140 percent of the respective populations."***

Despite Fraud, Republicans Must Honestly Evaluate the Future

Dick Morris, Michael Barone, and Karl Rove all got it wrong. They thought Romney would win. Reports after the election described Mitt Romney as being stunned at his loss. He and his advisors had practically declared victory before the voting. They clearly underestimated their opponent.

Republicans were too nice to Obama. Romney himself made certain topics off limits. In contrast, spending hundreds of millions of dollars, Obama set out to destroy the character of Mitt Romney. While telling stories about how Romney killed people and shipped their jobs abroad, Obama's team never once could find a trait they liked about Mitt Romney. The Republicans never reciprocated. I nearly choked when I heard speakers at the GOP convention talking about Barack Obama's good qualities as a father and man.

The leadership of the Republican Party is living in an alternate reality. **Barack Obama isn't a good man. He is evil and corrupt.** Romney didn't have the guts to say it. He didn't want to talk about Obama's associations with communists and socialists. Nor did he want to talk about Obama's associations with Islamists and the Muslim Brotherhood. Romney skipped over Obama's sketchy past, his fictional birth story, and his possible ineligibility to serve as president. And on Obama's receipt of corrupt and foreign election funds—Romney remained silent.

Yes the economy is bad, but there needed to be more. What about Obama's support for infanticide? What about his support for death panels? Whoops, Romney couldn't talk about them because he has been all over the map on these issues. First Romney was against abortion, and then he was for it, only to be against it again when it was politically expedient. Romney had the same problem on Obamacare. Romneycare passed with his support in Massachusetts, and it is a close cousin to the corrupt healthcare program of Obama.

But let's put Romney aside, there are significant problems inside the Republican Party that handicap any candidate.

The overly zealous foreign policy of the neoconservative movement is hurting the Republican brand. Americans were worried Romney might get us in another Mideast war. Americans are tired of spilling blood in Islamistan. As a result, Obama scored better than Romney on the question of dealing with a foreign crisis.

This doesn't mean that we support a pre-1940 style of isolationism, but Americans want our troops to come home after a decade of fighting, and they believed Obama would bring them home.

Americans are not pacifists, but they are realists in the mold of Ronald Reagan. Reagan kept the peace through strength, but he also reached out to his enemies with constructive proposals. The modern Republican establishment is too bellicose, and Romney adopted their militant ways, lock stock and barrel. Americans feared Romney would start another undeclared war.

America cannot fashion the world in our own image. And we especially cannot do it if our only persuasive tool is advanced weapons falling on others heads.

Next, the Republican Party has truly become corporatist. The next Republican to win the presidency must be a populist. He or she needs to know Americans distrust big banks as much as they distrust big government. A Wall Street allied financial engineer like Romney was not the best candidate when the last big scandal to rock the nation was in banking. To be the party of America, the GOP must stop coddling big business. Free trade is important, but it isn't so perfect as to be worshiped. Transnational corporations that care less about America than profits must be reined in.

Finally, what Rove and the GOP establishment did to conservative candidate Todd Akin will not be soon forgotten. **The establishment elite of the GOP must stop the war against conservative and Christian candidates lower down the ticket.** By wounding their own with harmful attacks, **the GOP establishment only ends up hurting the Republican Party and causes losses and defeats.** It's rather like shooting your own foot, but in this case, Christians are the heart of the GOP—and we are not amused.

America's and the GOP's real solution to problems will only come when we rediscover God is the Creator and Finisher of our nation and our world.

A Final Word

Regardless of who wins any election, **for an election to be successful in a free society, everyone needs to leave the polls feeling they have had a say, and the election was fair**. Distrust of elections will continue to heighten the tensions between parties and lead to the alienation of Americans who believe the outcome was rigged.

We are experiencing this type of alienation now in America. **What Obama's next four years will hold is truly frightening, and the distrust generated by a fraudulent and rigged election has only heightened tensions.**

For America to move forward, we need to seek some unity of common purpose. From what we've already seen, it is doubtful that the leadership of Obama's second term in office will achieve any unity.

With massive layoffs decimating America's family's finances, and Barack Obama demanding gigantic tax increases or else he will drive us over the fiscal cliff, I cannot help but day-dream about four years from now. I dream of days when Barack Obama will finally be retired, and his ignorance of economics will no longer plague our homeland.

Let's focus together on a brighter future which is possible once the blight of Barack Obama is gone. And to achieve a better tomorrow, we must be willing to look back and reclaim what is best about America.

But this is in fact **our next step forward: To choose to go back to, instead of, "In Government We Trust," to "In God We Trust."**

We desperately need real leadership from the White House, we need character and we need someone capable of making the hard choices. Back in 1964 America faced a similar time for choosing, and Ronald Reagan traveled the country on behalf of Barry Goldwater seeking the presidency. Reagan gave a speech called "A Time for Choosing" and it became a classic, joining the great speeches that have defined the American experience.

We must go back to the America of the American Revolution. As Ronald Reagan said in 1964:

> *"This is the issue of this election:* **Whether we believe in our capacity for self-government or whether we abandon the American Revolution and confess that a little intellectual elite in a far-distant capitol can plan our lives for us better than we can plan them ourselves..."**

> **"A government can't control the economy without controlling people. And they know when a government sets out to do that, it must use force and coercion to achieve its purpose. They also knew, those Founding Fathers, that outside of its legitimate functions, government does nothing as well or as economically as the private sector of the economy.**

It is again a time for choosing.

Obama may control the White House for the next four years, but **I hope you will stand with me and other Patriots to fight his every move, policy or action that hammers, carves and chisels away, further destroying America. Together we can stop his drive to fundamentally transform America, dead in its tracks. We can conserve America until 2016, when we have another opportunity to complete the task of America's Constitutional Restoration.**

SOURCES

1 Kimberley Strassel, The President Has a List, WSJ, April 26, 2012

2 http://abcnews.go.com/blogs/politics/2008/06/deconstructing

3 Sara K. Smith, "RIP Obama's "Enemies List", NBC News Miami, August 18, 2009

4 http://www.commentarymagazine.com/article/obamas-enemies-list/#

5 Andrew Malcolm, "Top of the Ticket: Transcript of President Barack Obama with Univision," Los Angeles Times, October 25, 2010, http://latimesblogs. latimes.com/washington/2010/10/transcript-of-president-barack-obama-with-univision.html

6 http://thehill.com/video/campaign/228509-cory-booker-walks-back-criticism-of-obama-tactics-as-nauseating-

7 http://www.nypost.com/p/news/national/bam_on_cory_he_dead_to_us_

8 Rabbi Brad Hirschfield, FoxNews.com, May 17, 2012

9 Peter Roff, Obama Campaign Tries Donor Intimidation Against GOP Funders," US News & World Report, May 17, 2012

10 Peter Wehner, Obama's Enemies List, Commentary, April 2012

11 Kate Hicks, "Donors Beware: Obama Posts Online 'Enemies List'", Townhall. com, April 27, 2012

12 http://www.liberallyconservative.com/tag/us-constitution/

13 Stephanie Mencimer, "Pyramid-Like Company Ponies Up $1 Million for Mitt Romney," Mother Jones, February 6, 2012

14 Stephanie Mencimer, "Pyramid-Like Company Ponies Up $1 Million for Mitt Romney," Mother Jones, February 6, 2012

15 Kim Strassel, "Trolling for Dirt on the President's List," WSJ, May 10, 2012

[16] http://www.theblaze.com/stories/romney-donor-finds-out-what-it-means-to-be-on-president-obamas-enemies-list/

[17] http://www.heritage.org/about/staff/c/rory-cooper

[18] http://communities.washingtontimes.com/neighborhood/tygrrrr-express/2012/feb/15/barack-obamas-enemies-list/

[19] THEODORE B. OLSON, "Obama's Enemies List," WSJ, February 1, 2012

[20] http://www.alec.org/

[21] http://www.cbsnews.com/2100-250_162-6196337.html

[22] CJ Ciaramella, "Liberal advocacy groups meet to plot conservative network's demise," Free Beacon, May 14, 2012, http://freebeacon.com/target-alec/

[23] Brendan Greeley, "ALEC's Secrets Revealed; Corporations Flee," Bloomberg Businessweek, May 03, 2012

[24] Karl Marx and Frederick Engles, *Manifesto of the Communist Party,*" English edition 1888, part I. Bourgeois and Proletarians

[25] CJ Ciaramella, "Liberal advocacy groups meet to plot conservative network's demise," Free Beacon, May 14, 2012, http://freebeacon.com/target-alec/

[26] WENDY GRAMM and BROOKE ROLLINS, "Why the Left Wants to Blacklist ALEC," WSJ, May 15, 2012

[27] Arthur Brooks, *The Road to Freedom: How to Win the Fight for Free Enterprise,* Basic Books, New York, 2012

[28] ARTHUR C. BROOKS, America and the Value of 'Earned Success', WSJ, May 8, 2012

[29] John Hawkins, "7 Reasons Liberal Economic Policies Don't Work," Townhall, May 08, 2012

[30] John Hawkins, "7 Reasons Liberal Economic Policies Don't Work," Townhall, May 08, 2012

[31] David Limbaugh, "Truth Is Major Obstacle to Obama's Re-election," Townhall.com, May 08, 2012

[32] Karl Marx and Frederick Engels, *Manifesto of the Communist Party,*" English Edition, 1888, pt. I. Bourgeois and Proletarians

[33] Mamet, David, *The Secret Knowledge,* Penguin Group, New York, 2011

[34] Edward Conard, *Unintended Consequences: Why Everything You've Been Told About the Economy Is Wrong,* Penguin Group, New York, 2012

[35] Adam Davidson, "The Purpose of Spectacular Wealth, According to a Spectacularly Wealthy Guy," New York Times, May 1, 2012

[36] Adam Davidson, "The Purpose of Spectacular Wealth, According to a Spectacularly Wealthy Guy," New York Times, May 1, 2012

[37] Mamet, David, *The Secret Knowledge,* Penguin Group, New York, 2011

[38] NICK TIMIRAOS And RUTH SIMON, "Borrowers Face Big Delays in Refinancing Mortgages," *Wall Street Journal,* May 9, 2012

[39] http://ecreditdaily.com/2012/05/demand-prolonging-average-refinance-timetable-70-days/

[40] NICK TIMIRAOS And RUTH SIMON, "Borrowers Face Big Delays in Refinancing Mortgages," WSJ, By May 9, 2012

[41] http://www.inman.com/news/2012/02/16/top-10-us-foreclosure-hotspots-9-in-california

[42] http://money.cnn.com/2008/06/05/news/economy/foreclosure/

[43] LAWRENCE B. LINDSEY, "The Sharp Pencil Test," *The Weekly Standard,* June 13, 2011

[44] Terry Jeffrey, "Obama's Stimulus: A Documented Failure," WSJ, May 09, 2012

[45] Terry Jeffrey, "Obama's Stimulus: A Documented Failure," WSJ, May 09, 2012

[46] Larry Kudlow, "Investor-Class Dead Heat," Townhall.com, May 8, 2012

[47] Michael Reagan, "Only Obama Is Better Off," Newsmax, May 9, 2012

[48] Michael Reagan, "Only Obama Is Better Off," Newsmax, May 9, 2012

[49] DANIEL HENNINGER, "Demolishing Paul Ryan," *Wall Street Journal,* April 12, 2012

[50] Remarks of the President, Associated Press Luncheon in Washington, DC, April 3, 2012

[51] Peter Ferrara, "Why Obama Hates Paul Ryan," The Spectator, April 11, 2012

[52] Peter Ferrara, "Why Obama Hates Paul Ryan," The Spectator, April 11, 2012

[53] IBD Editorial, "Welch Hits Finger-Pointer In Chief," *Investor's Business Daily,* 04/13/2012

[54] http://www.washingtonpost.com/2011/02/25/ABjfuEJ_category.html?blogId=fact-checker&tag=4%20Pinocchios

[55] Obama's Acceptance Speech, August 8, 2008, http://uspolitics.about.com/od/speeches/a/obama_accept_5.htm

[56] http://www.govtrack.us/congress/bills/112/s2230

[57] The Buffett Tax Loss, WSJ, April 13, 2012, 7:16 p.m. ET

[58] The Glenn Beck Show, September 22, 2011, http://www.glennbeck.com/content/blog/stu/eleve-ways-warren-buffett-is-lying-about-warren-buffett

[59] Stephen Ohlemacher, "FACT CHECK: Are rich taxed less than secretaries," Associated Press, September 20, 2011

[60] http://www.whitehouse.gov/the-press-office/2012/04/11/remarks-president-buffett-rule

61 Dana Milbank, "Rebuffing Obama's gimmicky 'Buffett Rule'," Washington Post, April 11, 2012

62 Mark Landsbaum, "Billionaire Buffett, get out your checkbook," Orange County Register, April 12th, 2012

63 http://www.issues2000.org/2012/Barack_Obama_Tax_Reform.htm

64 John Kartch, Americans for Tax Reform, http://atr.org/obama-thank-tax-hikes-families-making-a6834#ixzz1rqloTU3p

65 Joseph Farah, "Taxation without representation – it's back, again," WND, May 8, 2012

66 CHARLES DUHIGG and DAVID KOCIENIEWSKI, "How Apple Sidesteps Billions in Taxes," NYT, April 28, 2012

67 CHARLES DUHIGG and DAVID KOCIENIEWSKI, "How Apple Sidesteps Billions in Taxes," NYT, April 28, 2012

68 Me Carter O. Snead, "Obama's Freedom Deficit," First Things, March 1, 2012

69 Melissa Moschella, "Freedom of Conscience – Or Free Contraceptives," National Review, February 21, 2012

70 "ERLC Releases 'Fact Sheet' On Obama Mandate," Press Release, February 24, 2012.

71 Ken Blackwell, "Remarks On Religious Liberty," Family Research Council, May 29, 2012.

72 Steve Ertelt, "Obama Administration Weakens Protections For Pro-Life Workers," LifeNews.com, February 10, 2011.

73 Frederick Engels, "Draft of Communists Confession of Faith" 1847, Question 22, Answer

74 Karl Marx and Frederick Engels, "Manifesto of the Communist Party" English Edition, 1988, pt. II. Proletarians and Communists

75 Kimberly Atkins, "EEOC Transgender Ruling Could Open Door To Gay Bias Claims," LawyersUSA.com, May 8, 2012.

76 "EEOC v. Hosanna-Tabor Evangelical Lutheran Church And School, Michigan, (2010-Current), The Becket Fund, 2012.

77 Supreme Court decision, Hosanna-Tabor v. EEOC, October, 2011

78 http://cnsnews.com/news/article/chaplains-group-says-pelosis-wrong-about-need-protect-conscience-rights-chaplains

79 http://www.christianpost.com/news/pelosi-calls-chaplain-conscience-clause-a-fraud-75190/

80 "Franklin Graham Regrets Army's Decision To Rescind Invite To Pentagon Prayer Service," FoxNews.com, April 22, 2010.

[81] Ken Blackwell, Ken Klukowski, "Delta Force Hero Can't Speak At West Point Because Of His Christian Beliefs," Huffington Post, February 2, 2012.

[82] Connie Hair, "White House Censoring Christianity?" Human Events, May 5, 2010.

[83] Julia Duin, "Obama To Be Prayer Day No-Show," The Washington Times, May 6, 2009.

[84] "Obama Hosts Iftar For American Muslim," Daily News Egypt, September 2, 2009.

[85] Karl Marx and Frederick Engels, *Manifesto of the Communist Party* English Edition, 1888, pt.II. Proletarians and Communists

[86] Frederick Engels, *"Draft of Communist Confession of Faith"* 1847, Question 20, Answer

[87] Rush Limbaugh radio transcript, April 12, 2012

[88] M.J. Lee, "Sarah Palin: 'Mama Grizzlies Roar At Rosen, Politico, May 13, 2012

[89] "Hope, Change, & Lies: Orchestrated 'Grassroots' Smear Campaigns & The People Who Run Them," The Jawa Report, September 22, 2008

[90] Michelle Malkin, "Mr. And Mrs. Cranky Pants," Jewish World Review, January 27, 2012

[91] "Inside Media Matters: Sources, Memos, Reveal Erratic Behavior, Close Coordination With White House And News Organizations," The Daily Caller, February 12, 2012

[92] Kerry Picket, "Tactics Used Against Limbaugh And Others Described In Media Matters Strategy Docs," The Washington Times, March 8, 2012

[93] Vince Coglianese, "Inside Media Matters: David Brock's Enemies List," The Daily Caller, February 13, 2012

[94] "Newsweek's Queen Of Sleaze: Tina Brown Assaults 'Crazy' Conservatives," Media Research Center, Profiles in Bias, undated online report

[95] Glenn T. Stanton, "The Playground Attacks On Marcus Bachmann," National Review Online, July 19, 2011

[96] Marybeth Hicks, "Julia's Carefree Life Offers No Real Appeal," May 9, 2012, Townhall.com

[97] Lauren Fox, "GOP Offers Rebuttal Message To Obama's 'Julia,' May 3, 2012, U.S. News & World Report

[98] Allison Yarrow, "She-PAC Targets Democratic Misogynist Hypocrisy, Pushes GOP Women Candidates," The Daily Beast, March 20, 2012

[99] "Justice Department Files Suit Against Arizona Immigration Law," *FoxNews. com*, July 6, 2010

[100] "Justice Department Files Suit Against Arizona Immigration Law," *FoxNews.com*, July 6, 2010

[101] "Justice Department Files Suit Against Arizona Immigration Law," *FoxNews.com*, July 6, 2010

[102] Byron York, The Washington Examiner, June 22, 2010

[103] Jacob Laksin, "Supreme Court Showdown Over Arizona," *FrontPageMagazine*, April 25, 2012

[104] Neil Munro, "White House Loosens Border Rules For 2012," *The Daily Caller*, June 20, 2011

[105] Neil Munro, "White House Loosens Border Rules For 2012," *The Daily Caller*, June 20, 2011

[106] Jacob Laskin, "Obama's Race Pandering," *FrontPageMagazine*, January 13, 2012

[107] Mark Krikorian, How Obama is Transforming America Through Immigration, Perseus Books Group, Kindle

[108] Mark Krikorian, How Obama is Transforming America Through Immigration, Perseus Books Group, Kindle 65-68

[109] Mark Krikorian, How Obama is Transforming America Through Immigration, Perseus Books Group, Kindle 212-215

[110] Raymond Ibrahhim, "Mexican Jihad," *FrontPageMagazine*, May 15, 2012

[111] Ryan Mauro, "Hezbollah Sets Up Shop In Mexico," *FrontPageMagazine*, July 13, 2011

[112] Sara A. Carter, "Border Agents Dispute Claim That Illegal Immigrant Tide Is Slowing," *The Washington Examiner*, May 14, 2012

[113] Edwin Mora, "Border Patrol Has 'Controlled' Only 129 Miles Of 1,994-Mile U.S. Mexico Border, According to Federal Audit," *CNSNews.com*, February 15, 2011

[114] Edwin Mora, "Border Patrol Official: Drug Cartels 'Have Taken Control' of 'Several Areas Along Our Border'" *CNSNews.com*, July 21, 2011

[115] "Government Insurgency in America? Former Border Agent Details National Security Threats Spilling Into the U.S.," *TheBlaze.com*, February 7, 2012

[116] Sheriff Joe Arpaio, "Illegal Immigration: It's A Crime," SheriffJoe.org

[117] Jamie Weinstein, "Poll: Americans Overwhelmingly Support Arizona Immigration Law, Think Court Should Uphold It," *The Daily Caller*, April 24, 2012

[118] Brian Sussman, *Climategate*, WND Books, Washington D.C., page 173.

[119] United States Energy Information Administration, "Coal Reserves," February 2009.

[120] Ibid., "Coal Mining Productivity by State and Mine Type," September 2008.

[121] John Entine, "Coal and Climate Change—Can King Coal Clean Up?" American Enterprise Institute, March 9, 2009.

[122] Brian Sussman, *Climategate*, WND Books, Washington D.C., page 173.

[123] http://www.slate.com/blogs/weigel/2012/04/27/crucifying_oil_companies_for_fun_and_profit.html

[124] Press Release, "Salazar Meets with BP Officials and Engineers at Houston Command Center to Review Response Efforts, Activities," US Department of Interior, May, 6, 2010.

[125] Noelle Straub, "Interior approves drilling on 2 Beaufort Seas leases," *E&E News*, October 19, 2009, http://www.eenews.net/public/eenewspm/2009/10/19/3.

[126] "Goodlatte bill would push drilling off Virginia," *Augusta Free Press*, April 6, 2011, http://augustafreepress.com/2011/04/06/goodlatte-bill-would-push-offshore-drilling-off-virginia-waters/.

[127] United States District Court, Eastern District of Louisiana, Hornbeck Offshore Services versus Kenneth Lee "Ken" Salazar, et al., Case 2:10-cv-01663-MLCF-JCW, Document 67, Filed 06/22/10.

[128] United States District Court, Eastern District of Louisiana, Hornbeck Offshore Services versus Kenneth Lee "Ken" Salazar, et al., Case 2:10-cv-01663-MLCF-JCW, Document 67, Filed 06/22/10.

[129] "New moratorium applies to any deep-water floating facility," *Associated Press*, July 12, 2010, http://www2.tbo.com/content/2010/jul/12/122245/new-federal-moratorium-applies-any-deep-water-floa/.

[130] James Rosen, "Drilling Moratorium Crippling Gulf, Says Industry," Fox News, August 11, 2010, http://liveshots.blogs.foxnews.com/2010/08/11/drilling-moratorium-crippling-gulf-says-industry/.

[131] James Rosen, "Drilling Moratorium Crippling Gulf, Says Industry," Fox News, August 11, 2010, http://liveshots.blogs.foxnews.com/2010/08/11/drilling-moratorium-crippling-gulf-says-industry/.

[132] John M. Broder, "White House Lifts Ban on Deepwater Drilling," *New York Times*, October 12, 2010.

[133] "The Administration Is Slowly Reissuing Offshore Drilling Permits," Institute for Energy Research, March 23, 2011, http://www.instituteforenergyresearch.org/2011/03/23/the-obama-administration-is-slowly-reissuing-offshore-drilling-permits/.

[134] "The Administration Is Slowly Reissuing Offshore Drilling Permits," Institute for Energy Research, March 23, 2011, http://www.instituteforenergyresearch. org/2011/03/23/the-obama-administration-is-slowly-reissuing-offshore-drilling-permits/.

[135] "The Administration Is Slowly Reissuing Offshore Drilling Permits," Institute for Energy Research, March 23, 2011, http://www.instituteforenergyresearch. org/2011/03/23/the-obama-administration-is-slowly-reissuing-offshore-drilling-permits/.

[136] http://www.eia.gov/forecasts/aeo/pdf/0383er%282011%29.pdf http://www. redstate.com/vladimir/2011/03/24/obamasalazar-moratorium-has-crippled-domestic-oil-production/

[137] "Shell Will Not Drill Offshore Alaska in 2011, CEO Says," *Offshore Energy Today*, February 3, 2011, http://www.offshoreenergytoday.com/shell-will-not-drill-offshore-alaska-in-2011-ceo-says/.

[138] Barack Obama, during a meeting with the Editorial Board of the Keene Sentinel newspaper in New Hampshire, on Nov. 25, 2007, and reported in "Nuclear Power a Thorny Issue For Candidates", National Public Radio *Morning Edition*, July 21, 2008, by David Kestenbaum. Available on youtube.com "Sen. Barack Obama on nuclear power from SentinelSource.com"

[139] As of August 1, 2011.

[140] International Atomic Energy Association, http://www.iaea.org/ programmes/a2/index.html

[141] Joseph Mann, "Nuclear Power Given Green Light," *Sun Sentinel*, May 4, 2005.

[142] Senator Lamar Alexander, "Blueprint for 100 New Nuclear Power Plants in 20 Years," July 13, 2009.

[143] Cited in remarks made to the AFL-CIO by Admiral Frank L. Bowman, USN (Retired), President and CEO, Nuclear Energy Institute, April 15, 2008, http:// neinuclearnotes.blogspot.com/2008/04/skip-bowman-builds-on-nuclear-promise.html.

[144] Cited in remarks made to the AFL-CIO by Admiral Frank L. Bowman, USN (Retired), President and CEO, Nuclear Energy Institute, April 15, 2008, http:// neinuclearnotes.blogspot.com/2008/04/skip-bowman-builds-on-nuclear-promise.html.

[145] http://www.thegatewaypundit.com/2012/05/more-hope-and-change-obama-epa-officials-visit-man-at-home-for-inquisitive-email/

[146] Ken Klukowski, "Eric Holder Is At War With Gun Owners' Rights," Washington Examiner, March 20, 2012

147 Ken Klukowski, "Eric Holder Is At War With Gun Owners' Rights," Washington Examiner, March 20, 2012

148 Matthew Boyle, "Holder In 1995: 'Really Brainwash People' To Be Anti-Gun," The Daily Caller, March 18, 2012

149 Supreme Court of the United States, No. 07-290, DISTRICT OF COLUMBIA AND ADRIAN M. FENTY, MAYOR OF THE DISTRICT OF COLUMBIA, Petitioners, v. DICK ANTHONY HELLER, Respondent. ON WRIT OF CERTIORARI TO THE UNITED STATES COURT OF APPEALS FOR THE DISTRICT OF COLUMBIA CIRCUIT BRIEF FOR FORMER DEPARTMENT OF JUSTICE OFFICIALS AS AMICI CURIAE SUPPORTING PETITIONERS, Covington & Burling LLP, January 2008

150 Ken Klukowski, "Eric Holder Is At War With Gun Owners' Rights," Washington Examiner, March 20, 2012

151 David Kopel, The Volokh Conspiracy, November 20, 2008

152 David Limbaugh, "Katie Pavlich's 'Fast And Furious,' Washington Examiner, April 17, 2012

153 Katie Pavlich, "Barack Obama's Bloodiest Scandal," Townhall.com, April 16, 2012

154 Wayne LaPierre, "The Obama Administration Is Planning A Second Term Attack On Gun Rights," The Daily Caller, December 12, 2011

155 "Obama Pushing UN Gun Control While Senate Bill Would Cut Funding Of UN Small Arms Treaty, May 8, 2012

156 Karl Marx and Frederick Engels, "Manifesto of Communist Party" English Edition, 1888, pt. II Proletarians and Communists

157 Amanda Coyne, "ATF Should Explain Why Agents Want Gun-Shop Records," Alaska Dispatch, April 25, 2012

158 Rep. Don Young, "Rep. Young Demands Answers from ATF," April 25, 2012

159 Dan Freedman, "House Blocks Obama Rule On Border-State Rifle Sales," Chron.com., May 10, 2012

160 Tom Blumer, "AP's Babington Can't Understand Why Anyone Would Think Obama Doesn't Support 'Backburner Issue' of 2nd Amendment Rights," Newsbusters, April 14, 2012

161 John R. Lott Jr., More Guns, Less Crime: Understanding Crime and Gun Control Laws, Kindle 169

162 Ken Blackwell and Ken Klukowski. The Blueprint: Obama's Plan to Subvert the Constitution and Build an Imperial Presidency, Kindle 2263-2273

163 Ken Blackwell and Ken Klukowski. The Blueprint: Obama's Plan to Subvert the Constitution and Build an Imperial Presidency, Kindle 2407-2420

164 Ken Blackwell; Ken Klukowski. The Blueprint: Obama's Plan to Subvert the Constitution and Build an Imperial Presidency, Kindle 2192-2195

165 Will Bunch, "Recession Weighs Heavily On Young Workers," *Philadelphia Daily News*, April 9, 2012

166 Will Bunch, "Recession Weighs Heavily On Young Workers," *Philadelphia Daily News*, April 9, 2012

167 Shawn Hess, "America's Youth Has Had Their Dreams Crushed By Dismal Economic Conditions," *WebProNews*, May 4, 2012

168 Samuel Bain, "Obama's State Of The Union – Young People Aren't Buying It," *Fox News Digital*, January 25, 2012

169 Harry Graver, "Obama Tells Unemployed Youth To 'Persevere,'" The College Fix, May 23, 2012

170 Mark Steyn, *After America*, Regnery Publ,. Washington, D.C., pg. 62

171 Robert Costa, "Alexander: Obama's 'Soviet-Style' Takeover Of Student Loans," *National Review*, March 30, 2010

172 Karl Marx and Frederick Engels, *"Manifesto of the Communist Party"* English Edition, 1888, pt. II Proletarians and Communists

173 Maritza Vega, "The Obama Administration's War On For-Profit Schools Hurts People Like Me," *The Daily Caller*, December 29, 2010

174 Karl Marx and Frederick Engles, *"Manifesto of the Communist Party,"* English Edition, 1888, pt. II. Proletarians and Communists

175 "WE CAN'T WAIT: WHITE HOUSE ANNOUNCES NEARLY 300,000 SUMMER JOBS AND OTHER EMPLOYMENT OPPORTUNITIES FOR YOUTH AND NEW ONLINE TOOL TO HELP YOUTH ACCESS OPPORTUNITIES," US Fed News Service, Including US State News, May 5, 2012

176 "Minimum Wage Increase Leads To High Teen Unemployment Rate," *Wall Street Journal*, October 3, 2009

177 Matthew Boyle, "AARP Latest To Receive Obamacare Break," The Daily Caller, May 19, 2011

178 David Catron, "The Right Prescription: A Rationing Advocate To Head Social Security Advisory Board?, The American Spectator, November 18, 2011

179 David Catron, "The Right Prescription: A Rationing Advocate To Head Social Security Advisory Board?, The American Spectator, November 18, 2011

180 Henry Aaron, "IPAB Repeal Not Warranted," Politico, July 14, 2011.

181 Dan Halper, "Expert: IPAB 'Absolutely Will' Lead To Rationing," The Weekly Standard, March 6, 2012.

[182] John Mariotti, "Obama's 'Sneak Attack' On Senior Citizens," Forbes, February 24, 2012.

[183] "Medicare, Seniors – Jim Martin, "The Most Anti-Medicare President In History Has No Credibility With Seniors," Press Release, 60 Plus Association, May 25, 2012.

[184] Dan Weber, "U.S. Seniors Worst Affected By Fuel Prices, Says AMAC," American Association of Mature American Citizens press release, March, 2012.

[185] Gratzer, David (2009-11-10). Why Obama's Government Takeover of Health Care Will Be a Disaster (Encounter Broadsides) (p. 11). Perseus Books Group. Kindle Edition.

[186] Kenric Ward, "Obama Health-Care Hikes Hit Military, Spare Union; Vets Vow To Fight," SunShineStateNews.com, February 29, 2012.

[187] http://www.nationalreview.com/articles/302031/obamas-third-party-history-stanley-kurtz

[188] Rich Miller, "Americans Cling To Jobs As U.S. Workforce Dynamism Fades," Business Week, June 7, 2012

[189] Rich Miller, "Americans Cling To Jobs As U.S. Workforce Dynamism Fades," Business Week, June 7, 2012

[190] David S. Hilzenrath and N.C. Aizenman, "New Health-Care Rules Could Add Costs, And Benefits, To Some Insurance Plans," The Washington Post, 6/15/10

[191] Philip Rucker and David S. Hilzenrath, "GOP Eyes Rules That Firms Say Hurt Jobs," The Washington Post, 2/7/11

[192] Clyde Wayne Crews, "Ten Thousand Commandments," Competitive Enterprise Institute, 2012.

[193] Michael Barrera, "Challenges Faced By Small Businesses Due To Obamacare," FoxNewsLatino, December 26, 2011.

[194] John Vinci, "Obama Administration Signals That Small Businesses May Not Get To Keep Their Self-Insured Health Plans," Americans for Limited Government, June, 2012.

[195] Wayne Allyn Root, "Obama Bent On Destroying Small Business," NewsMax.com, December 7, 2010.

[196] http://www.gop.com/index.php/news/comments/icymi_highlights_from_conference_call_on_why_president_obamas_policies_are_

[197] State News Service, "Highlights From Conference Call On Why President Obama's Policies Are Bad For Job Creators," May 29, 2012.

[198] Memorandum, House Small Business Subcommittee on Investigations, Oversight, And Regulations," Rep. Mike Coffin, May 10, 2011.

[199] "Will Your Business Be Hit By The EPA's Top Five Job Killers?," National Federation of Independent Businesses

[200] Jim Hoft, "Good Grief: EPA Wants To Kill Off 183,000 Private Sector Jobs A Year With New Regs," *The Gateway Pundit,* September 26, 2011.

[201] Sen. Jim DeMint (R-SC), "Obamacare Creating Thousands Of Jobs. For Bureaucrats," demint.senate.gov. web site, April 17, 2012.

[202] Jim Hoft, "In 2007 Obama Warned He'd Make The U.S. Defenseless ... Now He's Cutting 80% Of U.S. Nukes," *TheGatewayPundit,* February 15, 2012.

[203] Robert Patterson, *Conduct Unbecoming: How Barack Obama Is Destroying The Military And Endangering Our Security,* Regnery Publishing, Washington, D.C, 2010, Kindle pp. 9

[204] Victor Davis Hanson, *How The Obama Administration Threatens Our National Security,* Perseus Books Group, 2010, Kindle pp. 255-256

[205] Karl Marx and Frederick Engels, *"Manifesto of the Communist Party"* English Edition 1848; pt.II. Proletarians and Communists

[206] Mike Brownfield, "Obama's Blockbuster Secrets," The Heritage Foundation, May 24, 2012.

[207] Rich Truzupek, "Obama's Wikileaks Problem," *FrontPageMagazine,* December 7, 2010.

[208] David Meir-Levin, "Obama's Knife In Israel's Back," *FrontPageMagazine,* April 5, 2012.

[209] John Bolton, *How Barack Obama is Endangering our National Sovereignty,* Perseus Books Group, 2010, Kindle pp. 78-81

[210] John Bolton, *How Barack Obama is Endangering our National Sovereignty,* Perseus Books Group, 2010, Kindle pp. 229-231

[211] Robert Patterson, *Conduct Unbecoming: How Barack Obama Is Destroying The Military And Endangering Our Security,* Regnery Publishing, Washington, D.C, 2010, Appendix 1.

[212] http://www.reuters.com/article/2012/04/12/us-usa-florida-shooting-poll-idUSBRE83B1BB20120412

[213] Walter E. Williams, "Media dishonesty and race hustlers," *Human Events,* April 11, 2012

[214] Walter E. Williams, "Media dishonesty and race hustlers," *Human Events,* April 11, 2012

[215] Bryan Llenas, Trayvon Martin: Parents Vow Justice, Suspected Racism Fuels Anger," *Latino Fox News,* March 22, 2012

216 Jelani Cobb, "What Got George Zimmerman Charged With Second-Degree Murder, *The Daily Beast,* April 12, 2012

217 Alan Dershowitz, "Zimmerman Arrest Affidavit "Irresponsible And Unethical", Mediate, April 4, 2012; http://www.realclearpolitics.com/video/2012/04/12/alan_dershowitz_zimmerman_arrest_affidavit_irresponsible_and_unethical.html

218 Excerpts from The Rush Limbaugh Show, April 9, 2012

219 Mamet, David, *The Secret Knowledge,* Penguin Group, New York, 2011, pg. 26

220 Deneen Borelli, *Blacklash*, Simon & Shuster, New York 2012

221 Deneen Borelli, *Blacklash*, Simon & Shuster, New York, 2012, pg. 14

222 Deneen Borelli, *Blacklash*, Simon & Shuster, New York, 2012, pg. 15

223 Deneen Borelli, *Blacklash*, Simon & Shuster, New York, 2012, pg. 17

224 Deneen Borelli, *Blacklash*, Simon & Shuster, New York, 2012, pg. 20

225 Deneen Borelli, *Blacklash*, Simon & Shuster, New York, 2012, pg. 49

226 Deneen Borelli, *Blacklash*, Simon & Shuster, New York, 2012, pg. 52

227 Steve Lopez, "Clooney's Obama party full of 'Hollywood hypocrites'," *Los Angeles Times*, May 10, 2012

228 http://www.politico.com/blogs/click/2012/04/jon-lovitz-goes-off-on-obama-121449.html?fb_ref=.T5iZ_qVQqac.like&fb_source=home_multiline

229 Rebecca Keegan, "George Clooney's Obama fundraiser uses star power with a twist," *Los Angeles Times,* May 10, 2012

230 Rebecca Keegan, "George Clooney's Obama fundraiser uses star power with a twist," *Los Angeles Times*, May 10, 2012

231 MIKE McINTIRE and MICHAEL LUO, "White House Opens Door to Big Donors, and Lobbyists Slip In," *New York Times*, April 14, 2012,

232 MIKE McINTIRE and MICHAEL LUO, "White House Opens Door to Big Donors, and Lobbyists Slip In," *New York Times*, April 14, 2012,

233 MIKE McINTIRE and MICHAEL LUO, "White House Opens Door to Big Donors, and Lobbyists Slip In," *New York Times*, April 14, 2012,

234 Ran Duchin, Denis Sosyura, "The politics of government investment" Ross School of Business, University of Michigan, May 2, 2012, http://www.sciencedirect.com/science/article/pii/S0304405X12000700

235 Matthew Boyle, "Obama bundler helps convicted, alleged financial criminals secure Virgin Islands tax breaks," *The Daily Caller*, April 13, 2012

236 *Washington Free Beacon Staff*, "Obama's "Wall Street Guy" has raised at least $500,000 for reelection campaign, March 23, 2012

[237] "Service Employees International Union," DiscoverTheNetworks.com

[238] Freddoso, David (2011-04-04). Gangster Government: Barack Obama and the New Washington Thugocracy (Kindle Locations 2136-2140). Perseus Books Group. Kindle Edition.

[239] Michelle Malkin, *Culture of Corruption: Obama and His Team of Tax Cheats, Crooks, and Cronies* (Kindle Locations 1875-1878)

[240] David Freddoso, *Gangster Government: Barack Obama and the New Washington Thugocracy* (Kindle Locations 2175-2177). Perseus Books Group, 2011

[241] Christopher Neefus, "UAW Bondholders To Receive More Equity In GM Than Others," *CNSNews.com*, June 1, 2009.

[242] Dave Boyer, "Obama Praises UAW At Gathering," The Washington Times, February 29, 2012.

[243] Byron York, "Uncovered: New $2 Billion Bailout In Obamacare," Washington Examiner, March 31, 2011.

[244] "Obama's Drivel: Empty Suit," Pittsburgh Tribune-Review, September 7, 2011.

[245] Mona Charen, "Obama's Education Hypocrisy – Again," PatriotPost, May 25, 2012.

[246] Wynton Hall, "NEA Has Signed Up 10,000 Teachers To Reelect Obama," Breitbart.com.

[247] 2011-2012 NEA Resolutions

[248] Bob Unruh, "Obama Imposing National School Curriculum," WorldNetDaily, February 20, 2012.

[249] Allison Meyer, "Obama's Education Takeover," The Heritage Foundation, March 6, 2012.

[250] Lindsey Burke, "States Must Reject National Education Standards While There Is Still Time," The Heritage Foundation, April 16, 2012.

[251] "NEA's Involvement In The Common Core State Standards," NEA.org., undated

[252] Kyle Olson, "Progressive Teacher Pustule: Pay Your School Taxes And Shut Up," Townhall.com, April 14, 2012.

[253] http://times247.com/articles/suspended-teacher-yelled-at-student-for-defending-romney?utm_source=twitterfeed&utm_medium=facebook#ixzz1xXhOpqUC

[254] Deneen Borelli, *Blacklash*, Simon & Shuster, New York, 2012, page 103

255 Conn Carroll, "Federal Workforce Continues To Grow Under Obama Budget," The Heritage Foundation, February 22, 2011.

256 Edward John Craig, "230,000 New Bureaucrats For The EPA, *The Daily Caller*, September 26, 2011.

257 Eshe Nelson, "EPA Justifies Spying On Farmers, Claims There Are No Drones," *The Daily Caller*, June 7, 2012.

258 Roy Bigham, "EPA Jurisdiction Questioned: Have You Ever Wondered Just How Much Authority The EPA Actually Has?" Pollution Engineering, February 1, 2012.

259 "Obama's Czars And Their Left-Wing Affiliations," *FrontPageMagazine.com*, May 16, 2011.

260 Steve Chapman, "President Obama, Czar In Chief," *The Washington Examiner*, January 8, 2012.

261 Lachlan Mackay, "Big Brother Obama Takes Off The Gloves," The Heritage Foundation, January 10, 2012.

262 "Obama's Internet Police; Administration Moves To Regulate Online Commerce," *The Washington Times*, March 7, 2012.

263 Aaron Klein, and Brenda J. Elliott, *The Manchurian President*, Midpoint Trade Books, 2010, Kindle pp. 189.

264 Karl Marx and Frederick Engels, *"Manifesto of the Communist Party"* English Edition, 1888, pt. II. Proletarians and Communists

265 Doug Powers, "List Of Those Who Don't Believe President Has Constitutional Authority To Suspend Deportations Includes … Obama?" *Michelle Malkin Online*, June 16, 2012.

266 Thomas Sowell, "Barack Obama: Socialist For Fascist?" *Jewish World Review*, June 15, 2012.

267 Mike Brownfield, "Socialism Rises Again," The Heritage Foundation, May 8, 2012.

268 Daniel Hannan (2011-03-01). Why America Must Not Follow Europe, Perseus Books Group. Kindle pp. 1-2

269 Michael Medved, "Obama's Achilles: Broken Promise of Bipartisanship May Sink Reelection," *The Daily Beast*, April 1, 2012

270 Peggy Noonan, "Not-So-Smooth Operator," WSJ, March 31, 2012

271 Michelle Malkin, "Scytl: Voter Fraud Facts and Fiction," Townhall.com, May 09, 2012